Patios
& Landscape
Construction
1-2-3®

Meredith® BOOKS

Patios and Landscape Construction 1-2-3®
Editor: Larry Johnston
Copy Chief: Terri Fredrickson
Copy Editor: Kevin Cox
Publishing Operations Manager: Karen Schirm
Senior Editor, Asset and Information Manager: Phillip Morgan
Edit and Design Coordinator: Mary Lee Gavin
Art and Editorial Sourcing Coordinator: Jackie Swartz
Editorial Assistant: Book Production Managers: Pam Kvitne,
    Marjorie J. Schenkelberg, Mark Weaver
Imaging Center Operator: Scott A. LaMar
Contributing Editor: Marty Miller
Contributing Proofreaders: Kristen Erickson, Gary Webster
Contributing Indexer: Donald Glassman

**Additional Editorial and Design contributions from
    Abramowitz Creative Studios**
Publishing Director/Designer: Tim Abramowitz
Graphic Designers: Kelly Bailey, Adam White
Photography: Image Studios
    Account Executive: Lisa Egan
    Photographers: Bill Rein, Dave Classon, John von Dorn
    Assistant: Mike Clines
    Technical Advisor: Rick Nadke
Illustration: Jim Swanson, Performance Marketing

Meredith® **Books**
Editor in Chief: Gregory H. Kayko
Executive Director, Design: Matt Strelecki
Managing Editor: Amy Tincher-Durik
Executive Editor: Benjamin W. Allen
Senior Associate Design Director: Tom Wegner
Marketing Product Manager: Brent Wiersma
National Marketing Manager—Home Depot: Suzy Emmack

Executive Director, Marketing and New Business:
    Kevin Kacere
Editorial Director, Marketing and Publicity: Amy Nichols
Director, Sales—Home Depot: Robb Morris
Executive Director, Sales: Ken Zagor
Director, Operations: George A. Susral
Director, Production: Douglas M. Johnston
Business Director: Janice Croat

Senior Vice President: Karla Jeffries
Vice President and General Manager: Douglas J. Guendel

Meredith Publishing Group
President: Jack Griffin
Executive Vice President: Doug Olson

Meredith Corporation
Chairman of the Board: William T. Kerr
President and Chief Executive Officer: Stephen M. Lacy

In Memoriam: E.T. Meredith III (1933–2003)

The Home Depot®
Marketing Manager: Tom Sattler
© Copyright 2008 by Homer TLC, Inc.
First Edition.
All rights reserved.
Printed in the United States of America/in China/in Mexico.
Library of Congress Control Number:
ISBN: 978-0-696-24111-6

The Home Depot® and 1-2-3® are registered trademarks of Homer
    TLC, Inc.

Distributed by Meredith Corporation.
Meredith Corporation is not affiliated with The Home Depot®.

Note to the Reader: Due to differing conditions, tools, and individual skills, Meredith Corporation and The Home Depot® assume no responsibility for any damages, injuries suffered, or losses incurred as a result of following the information published in this book. Before beginning any project, review the instructions carefully, and if any doubts or questions remain, consult local experts or authorities. Because codes and regulations vary greatly, you always should check with authorities to ensure that your project complies with all applicable local codes and regulations. Always read and observe all of the safety precautions provided by any tool or equipment manufacturer, and follow all accepted safety procedures.

We are dedicated to providing accurate and helpful do-it-yourself information. We welcome your comments about improving this book and ideas for other books we might offer to home improvement enthusiasts.

Contact us by any of these methods:
Leave a voice message at: 800/678-2093
Write to: Meredith Books, Home Depot Books
    1716 Locust St.
    Des Moines, IA 50309–3023
Send e-mail to: hi123@mdp.com.

How to use this book

A beautiful patio or landscape starts with good bones—secure foundations, fences, and gates; level surfaces; sturdy retaining walls; tight stonework; and adequate drainage. While these important elements provide functionality, they can also be attractive additions to the overall design.

Creating a patio or landscape structure involves basic construction techniques: working with materials such as stone, lumber, and concrete; and using many kinds of tools, from power augers to a hammer and tape measure. Successful installations mean:

- mastering some unfamiliar skills
- using the right tools and materials
- working safely
- doing the job right the first time

Patios and Landscape Construction 1-2-3 can help. It's accessible, easy to use, and full of the right information. Here's how to get the most value out of *Patios and Landscape Construction 1-2-3.*

Trust the wisdom of the aisles

A genuine desire to help people say, "I can do that!" is what the associates at The Home Depot® are all about. Landscaping experts from around the country have contributed their years of on-the-job experience and wisdom of the aisles to *Patios and Landscape Construction 1-2-3.* They've created a hardworking, accurate, and easy-to-follow guide to the basics of patio and landscape construction.

The organizing principle

Patios and Landscape Construction 1-2-3 consists of 10 chapters that provide detailed coverage of the most common styles and techniques.

Take a look inside!

- **Chapter 1:** Outdoor design and planning.
How patios and structures fit into your overall landscape design.
- **Chapter 2:** Building patios.
Brick and paver patterns, soft-set and hard-bed patios.
- **Chapter 3:** Landscape steps.
Timber, brick and concrete steps and ramps.
- **Chapter 4:** Fences and gates.
Installing a variety of fencing options.
- **Chapter 5:** Landscaping walls.
Constructing walls from the most common building materials.
- **Chapter 6:** Sheds.
Sheds from scratch or from kits.
- **Chapter 7:** Trellises and arbors.
Finishing touches that add beauty and functionality to outdoor spaces.
- **Chapter 8:** Electrical.
Supplying power outdoors.
- **Chapter 9:** Plumbing and drainage.
Bringing water outside; installing drainage.
- **Chapter 10:** Concrete.
Basics from slabs to special surfaces.

Doing the job step-by-step

All the projects include complete instructions along with detailed, step-by-step photography to ensure successful completion. You have everything you need to do the job right the first time following standards set by manufacturers and the trades–just like the pros.

Tips, tricks, and timesavers

Each page includes more than just how to do the job. To help you plan your project and to schedule your time, you'll find expert advice: how hard a job is, how

long it takes a pro, and how long it might take you.

At the beginning of each project you will find a materials list along with commonly needed tools.

Additional features on the pages are filled with specific information—**Safety Alert, Buyer's Guide, Work Smart, Tool Tip** and **Design Tip** are all there to help you work efficiently and economically. Whenever a project involves something special—whether it's safety or getting the right tool—you'll be prepared for whatever comes up. **Tool kits** at the beginning of each chapter show you the basic tools you'll need for the following projects.

Get the most out of your landscaping experience

To make the best use of what's inside, carefully read through each project before you begin. Mentally walk yourself through the steps from beginning to end until you're comfortable with the process. Understanding the scope of the job will limit unnecessary mistakes and help you avoid spending money to do things twice.

Take your time

If you're not a landscaping contractor, don't expect to work like one on your first project. What you learn on the job will make it easier as you go along. You'll encounter challenges but will find solutions. Don't be afraid to ask the experts and then listen to what they say. All you need is a willingness to try and a desire to learn.

And don't forget to take a little pride in what you accomplish with some good advice and a little old-fashioned elbow grease.

Support your local building inspector

Building codes are often confusing to the do-it-yourselfer, but they exist to enforce consistent methods of installation and, more important, to ensure the safety of your family. Sometimes the reason for code is common sense; other times the code may seem silly. However, you must follow codes, so find out what's required and do it from the start. This book is written to meet relevant national codes. But codes change, and local codes can sometimes be more stringent than their national cousins. Legally it's up to you to make sure the job you're doing meets code because the consequences can be serious. Aside from potential danger, an inspector can make you start over (which can get expensive), and you may not be able to sell your house until you fix the violation. Find out what local standards you need to meet and get some advice on how to best go about the job. Get a permit, do the job right, and sleep soundly at night.

Table of contents

Chapter 5: Landscaping walls

Chapter 6: Sheds

Chapter 7: Trellises & arbors

Chapter 8: Electrical

Chapter 9: Plumbing & drainage

Chapter 10: Concrete

CHAPTER 1

Outdoor design & planning

Outdoor spaces serve multiple purposes for you and your family. Well-designed patios and outdoor structures, such as fences, walls, and trellises, are all elements that enhance your landscape and improve your quality of life.

Patios provide spaces to entertain, to enjoy the garden and the view, and to provide safe play areas for children. Comfortable seating and convenient access to and from the house make them ideal retreat areas. Fences, walls, sheds, and trellises help define areas of your landscape and make both useful and aesthetic contributions to its design. Steps get you to and from landscape areas situated in different planes, making such transitions easy and attractive.

When carefully constructed of materials that are appropriate for your landscape, all these structures become accents and focal points, creating pleasant additions to your outdoor space. They are, in fact, outdoor rooms, and the process of designing them is much the same as for an indoor room.

This chapter provides information on the basics of design and planning, offering both design tips and installation examples for beautiful and functional additions.

You'll also discover how your choice of materials will enhance the overall impact of your design. Such choices are not merely aesthetic—they also hinge on questions of available space, the time you have, and your skill level.

Designing an outdoor structure is a process composed of many different parts. Using the concepts contained in this chapter, you'll find that unifying those parts and creating beautiful outdoor spaces is a process that's both fun and rewarding.

Contents

Consider aesthetics and practicality as you finalize your design.

Laying a patio or building any outdoor structure successfully evolves from careful consideration of several factors:

■ **How will the new structure fit the existing landscape?** Your home's surroundings should influence the choice of materials. For a formal look, consider a patio or wall with brick set in a traditional pattern, such as running bond or herringbone. For informal styles use natural stone set in random patterns or define an area with gravel or wood chips.

■ **Will the new structure be part of the public or private spaces surrounding your home?** Public

spaces are seen by passersby, and design choices will affect your neighborhood. If possible make choices that complement your neighbors' homes. Private spaces, such as backyards or areas enclosed by fences, offer opportunities to define a more personal style.

■ **Are you confident in your ability to handle both the design and installation of your project?** If you're not sure what you're looking for, consider getting design advice from a landscape designer or seek help from the lawn and garden department of your local home center. Installing an outdoor structure may involve working with heavy materials and can be labor intensive. Consider hiring out a portion or all of the labor.

Elements of patio design

Designing a patio requires familiarity with your landscape and a basic understanding of design principles. Together they will help you create an outdoor space that is not only beautiful and functional, but also long-lasting.

Installing a patio can be hard work. In many ways, however, coming up with a design that you will be happy with for years is even harder. Find inspiration wherever you can—in books and magazines, garden shows on television, your neighbors' yards, or displays in the garden department of home centers. Once you have some ideas about what you like, start looking at materials and get advice on the advantages and disadvantages of each, as well as the complexity of installation.

The following pages will introduce you to basic principles that will help you create a design and develop a plan to carry out to completion.

Form and function

A successful patio design is a perfect blend of form and function. It is attractive, comfortable, and well-fitted to its site. It is composed of materials that are in tune with the home and the surrounding landscape. And it is installed to be durable as well as easily maintained. If that sounds like a tall order, it is. Like any other major home improvement project, you can achieve your goals when you divide the work into manageable pieces and put the puzzle together one piece at a time.

▲ **Pavers work effectively** *in large spaces because of their uniform size and ease of maintenance. Shrubbery surrounding the patio defines boundaries and the entrance.*

▼ **The more accurately you map out your property** *the more successful your final design will be. Sketching on paper helps you think through the concept and will make installation easier.*

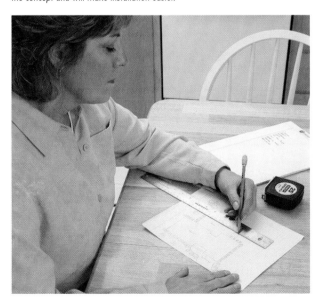

Putting the elements to use

In this chapter you'll learn how to get started. First you'll learn about the elements of design you'll need to create the right patio for you and your home. They include style, color and texture, pattern and form, scale and visual balance, unity, and variety. You already have some knowledge of these elements. You use them to analyze the objects you like around you every day. Being able to break down what appeals to you by using these elements will help you make wise design decisions.

Get it down on paper

Make a detailed sketch of your yard to scale, measuring as accurately as you can. Note the position of the house, front yard, backyard, driveway and sidewalks, other buildings, roads, trees, and such landscaping features as shrubbery and garden areas. Photocopy this sketch and use the copies to draft ideas about potential locations for the proposed patio.

With sketch in hand, find as many sources as possible for inspiration and ideas. Collect pictures and photographs of patios you like. Gather ideas and let them influence you as you finalize your own design.

Use resources in the garden area of your local home center, where knowledgeable associates and designers will give advice and answer questions. When you spend money to improve your home, foolish questions don't exist.

Elements of patio design (continued)

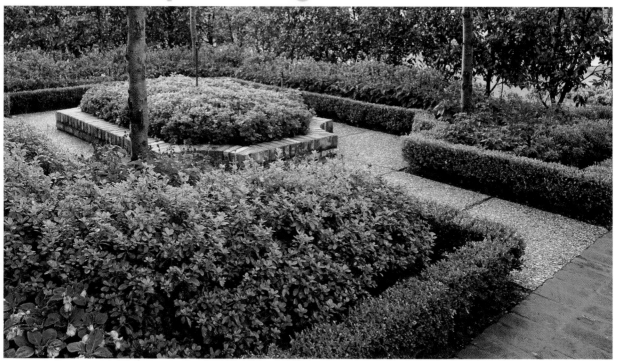

▲ **The simplicity of this patio** with a central planting space makes it a perfect setting for an abundant and immaculately styled garden.

Style

All design styles fall into two basic categories—formal and informal. Within the frame of formal and informal are motifs that can be defined as traditional and contemporary.

Formal and informal looks differ in how they achieve a sense of style with the use of materials, shapes, lines, and angles. Formal styles use formal geometry— straight lines, right angles, and strict geometric shapes. Bricks, pavers, and cut stone all fit well in a formal style. Formal designs also tend to have a symmetrical installation: When you draw a line down the middle of a formal patio, the sides are mirror images.

Informal designs are free-form, less dependent on geometry, and have pleasing curves and shapes that create asymmetrical balance between elements.

Traditional patio design attempts to control the environment with fountains, courtyards, and columns. Contemporary patios have more daring designs that use opposing materials and shapes, blending into the landscape to make a statement.

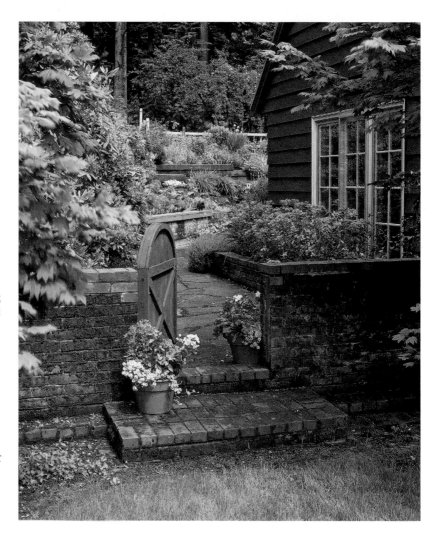

▶ **Brick walls and steps** and a rustic wooden gate enhance the country feeling of this backyard patio. Careful positioning of flowering containers welcomes visitors inside.

Color and texture

For your patio, choose colors that complement your home and that appear as part of the natural environment. Warm colors of stone and pavers tend to be red, rust, brown, yellow, beige, and orange. Cool tones include blue, black, and gray. Sand and mortar, which are used to fill joints, also add color to the patio. The green of grass and mosses that fill the joints of unsanded or unmortared paths offer color as well.

Texture is a matter of both design and safety. Polished materials such as stone or wood have smooth surfaces that can become slick when wet. Use them in enclosed spaces that are not subjected to the elements. The rougher textures of brick, pavers, and natural stone offer solid footing and a natural look. Concrete, the flattest stone surface, can be tinted and textured to make a dynamic design statement.

▲ *A concrete mold on a walkway* to simulate brick adds texture and shape to an otherwise uniform surface. Tinting the concrete adds color.

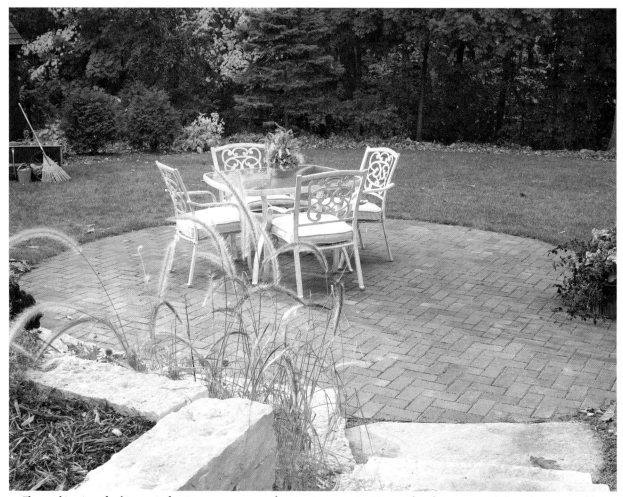

▲ *The combination of white patio furniture on a warm red patio creates an inviting outdoor living space.* The herringbone pattern of the patio emphasizes the variety of color in the pavers. Invisible edging between the patio and the lawn offers an uninterrupted connection between the two spaces.

Elements of patio design (continued)

▲ **A border of pavers along the edge of this walkway** enhances the herringbone layout and is a good example of how opposing patterns can create a sense of order. The border emphasizes the informal curving flow of the path.

Pattern and form

Pattern and form work together as dynamic patio design elements. Form refers to the shape of the individual materials that make up the surface of the patio or walkway. Shapes can be regular, such as brick or pavers, or irregular, such as natural stone.

Pattern refers to the arrangement in which the materials are placed. Rectangular pieces, such as brick or pavers, can be laid in a wide variety of patterns—running bond, basketweave, or herringbone, for example. These and other patterns are discussed in this book; you also can create patterns of your own. Patterns can be contained within borders to control visual movement in a space. Forms and patterns can be mixed to create visual interest. Consider mixing various shapes and colors of stone, for example, to create a dramatic pattern.

Natural stones have random shapes and are laid together in a free-form manner that creates a flowing, nongeometric design.

Scale and visual balance

Scale refers to how the size of the elements of a patio or the total installation relate to each other and to the overall design. Scale helps define the general feeling of a space.

With the proper use of scale, you can make small areas feel larger and large spaces more contained. The size, pattern, and type of the materials you choose for your patio help define scale. Large pieces of stone will emphasize the smallness of a modest space, while smaller stones will seem to fit more easily in the overall scale. Stones of the same size will offer an open and expansive feeling. Varying larger and smaller pieces, either in random pattern or as formal borders in a larger space, will draw attention to the surface and help contain it.

Two basic means achieve visual balance—symmetry and asymmetry. Symmetry occurs when forms of equal visual weight are arranged on each side of an imaginary centerline. Asymmetry creates balance by properly juxtaposing objects that vary in shape, size, and color. Walls or columns of equal height that frame the entrance to a patio create symmetry. A wall of shrubbery on one side of a patio and a stone wall on the other create an asymmetrical feeling although they can have equal visual weight.

◀ **The perfect symmetry of this patio,** with equally balanced elements on either side of an imaginary centerline, instantly creates a sense of formality and order.

Unity

As an element of design, unity means harmony. Harmony results in a unified interaction between each element of the design. Your patio should blend in with your home and the surrounding landscape in a harmonious and pleasing manner. In a unified environment, each element is unique but linked to everything else in terms of color, shape, line, and form. A formal 18th-century patio might be visually at odds with a contemporary home. On the other hand, a wood-chip walkway might seem out of place as the entrance to a formal stone patio.

Unity also rises out of elements that are arranged to lead the eye to a focal point—whether it be the furniture, a wishing well, or a fountain. A well-unified space exudes an inviting and comfortable feeling.

▶ **Rows of brick in this simply poured sidewalk** *echo the brick steps and link the sidewalk to the home's entrance level.*

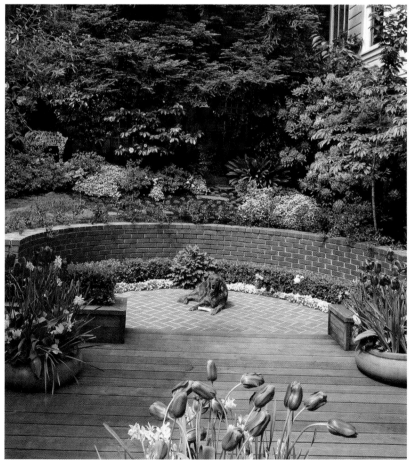

Variety

Variety is expressed by the use of different shapes, textures, or colors. A perfectly unified space can become predictable without a few elements that surprise and delight. A change in pattern, the addition of a border, interspersing different shapes of stone into an otherwise formal layout, creating a mosaic as a focal point—each adds variety to a unified design.

Alternating squares of different colored stones or using the same stone in different colors as a border both create variety. So does including a mix of shapes and textures in the pattern of a stone surface.

Proper use of variety allows the eye to continually relive the design and keeps it fresh over time.

◀ **Mixing various shapes, colors, and textures of pavers** *offers a means of achieving variety in design. This sunken patio uses three distinct pavers laid in different patterns to create a sense of flow and movement. The border of flowering plants at the base of the wall separates it from the patio and helps define the boundaries of the patio space.*

Practical considerations

Installation choices

There are three basic types of patio installation—soft-set, hard-bed, and wood. If properly installed, all are attractive and durable.

Soft-set installations are generally easier and faster for homeowners because they don't require a concrete foundation and the joints between the materials are filled with sand. The site is excavated and leveled, then a sand or gravel base is added and compacted. The materials are then laid on the base and the joints are filled with sand. Edging strips are often spiked in place around the perimeter to hold the bricks or pavers in place. Soft-set installations are more prone to shifting due to freeze/thaw cycles and require periodic maintenance. With proper care, however, they will last indefinitely.

Hard-bed installations will last a lifetime because they start with a concrete foundation on which paving materials are laid in a mortar base, and the joints are filled with mortar. The resulting patio is solid and resists shifting and fluctuations due to freeze/thaw cycles. Hard-bed installations are more labor intensive but require less maintenance over time.

Wooden structures in the form of boardwalks or raised platforms are attractive and, if well-maintained, long-lasting.

Siting patios and walkways

Some aspects of the landscape itself, as well as the terrain of your yard, will affect where you put your patio.

Access. No matter how perfectly a patio blends into the surrounding environment, it will receive limited use if access is restricted or difficult. A patio that serves as an outdoor entertaining space will be most effective located off easily accessible living spaces.

Stairs. Stairs transition from one level to another. If your patio is situated on ground that would make a walkway too steep for a straight run or require too many turns in a running path, consider steps or landings at various locations to ease the journey.

Slope. A patio entrance that is too steep or made of materials that become slippery when wet will limit enjoyment.

▲ *Simple concrete sidewalks are the most effective* especially when the path passes between two densely planted flower gardens as shown above. The simplicity of the pathway also helps focus attention on the ornately styled Victorian porch and home beyond.

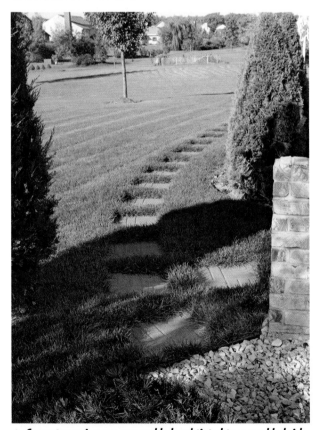

▲ *Concrete paving squares molded and tinted to resemble brick* are used to create a pathway around the side of this house. The sunken path marks a route commonly used by the homeowner's family and saves wear and tear on the lawn.

Locate starting points that are accessible from the house and that lead directly to an end point. Natural-feeling paths tend to follow the easiest course from the starting point to the end.

Drainage. Improper drainage can leave standing water on a patio, destroying your outdoor experience, the patio materials, and potentially the foundation of your home. Make sure that the patio slopes away from your home at a rate (approximately 1 inch for every 4 feet) that ensures runoff will be safely carried away.

Site a walkway so water flows toward a drainage system and not down the path. Gravel or wood chips can wash away on any surface, following the natural drainage of the terrain. Soft-set stone might be a better alternative.

The weather and patios

Successful patio design also needs to take climate and weather into consideration.

Sunlight and shade. Hot, bright sun bearing down on brick or stone can make a patio unusable. Too much shade can make it uncomfortable in cool weather. The ideal location for your patio is one that takes advantage of seasonal and daily changes. Orienting a patio toward the east will take advantage of morning light, but the patio will be cooler in the evening, making it a good site for those who enjoy dining outdoors.

West-facing patios will become quite bright and extremely warm in the afternoon unless properly shaded.

Southern sites will receive sun throughout the day and may also require additional shade during warm months. The sun will make the patio more useful during cooler months in areas with extreme climate shifts.

Northern sites receive far less sun and, consequently, will be shadier and cooler throughout the day.

Wind. The wind can either enhance the time you spend on your patio or limit its use. A gentle breeze is a pleasure, but areas with strong wind patterns require some sort of shelter. Select a location that will isolate your patio as much as possible. Patios are often partially or fully covered with roofs or retractable awnings, and some sides are enclosed with either solid walls or glass doors.

▲ *The gravel pathway through this garden* echoes the color and weathered texture of the bricks used on the house. Gravel is easy to install and maintain.

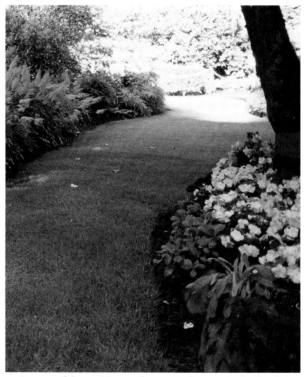

▲ *A successful transition can be as simple* as a strip of well-tended grass that connects two sections of a large yard to a patio. Create defining borders along the sides with a combination of flowering plants and shrubbery.

To attract or not to attract

The landscaping and flowers surrounding your patio are beautiful to look at, but they are also potential lunch for various members of the wildlife family, including squirrels, birds, deer, rabbits, and raccoons. Check with the garden department of your local home center for species of flowers and plants that are not favorites on their menus. However, birds can be delightful additions and enhance your outdoor pleasure. Attract birds with feeding stations placed near the site.

Practical considerations (continued)

Weather extremes. Rain and snow also are factors to consider solving with partial roofs or retractable awnings.

The style of your home, weather conditions, and the surrounding terrain are the best guides to the shape and position of your patio. Walk your property to look for patio sites and interesting routes for walkways to and from it. Great views can define a patio site, while the slope and flow of the land will offer insights into the siting of walkways.

Be aware of elements that would create unpleasant views from your patio, such as a neighbor's compost pile or rickety garage. If an unpleasant vista can't be concealed with fences, walls, or shrubbery, consider another site.

Defining patios

Where and how you locate your patio relative to your house will be determined by how you want to use it.

Attached. The majority of patios are attached in some way to the main dwelling, often with easy access from a family area or the kitchen. While one or more of the sides of an attached patio will probably follow the lines of the house, the area that extends into the yard offers the option of free-flowing lines.

Wraparound. Like wraparound porches on Victorian homes, wraparound patios offer access from more than one room of a home. Entrances can be accented or defined with short walls, planters, shrubbery, or lawn furniture. Wraparound patios tend to consume a great deal of area, and some ordinances will restrict patio size because of increased water runoff into sewer systems.

Detached. Detached patios should reflect the overall style and their surroundings, taking advantage of views that are not necessarily accessible from the area around your home. Detached patios can provide private, secluded settings. Provide access to a detached patio with a walkway that complements its design.

Courtyard. Courtyard patios are defined by the walls that surround them. They are good solutions for both rear and front areas of condos or townhouses. Walls, fences, or plantings can be added to create enclosed spaces. Contemporary homes often revolve around a centrally located courtyard patio that provides access from several points in the house and offers a secluded interior/outdoor space.

Defining walkways

Walkways are also generally categorized by their intended use.

Utilitarian walkways are designed to get you from one place to another easily and quickly. Although they can be constructed of a variety of materials, from the simplicity of concrete to elaborate paver or brick patterns, their function is to connect exterior spaces in a simple and straightforward manner. Utilitarian walkways should be as level and flat as possible to make movement as easy and efficient as possible. Therefore, they may require excavation and complex installation.

Free-form walkways are about the journey. Often they are sited to follow the natural contours that flow through the property or to simply define a path that has evolved naturally over time. If everyone takes the same route to the beach and the grass is showing signs of wear, it might be time to install stepping-stones or pavers. Consider benches or other seating stationed along the way to invite enjoyment of a particular view. Or concentrate garden elements, such as flowers or shrubs, in delightful spots to create new vistas.

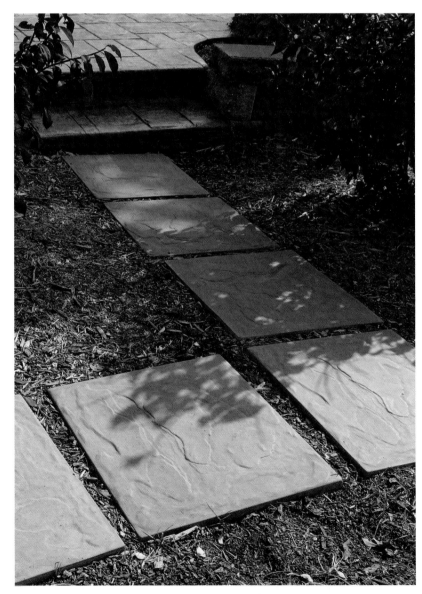

▶ **Form and function are combined effectively in this entrance walkway.**
Pavers make up the step and patio surface and slate tiles are laid to create the walkway. Combining elements creates focus and offers a visual reminder of the change in level.

Planning landscape structures

Retaining walls, fences, driveways, sidewalks, and pathways are the bones of the landscape or what contractors call the hardscape. These elements define the basic structure and many of the individual areas of your property. Once they are in place, you will begin to add landscaping details such as gardens, groupings of flowers and shrubbery, and structures that are primarily decorative, such as arbors and trellises. But first you must decide where the bones will go and how they will function.

Some of these elements may already be in place—driveways, for instance, or sidewalks, patios, and flower gardens. If so, your goals may be more specific than devising a plan for the entire landscape. You may want a retaining wall to protect an existing garden from runoff or to keep the side of the hill from ending up in your house.

A fence may help define the boundaries of your property, but it may also be needed to keep the deer from eating the vegetables.

If all you're looking for is security, a chain-link fence may be the answer, especially if the area you are protecting is on a private section of the property. In either case, as you make decisions about adding hardscape elements to your property, you should consider the differences between public and private spaces.

Public spaces

Public spaces are the areas of your property that are visible from the street—the front or sides of your home, the front yard, the driveway, and any paths or walkways that are in public view. Choices you make about public spaces will affect the entire neighborhood. Consider the impact on the neighborhood before you make a decision.

Private spaces

Private spaces are out of public view, but that doesn't mean they should be solely utilitarian. Private spaces such as back yards or patios should ideally be considered as another room in the house—inviting and comfortable for you and your family.

▲ *Retaining walls are good examples* of how form and function combine in a landscape design. A retaining wall adds variety and visual interest while keeping a hillside in place.

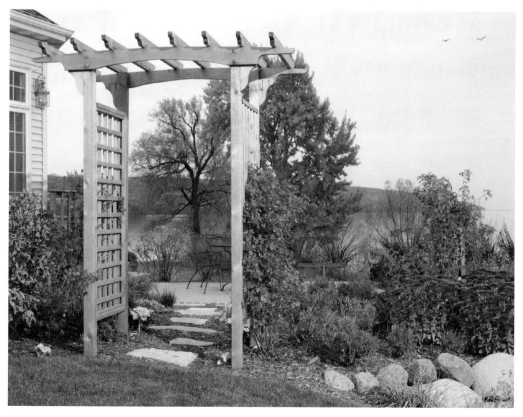

◄ *This graceful arbor* defines the entrance to a patio and provides a secure base for climbing plants. Choose a style of arbor that compliments the architecture of your home.

Planning landscape structures (continued)

Make a site map

Before you do anything you must have a plan. Maybe you already know where problem areas are, or maybe you have only a vague idea of the consequences of your design ideas. In either case, grab a long tape measure (100 feet), a pad, a pencil, and a helper and create a complete map of your property. Just as you would if you were designing a patio, include the boundaries and all fixed structures—the house, garage, and other buildings such as sheds. Chart the position of the driveway, sidewalks, patios, flower and vegetable gardens, groupings of shrubbery, trees, hedges, fences, and any other element or obstacle that may influence choices you will make.

Take your rough measurements and create a map in a scale that fits easily on a piece of paper. Make photocopies you can use to record ideas, and begin thinking about what you want to do. Spend some time walking your property, map in hand, so you can get a feeling for how your design will actually work when it's in place. This might be the time to consult a professional designer or, for a structural issue, a landscape contractor to review your ideas and make suggestions. They will usually do this for a fee, or if you hire them it will be part of the package.

Seek inspiration everywhere

Ideas come from many sources—books, magazines, friends, online, tours of finished landscapes that you like, garden shows on television, and in the garden departments of your local home center, to name a few. Research materials that suit the architecture of your home and are compatible with the surrounding landscape.

The ultimate goals

The ultimate goals in any landscape construction project are to solve problems, add functionality and beauty to your outdoor spaces, and equally important, to do so in a manner that creates a harmonious, unified result.

The more time you spend thinking and planning before you start digging, the less likely you'll want to pull the whole thing out and start over. Remember, you're going to live with your wall, fence, or arbor for a long time—be sure you're getting what you want.

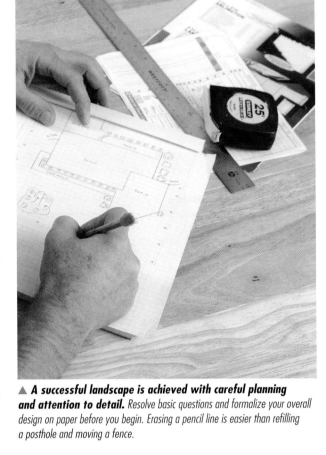

▲ **A successful landscape is achieved with careful planning and attention to detail.** *Resolve basic questions and formalize your overall design on paper before you begin. Erasing a pencil line is easier than refilling a posthole and moving a fence.*

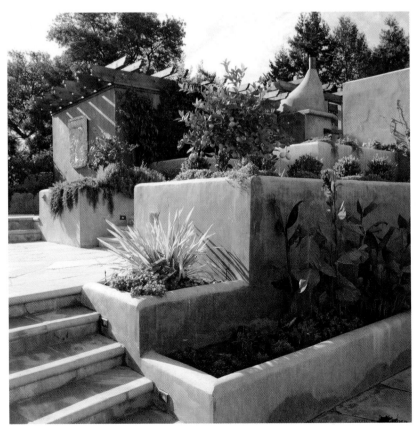

▶ **No matter how complex the design,** *landscape construction can be broken down into basic elements. Here the designer took advantage of a relatively steep hillside by combining stuccoed retaining walls and a series of stone terraces to create an inviting entrance to the outdoor living space situated at the top of the hill.*

Know the law

If you violate a local code or ordinance when you install any outdoor structure, and the local government discovers it, you'll have to alter your design or even its siting to comply. Saying, "Gee, I didn't know," won't get you very far with the inspector, and changes at the last minute can be costly. Factoring in the time involved in doing your project twice, determining what's acceptable before you begin is definitely worth the effort. Another issue to consider is whether deed restrictions that define the limits on what can be installed and what can't are in place in your neighborhood. Do your research before you begin work to ensure that you can enjoy your outdoor space in peace. Here are some issues to consider as you create your design:

Check building codes

Building codes exist to protect homeowners from potentially dangerous situations based on faulty construction methods and the use of unsafe materials. They're based on proven industry practices and are approved for safety and uniformity. Know and abide by local and national codes as you prepare and plan your project. Contact your local building inspector's office for codes that affect your home and property.

Research zoning ordinances

Zoning ordinances define how a piece of property can be used and how structures can be placed on it. For example, you usually won't be allowed to put up a gas station in the middle of a residential neighborhood even if it looks like the rest of the houses on the street. Residential zoning ordinances establish minimum setbacks from property lines, utility easements, and possibly size limits of a structure. Information will be available at your county clerk's office or your local government center.

Respect deed restrictions

Some communities have adopted deed restrictions in order to maintain control over local property values and architectural style. Restraints on the kind of outdoor structure you can build, including the style and the materials you choose, may exist. Some neighborhoods may have unspoken or informal restrictions on the kind of additions that can be installed to maintain the integrity of the neighborhood. While you may not be legally bound to follow these guidelines, it's not fun to be feuding with the neighbors. Take a good look around the area and talk to the neighbors before you install any outdoor addition.

Call before you dig

Utility and cable companies will visit your site and flag the position of underground lines. Call to have all utilities located before you dig. The placement of underground utility cables, such as electric, communication and telephone, and television, may affect the location of your patio, wall, or any landscape structure, even if the cables are buried deeper than you plan to excavate. Don't restrict access to them unless you're sure you'll never want to change. Sewer, water, and gas lines running to the house must also be considered.

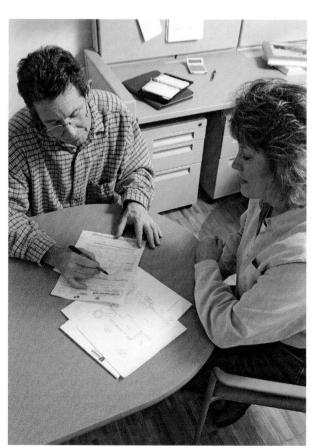

▲ **Once you've created your design,** review it with an inspector to make sure you're meeting necessary code and zoning requirements.

▲ **Know the location of buried lines** before you begin digging.

CHAPTER 2

Building patios

Patios are additional living spaces that offer comfortable areas to relax with family and friends or to spend a quiet moment of reflection. A patio that is properly sited, well-constructed, and easily accessible is a pleasure to use and will provide your family years of enjoyment.

Although most patios are situated adjacent to the home, a gathering space located in a secluded area somewhere else on the property and connected with a compatible pathway is a pleasing alternative.

Three basic patio options are available: soft-set, hard-bed, and wooden structures similar to decks but detached from the house.

Your choice of materials will depend on the landscape, climate conditions, terrain, and the style you seek to achieve.

As you design your patio, think about how the space will be used. If you entertain frequently, your patio should be large enough to accommodate a crowd and have plenty of comfortable seating and space for tables. Also consider making a place for a grill or outdoor kitchen. The patio should be easily accessible from the house, especially the kitchen.

In this chapter, you'll find information about some basic skills applicable to all patios, as well as more specific sections about constructing soft-set and hard-bed patios, brick, concrete, and other materials.

Contents

Working smart is easier than not

Building a patio, even a small one, is a large project. Once the design is in place, the materials need to be chosen, purchased, and transported to the site.

Here are some tips to help you get through the construction phase:

- **The project will probably take longer than you think,** even if everything goes smoothly. It's outdoor work, and you're at the mercy of the weather. Working in the rain is no fun, and concrete needs to be poured within a prescribed temperature range to cure properly. Allot yourself reasonably long work periods. A full day's work on Saturday and Sunday will get you a lot further than an hour here and there.

- **Don't push yourself.** These projects involve heavy lifting. Work slowly and take breaks as you need them. Consider wearing a back brace to support your back.

- **Wear the proper clothing and protective gear** while you're working. Long-sleeved shirts and gloves are essential when handling concrete or cutting pressure-treated lumber. Also recommended for these tasks are a respirator, safety goggles, and a hat.

- **If you're using power tools with which you're unfamiliar,** such as a masonry saw or a power auger, get instructions on safe use, and practice with the tool until you're comfortable.

- **Recruit a friend** or hire some labor to help with the heaviest lifting.

- **Work methodically** and review the overall project as you go to eliminate surprises and mistakes.

Building patios tool kit

3-pound sledgehammer	Circular saw	Darby	Hand tamper	Power tamper	Sponge
Bead blaster	Cold chisel	Drysaw	Handsaw	Putty knives	Straightedge
Brick chisel	Concave jointer	Dust mask	Levels	Rubber gloves	Trowels
Broom	Concrete edger	Framing square	Mattock	Rubber mallet	Wetsaw

Caulk gun	Concrete float	Garden rake	Paintbrush	Safety glasses	Wheelbarrow

Chalkline	Control jointer	Grout bag	Plumb bob	Shovel and spade	Work gloves

Pavers

Pavers are different from bricks, though the two often look alike. Bricks are made of clay that has been baked in a kiln until it's hard. Pavers are made of concrete that has been molded into shape. They come in countless shapes and are dyed several different earth tones.

Pavers are the perfect do-it-yourself product. No mortar is needed between the joints, and pavers are laid over a sand-and-gravel bed rather than the concrete pad that mortar requires. In place of mortar, sand is swept into the joints. Most pavers have small tabs on their sides so that the space between them is uniform. Many patterns are available in both full and half pavers, minimizing (but not eliminating) the need to cut them to fit.

A paver patio is really a four-part system: The pavers sit on a 1½- to 2-inch layer of sand, which sits on a 4-inch layer of gravel for drainage. The whole formation is held in place by edging, which prevents the pavers from shifting away from each other.

▲ **The beauty of pavers is their uniformity of size** and consistency of shape, which make installing patios quicker and easier than when using bricks or natural stone.

Sand and gravel

You'll want two kinds of sand for a paver patio. Most of the sand you'll need is bedding sand. The pavers sit on a layer of bedding sand, which has sharp edges that won't compact once you bed and compact the pavers into it. The sand that usually goes between individual pavers is mason's sand. It's finer and easier to sweep into the spaces between pavers.

The gravel that goes under the sand should be a gravel approved for use as a bed under asphalt paving. It's a mixture of different sizes of stones that compact and stay compacted so that once in place, the pavers don't settle. (For more on gravel, see page 24.)

Most projects require a large number of pavers, and large numbers of pavers are heavy. You'll also be working with large quantities of sand and gravel. Plan to have the pavers, sand, and gravel delivered. If the job is big, consider hiring someone to excavate and perhaps to put in the sand-and-gravel bed.

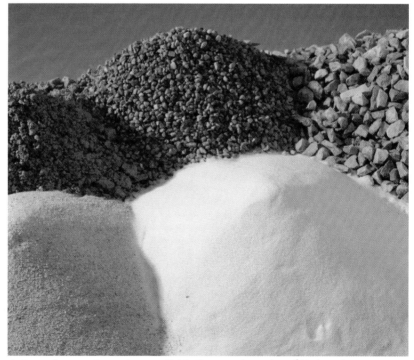

▲ **Several types of gravel are available; four are shown here:** ¾-inch gravel (top right) is stones that fit through a ¾-inch grid; ¾-inch with fines (top left) is the same gravel with finer stones mixed in. In between the two gravels is a bagged all-purpose gravel. Underneath patios, use whichever gravel the local road department approves for an asphalt bed. Bedding sand (lower left) compacts nicely underneath bricks and pavers. Mason's sand (lower right) is finer and is used to fill the spaces between bricks and pavers.

Stone

Stone comes in a variety of shapes, sizes, and textures. Those used in outdoor construction include limestone, sandstone, slate, fieldstone, and granite. Any stone will work, and no one stone is better than another, though some are more expensive. In addition to types, stone is sold with different surfaces: Flagstone has been split into sheets or tiles from thicker slabs; ashlar has been milled into faceted or roughly rectangular blocks; rubble is stone as it's found in the field or as it's blasted out of the quarry.

Limestone is a soft stone that is usually gray or reddish brown. Soft is a relative term in reference to stone. Limestone is plenty hard: The homes that German farmers in Pennsylvania made from limestone in the 1700s are strong and sturdy to this day. Limestone is a sedimentary stone, made of countless shells that formed in huge layers on the sea bottom. You'll often find a small fossil embedded in the surface.

Sandstone is formed by a combination of fine quartz particles (sand) bound together by a cementlike calcium carbonate. It is softer than limestone but strong enough to be used in walls and walkways. Colors range from beige to brown and even bluish gray or greenish. Generally speaking, the darker the color, the more durable the stone.

Slate is clay or shale that has been compressed by the earth above it to form a smooth, abrasion-resistant rock that was once used for blackboards and shingles. Slate splits easily into sheets, making it perfect for patios. You can buy it in sheets up to 2 inches thick for use as a flagstone walk or in thinner, smaller tiles for use on patios.

Granite is a volcanic rock packed with particles of quartz. It's the hardest and heaviest of the stones listed here. When milled and highly polished, it is extremely shiny, and it is used for countertops and monuments. In outdoor construction it's seldom given such a shiny finish. It's often milled into semirectangular blocks, however, and used in walls. In areas where granite is common, it is also used in curbs and sidewalks.

Fieldstone characteristics derive from the field in which it was found. Its chief quality is not its geologic content but its shape. In areas that were washed by rivers or glaciers, it may be smooth; in other areas, the surface and edges may be more angular. It's well suited to making walls but is seldom flat enough for patios.

Gravel. Anything between a ¼-inch and a 3-inch stone can be included in a gravel mix. (A ¼-inch stone will pass through a sieve with ¼-inch squares; a 3-inch stone will pass through a sieve with 3-inch squares.) What you want depends on what you're doing with the gravel, and you need plans to be well thought out.

▲ **Stone is used either as it's found or after it has been milled.** Ashlar is a rectangular stone milled for use in walls. Stone tiles (top left), are best used indoors.

For a gravel walk, get between ¾- and 1½-inch stones. Larger stones can be difficult to walk on; smaller stones can mush around underfoot like dry sand on the beach and make walking uncomfortable. The grains of gravel are usually jagged, making it easy to compact but uncomfortable to walk on barefoot. River gravel has been washed smooth over time and is more comfortable to walk on barefoot. It does not settle into a smooth surface the way other gravel does, however, and it also may tend to compact underfoot.

If you need gravel for a drainage bed under brick, pavers, or concrete, ask for a gravel mix that's approved for use under asphalt pavement. The mix varies from area to area and sometimes from town to town. In simplest terms, the specifications will be something like this: 70 percent of the stones must pass through a ¾-inch grid, 50 percent must pass through a ⅜-inch grid, 35 percent must pass through a No. 4 (12 mm) grid, and so on. Don't worry about the specifics. Just ask for the gravel that the local road department uses.

▶ **Gravel is available in a range of sizes** to accommodate a variety of needs. Gravel walkways are usually composed of stones between ¾ and 1½ inches.

Brick

To the eye, one brick looks much like the next. Sizes vary, some have holes in them, and some are yellow instead of red. If the differences stopped there, you could be sure that whatever you bought would work wherever you put it.

There are, however, two broad categories of bricks—those used as pavers and those used in walls. In addition, each type comes in three categories (SX, MX, and NX), each designed for a different degree of exposure to the weather. All of these bricks look similar, so make sure you tell your retailer what you need.

Paver bricks. You don't want to use a wall brick as a paver: Paver bricks are tougher and designed to resist abrasion. Type III pavers are for home and patio use; Type II is for high-traffic areas, such as stores; Type I is for driveways.

Wall bricks. If only a wall brick were just a wall brick, life would be good. But once again you have choices. A face brick has a uniform surface; a hollow brick is a face brick that has large holes running from top to bottom, making it lighter to work with and easier to manufacture. Either is fine for walls. (The exposed top row of a wall will require a face brick.) A building brick has a less than perfect surface and is designed for uses where it won't be seen or in designs featuring rustic accents.

Weather ratings. Pavers, face bricks, and building bricks all come in three grades based on what their exposure to the weather extremes will be.

SX bricks are for exterior use where the brick is in contact with the ground and may freeze during the winter. MX bricks are for exterior use where freezing does not occur during the winter. NX bricks are for interior use, where the structure itself shelters the brick from freezing.

What to get. What you need depends on where you are and what you're doing. If you're building a patio in Maine, you'll want an SX Type III paver. In Arizona you'll want MX Type III pavers. Wall builders in the North will want SX face or hollow bricks; in the South, look for MX face or hollow bricks.

▲ *Bricks come in several sizes, shapes, and colors. Bricks with holes in them are meant for wall construction and are unsuitable for patios. Not all solid bricks, however, are meant for patios. Get a brick called a paver brick, which stands up to wear. Ask for an SX paver brick if you live in an area with severe winters. MX pavers are fine for use in areas with milder winters.*

Edging

Edging is an important part of any paver installation, or any patio material set on a sand-and-gravel bed. The paving, sand, and gravel combine to give you a firm, well-drained surface, but without edging, the surface wouldn't stay put. Use, abuse, and weather slowly would push the surface apart. Eventually the pavers would have enough room to tip and tilt, and in a few years the surface would resemble rubble more than a patio. Edging locks patio paving in place, and the sand between the joints combines with the pavers to make a rigid, durable surface.

Edgers fall into two groups: those that are self-anchoring and those that need extra anchoring. Avoid garden edging designed to keep grass away from flower beds; it is not strong enough to contain the materials used in a patio.

▲ Some types of edging are strong enough that all you need to do is anchor them into the ground. **Landscape ties,** for example, need only be held in place with landscape spikes. Use ties that are a minimum of 6×6; smaller lumber is likely to warp. **Bricks** can be put on end in a trench alongside the patio to hold the pavers in place. Commercially-made polyethylene is one of the most popular edgings. Use **rigid polyethylene** for straight runs and **flexible polyethylene** for curves. (Flexible polyethylene is not available in all regions. Consult with your local home improvement center for a suitable alternative.) Both are designed so that when installed, they come only partway up the side of the paver. When you finish the patio and fill in around it, the edging is hidden underground, held in place by metal stakes.

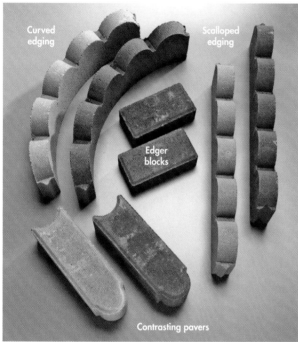

▲ To stay put, precast concrete edging needs to be as tall as the combined thickness of the sand, gravel, and paver. Use shorter edging like that shown here to dress up the edges of your patio, but anchor it firmly with another edging. Polyethylene is a good choice. **Scalloped edging** is designed primarily for use around gardens but can also be used along sidewalks. **Curved edging** can be used along the edge of a curved patio if the radius is right. **Edger blocks** can be laid in a straight line or curve. **Contrasting pavers,** or pavers put at a right angle to those in the pattern, look like edging but are really a pattern variation that needs to be anchored by some other type of edging material.

▶ Some types of edging work well in the lawn but aren't strong enough to hold pavers in place. Among the edgings that won't work with pavers are edgings like **black polyethylene** which is designed to be an edging between the lawn and garden.

Mortar, concrete, and grout

Concrete, grout, and mortar look much the same, do much the same thing, and come in bags that look pretty much the same. Concrete is used to make concrete patios or the base for a mortared installation; mortar holds bricks to each other or to a concrete pad; and grout is put between tiles once the patio is laid. Here's a quick look at what goes into each:

Cement is made by grinding a naturally occurring limestone that contains clay. Portland cement is made by baking cement at 2,700 degrees then pulverizing it. Neither cement is strong enough on its own, and both are mixed with some combination of sand, gravel, and lime to make concrete, mortar, and grout.

Concrete is made of cement and fine and coarse aggregates; the fine aggregate is sand and the course aggregate is gravel.

Although concrete is hard, as anyone who has ever scraped a knee knows, it's also brittle. A metal mesh usually runs through the middle of the pad to knit it together if it should ever crack.

Mortar is a mixture of cement, lime, and sand. Masons often refer to it as an adhesive, but it doesn't come in a bottle or can, and it is neither a glue nor a mastic. It's a cement-based mixture designed to adhere a brick, stone, or paver to a similar object or to a concrete pad.

Grout is a 1:1 mixture of cement and sand; it also may contain lime. It's finer than mortar to create a smooth surface between tiles on a floor or wall. Although similar in content to mortar, the proportions are different, and grout would not work well if you tried to use it as mortar.

▲ **Cement** is a naturally occurring limestone that is the basis for most of the mixes used in masonry. **Concrete** is a mixture of cement, sand, and gravel. **Grout** is made of equal parts of cement and sand and is used to seal between tiles. **Mortar** is a mixture of cement, lime, and sand and is used to hold brick, stone, and tile in place.

Cutting brick, tile, pavers, and stone

Skill level:	Time to complete:	Materials: Tile	Tools: Wetsaw or drysaw, chisels, square, pencil, grease

Skill level:
★ ☆ ☆ ☆

Time to complete:
Experienced 1 min.
Handy 1 min.
Novice 1 min.

Materials: Tile

Tools: Wetsaw or drysaw, chisels, square, pencil, grease pencil, 3-pound sledgehammer, dust mask, safety glasses, ear protection

Patio edges often have to be cut to fit. You can make the cuts several ways, and the technique is similar regardless of the material. The most inexpensive tool (called a wetsaw) looks like a mini-tablesaw that cuts with a diamond blade bathed in water.

Most pros use a heavier-duty saw with a top-mounted blade, which looks somewhat like a power miter saw. It, too, cuts with a diamond blade that is bathed in water, but it is more powerful than the small version.

Many patterns—such as a running bond—start or end each row with a half-brick. A lot of cutting is involved, and often the best way is to make the cuts after the bricks are laid, using a tool called variously a drysaw, cutoff saw, or quicksaw. This saw can be run dry or wet depending on the material you're cutting. When cutting pavers or brick, the drysaw (which is how it will be referred to in this book) is used without water to prevent staining the surface material. Whatever name you choose to call it, the tool looks like a large circular saw but is usually gasoline powered. Guide it along the intended edge of a patio after all the bricks, pavers, or stones are in place.

Power tools make quick work, but hand tools have their place too. For example, you'll need brick chisels and hammers when cutting stone pieces that may not fit on a power tool and that look best with a slightly ragged edge. Each cutting method is covered on the following pages.

A drysaw speeds installation of patios. Unless you're doing a very large installation, it's probably a good idea to rent the tool. A drysaw operates much like a circular saw, but you need to take some lessons on safety and operation from the rental store and practice with the tool before you start using it for your project.

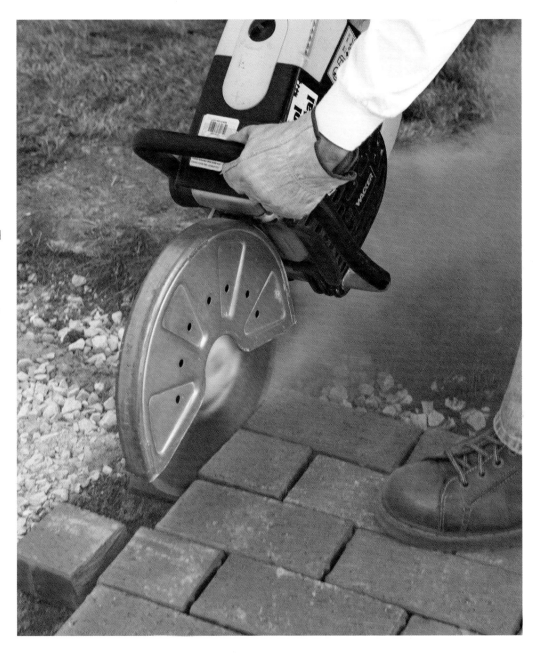

Using a tile saw with a bottom-mounted blade

1 Lay out the cut. Saws with a bottom-mounted blade have a limited cutting depth, approximately 1 inch deep, and are generally designed for cutting tile only. Draw a layout line with a grease pencil, marking where you want to make the cut. Subtract the width of the joint from the overall size of the tile.

2 Make straight cuts. Put water in the tub below the saw. Set the fence so that the layout line on the tile is lined up with the blade. Push the tile into the blade with slow, steady pressure.

3 Cut angles. A miter gauge cuts angles. Loosen the knob and turn the miter gauge until the layout line aligns with the blade. Put the brick, paver, or tile against the angle guide or miter gauge. Tighten the knob to lock in the angle and push the miter gauge forward to cut with slow, steady pressure.

Cutting with a saw with a top-mounted blade

1 Lay out the cut. An overhead saw makes deep cuts, as much as 3¾ inches. The saws for brick and tile are different, largely because of cutting depth; make sure you rent the one you need. Whichever you have, fill the tub with water. Put the brick, paver, or tile in place and draw a layout line to mark the cut. Subtract the width of the joint from the overall size of the tile.

2 Make straight cuts. With the saw off, put the paver, tile, or brick against the lip on the sliding table. Ease the table toward the blade. Align layout line with the blade and fasten the rip guide next to it. Turn on the saw and push gently and slowly to make the cut.

3 Cut angles. Align the layout line with the blade. Put the miter gauge attachment on the table, set it to match the angle of the brick, paver, or tile, and lock it in place against the material you're cutting. Turn on the saw and feed the table toward the blade to make the cut.

Cutting pavers with a drysaw

Use a drysaw to cut straight lines or curves after the paving surface is in place. Because you can cut more than one brick, tile, or paver at a time, it's efficient, and as long as you can follow your layout line, you're less likely to make small measurement mistakes.

The saw raises an incredible amount of dust. Make sure to wear a dust mask, close windows in the house, and move cars and items that can be damaged with dust away from the job site. Because of the dust raised, make sure you're cutting to a layout line that is highly visible—bright chalk works well. Spray the line with lacquer before you cut so the dust doesn't erase it as you work. Sweeping and compacting sand into the joints will remove both the lacquer and the chalk.

1 Lay out the edge on the ground. Snap a line on the ground showing where the paving will end. Lay pavers or brick up to the line. If a paver needs to be trimmed to fit, put it in place without cutting it.

2 Lay out the edge on the pavers. Putting the pavers in place covers the layout line, so snap the cut on top of the pavers. Spray lacquer on the line to keep it intact as you work.

3 Angle the saw slightly. Most drysaws can be run wet or dry. Run it dry so that the combination of dust and water doesn't stain the surface of your work. Start the saw and hold it at a slight angle so the bottom of the paver or brick will be cut a bit shorter than the top.

4 Make a first cut. Guide the saw along the layout line, cutting into the surface. Don't try to make the full cut in a single pass. Let the saw cut as deep as it will go on its own. Cut along the length of the entire line.

5 Make a second cut. Guide the saw along the first cut, holding it at the same angle and letting it cut as deep as it wants to go. Repeat until you cut entirely through the brick or paver.

Cutting brick or flagstone by hand

1 Lay out the cut. Mark the cut line on the material with a pencil or scratch it on the surface with a nail. Make sure the size of the line takes the space between the flagstone or brick into account.

2 Score along the top face. Guide a chisel along the layout line, striking the chisel, moving it, and striking again. To make sure the line is straight, strike the first blow at one edge of the material and the second blow at the opposite edge. Alternate back and forth until the line meets in the middle.

3 Score the sides. Draw lines on the edges of the material, showing where you want to cut it. Use a straightedge to guide the layout lines. Angle the lines slightly, a bit smaller at the bottom than at the top of the material so it will fit snugly against the edging. Score along the lines.

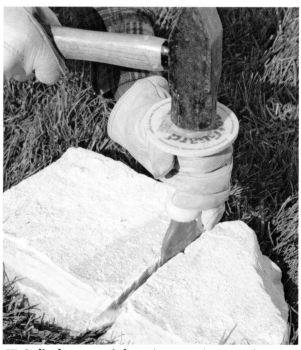

4 Score the back. Draw a line on the back, connecting the lines you drew on the sides. Score the line the same way you scored the line on the front of the material.

5 Split the material. Put the material you're splitting on the ground, which will absorb the shock. Put the chisel in a score line and strike with a 3-pound sledge. Move the chisel along the line, striking until you split the material.

Removing old concrete

Skill level:	**Time to complete:**		**Materials:** None	**Tools:** Jackhammer with chipping and cutting bits, safety glasses, dust respirator, work gloves, ear protection, wheelbarrow
★★★☆☆	Experienced	5 hrs.		
	Handy	6.5 hrs.		
	Novice	8 hrs.		

If an existing concrete pad is sound, you can often put a brick, stone, or paver patio on it. But cracks, holes, flaking, or an uneven surface are problems that will eventually work their way through a new surface. A new crack will eventually reappear right above the old one no matter how much repair work you do in advance.

To correct problems between control joints—lines cut through the surface at regular intervals when the concrete is wet—you may be able to limit the concrete taken out to the area between the joints. If not you'll have to remove the entire surface.

Removing concrete is just plain hard work, and you may want to hire someone to do it. To do it yourself, rent a jackhammer, at the very least, and have a plan to get rid of the broken-up material.

Jackhammers are simple to operate, and electric models don't require the expense, noise, and bother of big compressors required for pneumatic hammers. Technically, jackhammers are demolition hammers. (Chipping hammers are smaller and designed for work on walls and concrete ceilings. Rotary hammers are smaller yet and are little more than drills that twist as they pound.) Rent a 40- to 50-pound electric demolition hammer and let the weight of the tool do the work.

The biggest problem you're likely to face in removing concrete is the wire mesh that runs midway through the slab, which is put in as the concrete is poured in order to tie the concrete together. You'll have to cut through it with the hammer in order to break the concrete into manageable chunks.

▼ **A jackhammer makes short work of demolishing a concrete pad,** but it's noisy and provides a real workout. Take the time to learn how to use it and follow all safety instructions.

⊘ SAFETY ALERT
CUTTING CONCRETE SAFELY

A jackhammer is designed to demolish material, so treat it with respect. Wear a dust mask to keep the dust out of your lungs and goggles to protect your eyes. Wear ear protection to shield your ears from the noise.

Don't operate a jackhammer in the rain or on a wet surface. Not only is the surface slippery, the water may damage the tool or cause an electrical shock. Make sure you will not be cutting through live electrical wires or conduit.

Use only an extension cord rated for outdoor use and one that is rated to handle the amperage drawn by the hammer. Plug the machine into a properly installed GFCI to lessen the possibility of shock.

☑ WORK SMART
GETTING RID OF THE DEBRIS

Concrete is heavy and results in a lot of weight and jagged pieces when it's broken up. Use a jackhammer to break the concrete into manageable chunks that won't strain your back when you load them into a wheelbarrow or pickup. Be reasonable when loading a wheelbarrow or pickup and do not overload it.

The old concrete can be used as landfill if you need to fill a hole or build up a berm. It also can be disposed of at a municipal waste facility for a fee. Check with local codes to make sure you are aware of the restrictions on disposal in your community.

Operating a jackhammer

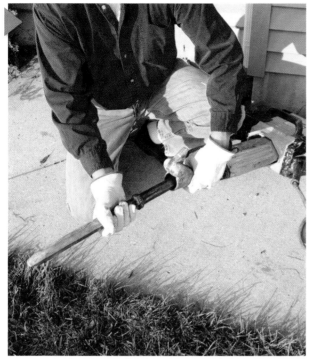

1 Insert the tip in the hammer. Make sure the hammer is unplugged. Swing the retaining arm back toward the handle. Put the cold chisel tool or the cutting point in the socket and swing the arm back in place. The cutting point usually works best when pounding through an old surface.

2 Set the chisel on the surface. Plug in the tool and put the cutting edge near an edge or near the damaged area of the surface you want to remove. Most tools have a "no load" striking safety that keeps the hammer from running unless it's on a surface. You may have to push down firmly on the tool to start its motion.

3 Break up the concrete. Let the weight of the tool do the work—trying to push on it will wear you out without getting the job done any sooner. Move across the surface, breaking it and creating new cracks as you go. Follow the cracks with the jackhammer to break up the concrete more quickly. About 2 inches into the pad, you'll run into the wire reinforcing mesh. Cut through it with the jackhammer, switching to a wider tip, if necessary, to break the concrete into manageable pieces.

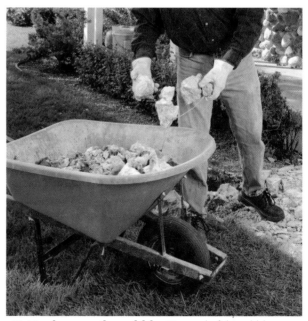

4 Haul away the rubble. Disposal of the rubble will be your hardest job. You can use it as clean fill somewhere in your lot or have it hauled away on a truck. Load the rubble into a wheelbarrow and haul away.

Laying out a site with batterboards

Skill level:	**Time to complete:**	**Materials:** 2×4s, 2×2s, mason's line, 10d (3-inch) common nails, masking tape, powdered chalk	**Tools:** Tape measure, circular saw, hammer, plumb bob, 3-pound sledgehammer, line level, garden hose, safety glasses
★★★☆☆	Experienced `1 hr.` Handy `1.5 hrs.` Novice `2 hrs.`		

Laying out straight edges

Batterboards and mason's line make handy tools for fool-proof layout. By sliding the line along the horizontal bar of the batterboard, you'll be able to bring the sides of the site into square. Batterboards are positioned 1 or 2 feet outside the area for the patio so they don't get in the way of excavation.

When you work with batterboards, make sure they're level with each other. If they are, the lines are also level, and you can measure down from them to determine the slope of the ground and the slope of the surface that results from digging.

 Build the batterboards. Build two batterboards for each corner you lay out. Cut points on two 2-foot-long 2×4s. Then nail a 2×4 crosspiece between them a couple of inches below the top.

 Position the batterboards. Drive a pair of batterboards at right angles to each other a foot or so beyond where you estimate each corner will be.

---

3 **When you lay out a patio next to a house,** drive a nail into the siding to mark one corner of the excavation. If the patio will follow the length of the house, drive a second nail in the siding at the opposite end, positioning it with a line level so that it's level with the first nail.

4 **Tie mason's line to the crosspieces.** Run line between the batterboards to lay out the approximate sides of the excavation. If the patio butts against the house, run line to the nails you drove into the siding.

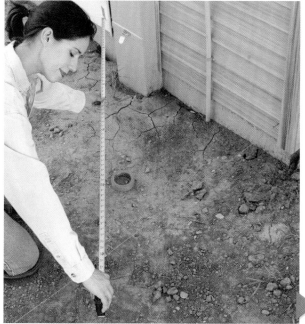

5 **Level the lines.** Hook a line level onto a line. Level the line by driving a batterboard farther into the ground. Repeat on adjacent sides until all four sides are level with each other.

6 **Square a corner.** At one of the corners formed by the lines (use the house as one of the sides, if possible), check for square with a 3-4-5 triangle: Mark one line 3 feet from the corner with a piece of tape. Mark the adjacent line 4 feet from the corner. The corner is square when the distance between pieces of tape is 5 feet. Slide the line along the batterboard, if necessary, until the lines are square.

7 **Square a neighboring corner.** Square neighboring corners with a 3-4-5 triangle. If you have to reposition one of the lines, move one other than the one that was used to create the first corner.

8 **Lay out the remaining side.** Mark the desired length of the patio on the two parallel lines with masking tape. Run mason's line between the batterboards so the line crosses the pieces of tape on the two sides. Check both corners for square with a 3-4-5 triangle.

9 **Double-check for square.** Check the entire layout for square by measuring diagonally across the area from opposite corners. The length of the diagonals should be equal. If not, repeat Steps 6 to 8.

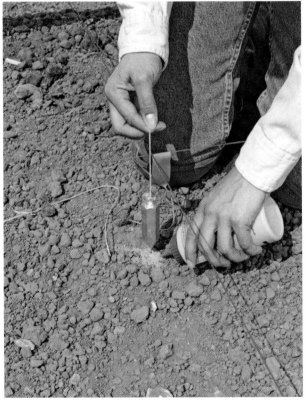

10 **Mark the corners on the ground.** Once all the corners are square, drop a plumb bob from each and use chalk to mark the patio corners on the ground. Mark the batterboards to show the location of the strings.

Laying out a slope

Drainage in the form of a slight slope away from the home is essential to keep water away from the foundation of the house and to keep standing water from building up on the patio surface. Patios should slope away from the house a minimum of ⅛ inch every foot. Very wet climates require a slope of ¼ inch every foot. Check local building codes to find out what's required where you live.

Lay out the slope with stakes and mason's line to help you excavate at the right slope. Start with a level batterboard layout, as explained on pages 34–35. Then drive stakes, stretch lines between them below the lines on the batterboards, and measure to create the proper slope.

Once you lay out the slope, drive in more stakes at 6-foot intervals. Stretch line between them to lay out a grid that you can use to check the excavation depth.

1 Drive two stakes at each corner. Drive a 2×2 stake between each batterboard and the chalk mark at the patio corner just outside the stringline. Use a plumb bob to make sure the lines still cross over the chalk mark.

2 Stretch line between the stakes. Run mason's line between the stakes. For now, the lines on the stakes should be parallel to and below the lines on the batterboards. Measure down from the line on the batterboards and slide the line up and down the stakes until the distance between the lines is the same at each corner. Use a plumb bob to make sure the lines cross over the chalk mark.

3 Lower the lines. To lay out the slope of the patio, lower the lines on the stakes farthest from the house by a minimum of ⅛ inch per foot. (Check to see what's required locally.) With a ⅛-inch slope, the outside edge of an 8-foot patio would be 1 inch lower than the edge at the house, for example. Mark the desired drop distance on the corner stakes farthest from the house, then lower the lines to the mark.

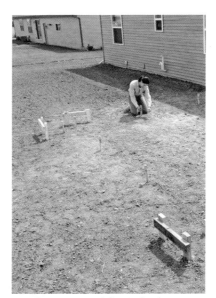

4 Create a grid. Mark where the lines meet the batterboards and remove the lines, leaving the batterboards. Drive stakes every 4 feet along the patio outline. Run lines between the stakes to lay out the grid. The grid will make it easy for you to excavate the area to the proper depth later by providing frequent reference points.

5 Measure as you dig. Dig trenches along edges and grid lines. Measure to make sure the bottom of the trench and the lines are the same distance apart along the entire length of each. Then excavate between the trenches, using a level and a 2×4 to make sure the patio is level from side to side.

Using a builder's level

Skill level:	**Time to complete:**		**Materials:** Batterboards, stakes, mason's line	**Tools:** Builder's level, leveling rod, tape measure, plumb bob, tape
★☆☆☆	Experienced	20 min.		
	Handy	30 min.		
	Novice	1 hr.		

Landscapers—who have bigger projects, and more of them, than average do-it-yourselfers—lay out the shape and grade of their projects with a builder's level. It's a simple tool to master, and it's accurate, quick, and available at most rental centers. Unless you lay out work frequently, renting is more economical than buying.

A builder's level is often called a transit, even though these are two different tools. On a builder's level, the scope turns from side to side. A transit has a scope that can be angled up and down as well as turned from side to side—a feature you don't need for patios. A builder's level is also less expensive to rent and less confusing to use.

The design of a builder's level varies by manufacturer and model. One level may have three wheels that level the scope; another may have four wheels. The small level used to level the tripod may be a tube or it may be a small circle. Make sure you get an owner's manual when you rent so you know what and how to adjust it. Once you get started, the use of the level is the same no matter which one you have.

It pays to be accurate when you lay out the slope of a patio. A builder's level is a quick and easy way to ensure accuracy.

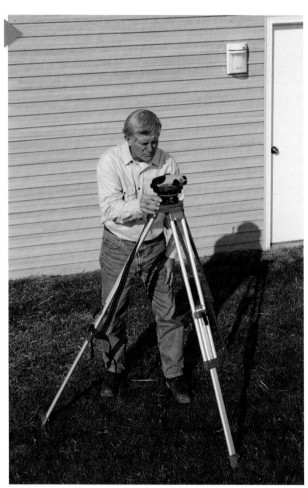

1 Set up the builder's level. Put the level near the middle of the excavation. Level both the tripod and the scope.

2 Drive stakes around the excavation. Drive stakes every 4 feet about 12 inches beyond the edge of the excavation.

3 **Find the high end.** Have your helper stand next to a stake at the high end of the excavation while holding the leveling rod or rule. Turn the scope so you can see the rod, and note the measurement in the crosshairs. Repeat at the other stakes at the high end. The stake with the smallest measurement is the highest stake.

4 **Mark the first stake.** Have your helper stand next to the high stake with the telescoping leveling rod. Mark the rod with a piece of tape to indicate the reading in the crosshairs. Then make a mark on the high stake to show where it meets the 6-inch line on the leveling rod.

5 **Mark the second stake.** Have two helpers stand at another stake along the high side of the excavation and lift the stick off the ground until the tape marker is in the crosshairs. Mark the stake at the 6-inch mark. The marks on the two stakes are now at the same level. Repeat for all the stakes at the high end.

6 **Mark the low end.** Without moving the tape marker, repeat the process for the stakes at the lower end. These marks are level with each other and those at the high end. Measure down at the low end by the amount you want the patio to slope ($1/8$ to $1/4$ inch per foot). Make a second mark, as shown in the inset. Snap chalklines between this mark and the mark on the corresponding stake at the upper end, and mark any stakes in between.

Excavating

Skill level: ★★★☆☆

Time to complete:
Experienced 5 hrs.
Handy 7 hrs.
Novice 9 hrs.

Materials: 2×4s, mason's line, powdered chalk

Tools: Garden edger, sod lifter, mattock, spade, shovel, 4-foot level, straightedge, gloves

Excavation simply means digging. Use the right tools to make the job as efficient as possible. A garden edger quickly cuts a straight line through sod. A shovel with a curved blade is for digging; don't confuse it with a spade, which has a flat back and is designed to cut the edge of a trench. To remove sod, break up the surface with a mattock, which looks like a pick. If your patio is large, you might want to use a sod lifter, which has a curved handle and will save you much bending. When excavating, make sure you dig out all roots and organic material, which tend to decay, collapse, and undermine your patio. The depth you dig depends on the type of patio: 8 to 9 inches for bricks or pavers set on a sand-and-gravel base, 8 to 9 inches for a concrete slab patio, and 11 to 12 inches for bricks or stones set in mortar on a concrete slab.

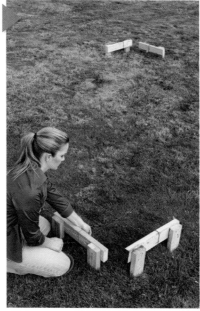

1 Lay out the shape. Set up batterboards and use mason's line to lay out the outline of the patio. Use powdered chalk to mark the outline of the installation.

2 Step on the edger to cut straight into the sod. Work your way along the layout lines. To remove wide areas of sod, cut 1-foot strips with the edger. Lift the sod with a shovel or sod remover. Hold the blade at a low angle. Put weight on the top of the tool to cut between the soil and the roots and pry it loose.

⚠ **SAFETY ALERT**
DEPTH CHECK

Check for any septic system, gas, water, phone, cable, and electrical lines before digging.

☑ **WORK SMART**
HOW TO USE A MATTOCK

In small areas, rolling up the sod can be a quick way to remove it. If you're excavating for a large patio, however, it may be easier to break up the sod and toss it in the wheelbarrow with the rest of the dirt. The tool to use for this job is a flattened pick called a mattock. Let the tool do the work. Swing the blade up, bring it downward with some force but loosen your grip slightly, and let it hit the ground under its own steam. You'll get "mattock elbow" if you try to slam the tool into the ground. Medically speaking, it's the same as tennis elbow, and it hurts.

Checking the slope

Patios should slope away from the house so they don't channel rain toward the foundation. The typical slope is 1/8 inch to 1/4 inch per foot, depending on rainfall; ask your local building officials for the required slope in your area. Check the slope by propping a wedge underneath one end of a level.

If the slope should be 1/4 inch per foot, for example, the wedge would be 3 × 1/4 or 3/4 inch thick on a 3-foot level. It would be 4 × 1/4 or 1 inch thick on a 4-foot level.

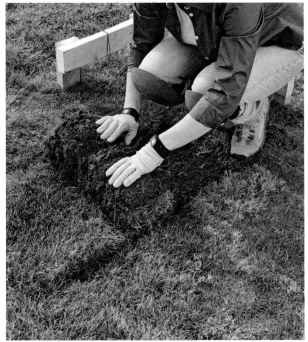

3 **Remove the sod from the excavation.** Roll the sod and remove it from the area to be excavated. Put at least some of it in a cool, shady place and use it to patch the lawn when you finish the project.

4 **Dig a trench.** Work along the layout lines, measuring down from them to dig a trench to the desired depth of the excavation. Usually the excavation slopes as it runs away from the house and is level from side to side. The directions for individual projects later in this chapter state the proper slope. Dig the trenches at the recommended slope.

5 **Check with a level.** Rest a level on a straightedge and check to see if the trench is level. If the excavation is supposed to slope for drainage, put a wedge between the straightedge and the level equal to the desired slope over the length of the level.

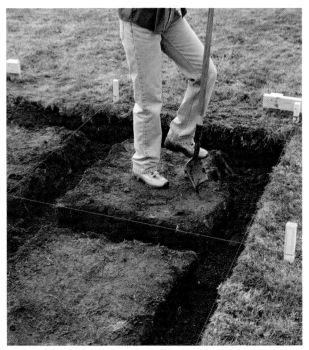

6 **Dig between the trenches.** Large excavations, such as those for patios, will have a grid of layout lines, and you should dig a properly sloped trench under each one. Once you have, dig out the space between the trenches. Smooth by pulling a 2×4 along the surface and check with a level, as in Step 5. Regrade as needed and compact.

Laying a running bond pattern

▲ **Laying bricks is similar to laying pavers,** except you need to pay more attention to alignment. A running bond is one of the simplest patterns to create. Every second row begins with a half brick, offsetting the joints from row to row.

1 Stretch a guideline. Put a brick at the beginning and end of the first course. Stretch a line along the edges of the brick as a guide, anchoring the line with another brick, as shown.

2 Lay rows of bricks. Lay a row of bricks or pavers. If they have no tab on the edges to space them, cut thin pieces of plywood to use as spacers. Embed the bricks in the sand with a rubber mallet. Start the next row with a half brick to stagger the joints. Alternate, starting one row with a full brick and the next with a half brick. Check for high or low spots with a 2x4 and add sand or tap bricks in place as necessary.

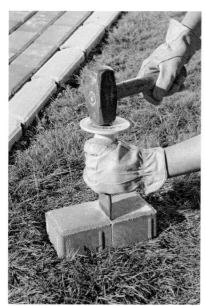

3 Trim bricks to fit. To cut a brick, score a line around the entire brick with a brick chisel and a 3-pound sledgehammer. Position the brick chisel in the scored line, then snap off the cut with a sharp blow of the hammer. **Always wear safety goggles and work gloves when cutting brick or pavers.**

4 Fill the joints with sand. Once all the bricks are laid, sweep a layer of fine sand, often sold as mason's sand, over the surface with a broom or stiff brush to pack the joints between the bricks.

5 Compact the surface. Compact the entire surface with a power tamper. Some manufacturers recommend that you spray the surface with water to wash and fill the sand into the joints.

Laying a basket-weave pattern

▲ **Basket-weave patterns** require no cutting if you plan the borders correctly. Start in the middle of an edge and lay three short rows to create a stepped pyramid. Once the rows are laid, work diagonally, filling in the steps until you cover the surface.

1 Snap a line down the middle. Lay out the patio, put the edge restraints in place, and install and level the sand bed. Snap a chalkline down the center of the sand bed.

2 Begin layout at the center line. Put the first brick in place against the edging, with the long edge on the centerline. Make sure it's square. Lay six bricks on each side of the line in the pattern shown, alternating the orientation of each pair.

3 Lay the second row. Begin the second row before you finish the first. Starting at the centerline, place the bricks following the pattern, laying only four bricks on each side of the line, making sure that the orientation of each pair is perpendicular to the bricks in the first row.

4 Lay the third row. Install two bricks on each side of the line to create a stepped pyramid pattern. From now on you'll lay bricks in the steps, which will keep the bricks aligned and square.

5 Follow the pattern. Start at the edge restraints and nestle two bricks in the corner created by the restraints and the bricks already laid. Work your way up the stepped sides of the pyramid on each side. Continue laying in a stepped pattern to lay the entire surface. Cut end pavers as needed to fit against the restraints.

Laying a herringbone pattern

▲ **Herringbone is fancier than running bond** but no harder to lay. It is, however, more time-consuming because so many bricks need to be cut. The finished effect is eye-catching, and many do-it-yourselfers feel the result is well worth the trouble. Measure to make sure you get the right size of brick: The true (rather than the nominal) length of the brick must be twice the true width for the pattern to work.

1 Start in a corner. Lay out the patio site with batterboards or a builder's level. (See pages 34 and 38.) Set a trial run along each edge to make sure the bricks or pavers fit and adjust the borders if necessary. Starting at one corner, lay a pair of full bricks at right angles.

2 Continue along the edge with half pavers or bricks. Install half bricks next to the full pavers in the corners, as shown. Spread piles of pavers along the path so you don't have to make trips back and forth as you lay the pattern.

3 Lay perpendicular bricks. Lay a leg of full-length bricks or pavers at right angles to each other in a stepped pattern, as shown. Once a leg is properly laid, bed the bricks in the sand with a tap from a rubber mallet.

4 End the first leg and start the next. End the first leg along the perimeter with a half brick. Then lay another stepped leg of full bricks, alternating their long and short sides at right angles to each other.

5 Continue laying stepped legs, finishing each end of every other leg at the perimeter with a half brick. After the patio is laid, sweep sand in between the bricks. Then compact the patio with a power tamper to embed the bricks and spread the sand between the joints.

Laying a diagonal herringbone pattern

▲ *Diagonal herringbone* is a more complicated pattern to lay. It involves cutting numerous bricks or pavers to fit. Lay the pattern using full bricks, then make all the cuts to fill in at the edges. Measure carefully for the location of the starter row and check your work constantly as you proceed.

1 Lay a small sample. Lay nine pavers as shown. To make sure the layout is square, draw a line at a 45-degree angle across one brick, as shown, and connect the corners of the other bricks in a straight line. Measure the distance between the two lines. Stretch a mason's line this distance from the edge.

2 Lay the first four bricks. Make sure the line you stretched in Step 1 is parallel to the edge restraints; reposition if necessary. Lay two bricks, as shown, so that the outside corner of one and the inside corner of the other fall along the line. Lay two more and make sure they are square.

3 Continue the starter rows. Snug two bricks up against the first bricks, aligning the corners as in Step 2. Follow the line all the way across the surface you're covering.

4 Lay single rows. The next row and all subsequent rows are single rows. Align them by tucking the second brick of the row in place. Next lay the first brick of the row, then lay the remaining bricks in the row.

5 Check against a straightedge. Lay two rows, then stretch a line across the surface. The corners of each block should just touch the line. If not, adjust the bricks so that they do. Continue laying rows and checking the alignment until the surface is covered with whole bricks. Cut bricks to fill in the spaces at the edges of the pattern.

Laying octagonal pavers

▲ **Octagonal pavers are really key shapes.** A square extends from the octagon. These are difficult pavers to lay, and laying them involves much trimming. To fit them, use the open-field method, in which you put in the edge restraints on two sides and cut the pavers to fit them. On the other two sides, lay all the stones, cut a straight line in them while they're on the ground, then install the restraints against the pavers. Brick pavers are often installed between the pavers and the edge restraints as a border.

1 Lay out cuts on the first two pavers. Put edging on two adjacent sides of the patio and mark the other sides with layout lines. Some manufacturers make half pavers that simplify trimming. If you can't get them, lay out cuts on two pavers. To mark the first cut, lay a straightedge along the side of the square extension and draw a line across the octagon. Put the straightedge on the second paver so that it connects the bottom chamfers of the pavers, and draw a line.

2 Put the pavers in the corner. Cut the pavers along the layout lines. Put them next to each other in the corner of the installation.

3 Lay out and cut the second row. From now on all the pavers will be laid in a diagonal direction across the site. Trim the first paver of the second row and put it in place. Lay full pavers next, working diagonally across the patio.

4 Lay the third row. Begin the third row with a trimmed paver and work diagonally to the other edge. Trim the last paver to fit. Continue laying diagonal rows until you have filled the patio and reach the layout lines along the other side. You should have no empty spaces along the layout lines, and parts of some pavers will extend across them.

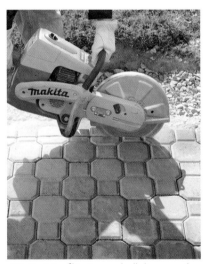

5 Cut to fit. Snap chalk lines on the surface of the pavers to mark the edges of the paved surface. Cut along the lines with a drysaw. Remove the scraps and install the border, if any. Then install the edge restraints. Using a drysaw to cut bricks or pavers takes a little practice. Take some trial runs to get the hang of it before you make cuts on your pavers.

Laying multiweave pavers

Multiweave pavers have zigzag edges. The pavers nestle perfectly against one another, making installation easier; however, they can be hard to check against layout lines, and the shape requires some extra cutting. Most manufacturers sell half pavers that you can use instead of cutting your own. It's worth figuring out how many you'll need.

Any pattern that will work for rectangular pavers will work for multiweave pavers, and once installed the zig-zag edges make the pattern appear more intricate than it actually is.

Because of all the cutting involved, multiweave patterns are a perfect candidate for the open-field method: Install edging on two adjacent sides and lay the pavers so that each one either meets or goes past your layout lines. Rent a drysaw with a diamond blade, snap new layout lines, and cut along them with the saw.

▲ **Running bond.** *Laying this pattern will be simple if you put a border on the edges perpendicular to the long side of the bricks. Once you have, start the pattern with one of the half pavers sold separately with most multiweave patterns. Then lay full bricks against the border, completing the first row. Install the second brick of the second row, then cut the first brick to fit.*

▲ **Basket weave.** *Like basket weave with other bricks, the trick to successful layout is to plan so that the total size of the patio is an exact multiple of the paver size. Measure the overall size, which includes the face of the brick and the tabs along the side that keep the pavers a constant distance apart.*

▲ **Alternate basket-weave pattern.** *This is another pattern in which the patio should be a multiple of the size of the paver. If it's anything less, you'll have to do a lot of trimming to get the blocks to fit along the edge.*

▲ **Diagonal herringbone** *is another candidate for the open-field method, in which you put in only two adjoining edge restraints. (If you put in all four restraints at the outset, expect to cut at odd angles to get the pavers to fit.) To lay an open-field patio, start pavers at the restraints. Lay the entire surface, continuing up to the lines marking the unrestrained edges. Then cut along the lines using a drysaw and install the edge restraints.*

Laying a paver patio

Skill level:	Time to complete:		**Materials:** Batterboards and mason's line, powdered chalk, tape, spray paint, gravel, bedding sand, joint sand, landscape fabric, interlocking pavers, edging, clear lacquer.	**Tools:** Tape measure, line level or water level, plumb bob, straightedge, spade, shovel, garden rake, rubber mallet, power tamper, level, broom, 3-pound sledgehammer, plywood-and-2×4 screed, paver splitter, wetsaw or drysaw, work gloves, safety glasses, dust mask, ear protection
★★★☆☆	Experienced	20 hrs.		
	Handy	26 hrs.		
	Novice	39 hrs.		

The design of patio pavers is a brilliant one. Even beginning do-it-yourselfers can master laying pavers without mastering the techniques of mixing and pouring concrete. And because no concrete is involved, you can start one day and finish another. Most pavers even simplify the job of spacing them correctly—they come with tabs molded on their sides to separate them at a consistent distance.

Here's how it works: The pavers lie on a 5½- to 6-inch bed of sand and gravel. The bottom 4 inches is gravel to provide drainage. The top 1½ to 2 inches is bedding sand that helps hold the pavers in place once they're compacted into it. Finer sand, sprinkled between the pavers, keeps them from shifting. Edging around the outside of the patio holds the pavers in place.

Because no system is foolproof, pay attention to details. Lay out the site using the techniques shown on pages 34-39, sloping it away from the house at a rate of ⅛ to ¼ inch per foot to keep water from working its way into the house. Check local codes to see what slope your conditions require.

Make sure you compact the gravel in 2-inch layers. If you don't, the top will be hard but the surface beneath it will be soft. It will shift, creating ripples in your patio. Use the right sand in the right places and make sure the edging you use is designed for pavers, not gardens. Garden edging isn't strong enough. If you take more than a day to lay the patio, cover the bed with tarps between work times to retain consistent moisture content throughout the entire bed.

▲ **Because pavers are cast, they are uniform in size, thickness, and color.**
This uniformity makes them easier to install than brick, which can sometimes vary in size and shape. Paver patios are extremely durable and require very little maintenance.

Installing the edging and sand bed

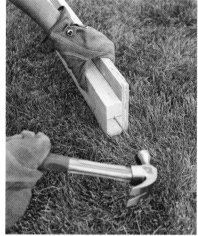

1 Install edging. Use a house wall as the edge restraint for one side of the patio. After you build the gravel base, Put edging along one of the adjoining sides. (You'll put in the rest of the edging after the pavers are installed.) Use the layout lines as a guide for both the proper location and slope of the pavers. Use edging designed for pavers rather than garden edging, and follow the manufacturer's directions. The plastic edging shown is held in place by landscape spikes driven into the compacted gravel.

2 Put down bedding sand. Shovel bedding sand on top of the gravel to create a layer about 1½ to 2 inches deep. Rake the bedding sand smooth.

3 Make a screed. A screed is a straightedge, usually a piece of wood, that you pull along the sand to smooth it. Have a home center or lumberyard cut a straight piece of ¾-inch plywood 8 feet long and about 3 inches wide. Reinforce it by screwing a 2×4 to the back. Drive a nail in each end of the 2×4 so the distance between the nail and an edge of the plywood is the thickness of a paver.

4 Adjust the sloped lines. Remove all the lines perpendicular to the slope except the one at the edge. Remove every second sloped line so there are lines at the edges of the patio and every 8 feet in between. Slide the sloped lines down the stakes. Move each line an equal distance until it is at the same level as the intended top of the patio.

5 Screed. Work with a helper to smooth the sand by guiding the nails along the top of the mason's lines. Use the lines as a guide only and be careful not to move them by pushing down on them with the screed. Have a second helper add sand to the low spots and remove sand that builds up in front of the screed. Repeat until the surface is smooth. After you screed the sand, screed it again, starting at the end where you finished and working in the opposite direction across the patio.

BUYER'S GUIDE

$ SAND, UP CLOSE AND PERSONAL

Sand comes in varying sizes, shapes, and degrees of hardness, not all of which work well under pavers. When buying sand for the bed, ask for bedding sand. You'll get coarse, hard sand with symmetrical particles and sharp edges. Stay away from limestone screenings, which are often touted as a substitute for bedding sand. Limestone is too soft and will dissolve from moisture and abrasion, eventually creating a wavy surface on your patio.

After you've laid the pavers, you'll fill the cracks between them to keep them from rocking. Bedding sand, however, is too coarse to readily fill the cracks. Use either concrete sand or mason's sand for the job. Mason's sand, which is finer, works best.

Laying a paver patio (continued)

Laying the pavers

1 **Stretch guidelines.** Lay a sample row of pavers on each side of the patio and stretch lines to mark the ends of the rows. Remove the pavers and use the lines as a reference while laying the pavers to make sure you are laying them in straight lines.

2 **Lay the first paver.** This patio, which is a running bond pattern, begins by putting the first paver in a corner of the patio. Exactly where the first paver goes depends on the pattern you use. (See pages 42–47 for more information.)

3 **Lay the second paver.** Cut a paver in half and put it next to the first one. Depending on the pattern, you may be able to cut pavers in place or wait until the end and cut most of the partial pavers at once. The running bond pattern requires a half paver. Cut it with a wetsaw, drysaw, or paver splitter.

SAFETY ALERT
CUTTING PAVERS

Wear ear protection, safety glasses, and a dust mask when cutting pavers.

WORK SMART
CLICK IT

Many pavers have built-in spacer tabs for positioning. If yours don't, use the click-it method. Hold the paver by its top edges about an inch or so off the ground and bring it against its neighbor just hard enough to make a clicking sound but not hard enough to displace it. Drop the paver into place at the sound, and you'll get the proper spacing.

4 **Finish laying the first row.** Lay the rest of the row, alternating full pavers and half pavers for running bond. (To lay other patterns, see the directions on pages 42–47.)

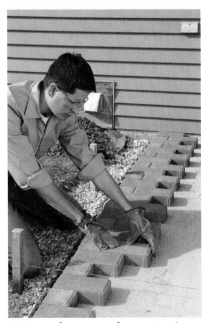

5 **Lay the second row.** Lay the row according to the pattern you're using. For running bond, this row and all but the last row are composed of full pavers.

6 Check the pattern alignment. Lay pavers, checking them against the staked lines as you go. Periodically stretch a line, as shown, to check that the ends of the pavers align. Make corrections as necessary while laying the pavers.

7 Continue laying past the edges of the patio. Continue laying pavers as called for by the pattern to the edges of the patio. If a brick is too long, lay it anyway and save your cutting until you've laid the entire patio.

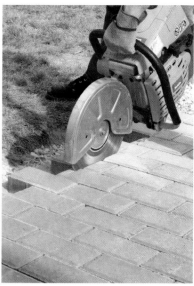

8 Cut the pavers on the ground. Snap a chalkline where the edge of the patio should be and spray it with a clear lacquer to keep it from blowing off while you work. Cut along the line with a drysaw and remove the scraps. Compacting the joint sand will rub off the lacquer and the chalk line.

9 Install the edging. Put edging along the side of the patio you just cut and along the bottom edge of the patio. Drive landscape spikes through the holes to fasten plastic edging. If you use 4x4s, drill holes for the spikes first. If you use 2x4s, put them in place, drive stakes behind them, and nail the stakes to them.

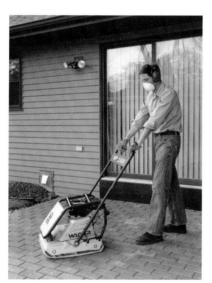

10 Compact the surface. For stability the pavers must be compressed into the bedding sand. Using a power tamper, compact the edges first, then the middle. Repeat, compacting in passes perpendicular to the first ones. Keep an eye out for pavers that crack during compacting. As you work, mark any cracked pavers with a permanent marker to make finding them again easier. Remove and replace the damaged pieces and run the power tamper over them.

11 Spread and sweep sand across the patio. Spread mason's sand across the pavers and sweep it into the spaces between them. Mason's sand is fine and works its way easily into the cracks.

Run the power tamper again over the patio, first along the edges, then down the middle. Have a helper sweep sand to refill the joints, and compact again. Keep sweeping and compacting until the joints are full. Shovel soil into the edges of the excavation to cover the edging, and plant the soil with grass or flowers.

Laying bricks on a sand-and-gravel base

Skill level:
★ ★ ★ ☆ ☆

Time to complete:
Experienced 8 hrs.
Handy 10 hrs.
Novice 12 hrs.

Materials: Bricks, bedding and mason's sand, gravel, landscape spikes, landscape fabric, edging

Tools: Mason's line, rubber mallet, framing square, level, 3-pound sledgehammer, brick chisel, brush or broom, power tamper, garden hose, safety glasses, work gloves, knee pads, dust mask, ear protection

A base of sand over gravel supports concrete bricks as well as it supports concrete pavers. The bed for brick, however, is slightly different: The landscape fabric goes over the stone rather than under it.

Use a paver brick (as opposed to a building brick) that is rated for outdoor use. Use SW brick in areas that freeze and MW brick in areas that don't.

Paver bricks come in various sizes. Each is smaller than its given size by the thickness of a mortar joint. Measure the paver you intend to use and design the length and width of your patio accordingly.

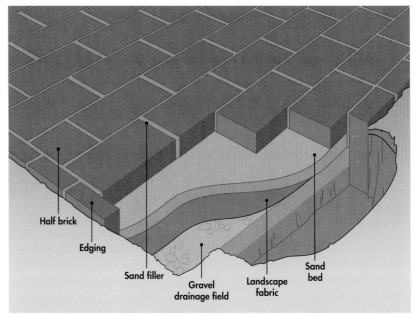

Half brick

Edging

Sand filler

Gravel drainage field

Landscape fabric

Sand bed

A brick patio begins with a 4-inch layer of stones, which provide drainage. A layer of sand provides a smooth bed for the bricks. Make sure you use a paver brick rated for outdoor use. Fill joints between bricks with sand to help lock them in place.

Lay bricks

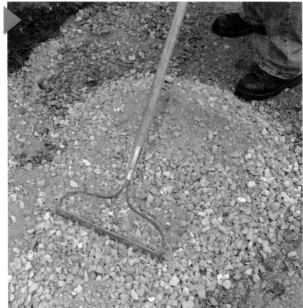

1 Lay a gravel bed. Lay out and dig a bed that is 5½ inches deep plus the thickness of a brick, sloping the bed ¼ inch per foot away from the house. Compact the soil with a power tamper. Spread a 2-inch layer of gravel, and compact. Add and compact gravel in 2-inch layers or less until the bed is 4 inches deep. The bed is firm enough when you can't drive a spike into it with anything less than a 3-pound sledgehammer.

2 Install landscape fabric, a sand bed, and edging. Spread a layer of landscape fabric on the gravel to keep the sand from filtering into the gravel. Overlap rows of fabric by 12 to 18 inches. Install edging, anchoring it as directed by the manufacturer. Spread a 1½- to 2-inch layer of sand and flatten it with a screed.

3 Lay a border. The finished patio will look best if you lay a row of bricks around the edges. Lay the bricks lengthwise against the edging. Plan so you won't have to trim any bricks to width while laying the final row.

4 Lay the first row. Start laying the bricks from one corner, spacing them 1/8 inch apart or less. On a large patio, run a mason's line across the patio to mark the edge of the bricks.

5 Bed the bricks. Use a rubber mallet to tap the bricks into place on the sand bed. Use a level to make sure the bricks are the same height as the edging. If a brick is too high, remove some sand from under it. If a brick is too low, use extra sand to fill the depression.

6 Continue laying the pattern. On the running bond pattern used here, the first brick of every other row is a half brick. Lay out the cut for the half brick and cut several in advance so you can work without pausing to cut. Lay them as you go. Herringbone and other patterns require even more cutting.

7 Check for flat. As you lay rows, keep checking the patio surface for high and low spots by putting a straight 2×4 or a level across the bricks. Seat high spots with a tap from the rubber mallet. Add sand to shore up low spots. Continue laying bricks as described in Steps 4–6.

8 Seat the bricks. Pass over the patio with a power tamper. Then pour fine sand—sold as mason's sand—across the patio and sweep it into the joints between bricks. Tamp, sweep more sand, and repeat until all joints are filled.

Laying a curved edge

Skill level:	Time to complete:		**Materials:** Gravel, sand, edging, pavers, landscape spikes, clear lacquer, powdered chalk	**Tools:** Mason's line, garden hose or PVC pipe to lay out curve, tape measure, drysaw, power tamper, 3-pound sledgehammer, shovel, rake, knee pads, gloves, safety glasses, dust mask, hearing protection
★★★☆☆	Experienced	Variable		
	Handy	Variable		
	Novice	Variable		

Even though bricks and pavers are rectangular and tape measures are straight, your patio can have curves and angles.

After you've laid a patio, you can use a handheld portable masonry saw to shape the edges.

Before laying the patio, however, lay out the curve on the ground using one of the techniques described below.

Lay the patio as you normally would, setting the bricks right up to or just past the layout line. Cut the edge to shape and install the edge restraints as the final step.

Curved edges break up the square lines of a patio and add a little drama to a geometrical layout. Curves can follow a prescribed arc, as shown here, or undulate in a more free-form manner.

 ## Options for laying out curves

PVC pipe is a low-tech tool. Hold the center of the pipe over the spot on the ground that will be the center of the curve. Have two helpers grab the ends and flex the pipe until it reaches the ends of the curve. It won't necessarily be a perfect arc, but it will be a smooth curve that connects the critical points along the edge of the patio.

A garden hose is the perfect tool to form curves. Lay the hose on the ground in whatever shape you like, keeping the curves gentle. The smallest curve a drysaw can cut is on about a 4-foot radius. Pick several key spots in the curve and measure their distance from each of the straight edges. You'll use the measurements later to re-create the curve.

1 Install edge restraints on two adjoining straight sides. The curve may be the focal point, but the work begins on the straight sides. After you excavate for the patio and fill and level the foundation, put in edge restraints along two adjoining straight sides. Check that they're square using the 3-4-5 triangle method. (See page 35.)

2 Lay out the curve (one method). Lay out the curve with a compass made of mason's line, a landscape spike, and a squeeze bottle of powdered chalk. Using the compass will give you a perfect arc—each point on the curve will be the same distance from the center of the patio.

Options. Other methods require you to mark the ground in a separate step. You can sprinkle chalk or flour along the pipe or hose to mark the ground. Gardeners like to lower the pH of the ground by marking it with lime. You can also buy marker spray paint, which comes in a can designed to be held upside down. It works well, but expect to get some on the hose.

3 Lay the pavers. Start in a corner of the patio and lay pavers as you ordinarily would. Snap a few reference lines across the surface before you begin so you know if the pavers are staying in a straight line.

4 Continue past the edge. Don't try to cut the pavers to match the curve. Lay pavers so they either reach the layout or go just past it, as the pattern dictates. In a couple of steps, you will cut the curve while the pavers are on the ground.

5 Lay out the curve again. Your work has covered up the layout line, which you'll need to cut the curve. Lay out the curve the way you did before and mark it in pencil, which gives you a more distinct cut line.

Laying a curved edge (continued)

6 Spray with lacquer. Spray a clear lacquer over the layout line so it won't rub off before you finish cutting. The lacquer will wear off with use and when you compact the pavers into the sand bed.

7 Cut with a drysaw. Rent a drysaw with a diamond blade. If the saw has a hose connection for running water to cool the blade, don't use it. Run the saw dry so the water and paver residue don't stain the surface. The saw creates a lot of dust, so wear safety glasses and a mask. Avoid working when the wind will blow the dust through house windows or onto cars.

8 Install flexible restraint. After you cut the curve, put edge restraints around it immediately. Get flexible restraints and bend them to the shape of the curve, one short section at a time.

9 Spread sand and compact. Spread sand across the surface of the pavers and compact it with a power tamper to fill the spaces between the pavers.

Including a fire pit or decorative opening

Skill level: ★ ★ ★ ★ ★

Time to complete:
Experienced — Variable
Handy — Variable
Novice — Variable

Materials: Batterboards and mason's line, powdered chalk, tape, spray paint, gravel, bedding sand, mason's sand, landscape fabric, interlocking pavers, edging

Tools: Tape measure, line level or water level, plumb bob, straightedge, spade, shovel, garden rake, rubber mallet, power tamper, level, broom, 3-pound sledgehammer, plywood-and-2×4 screed, paver splitter, wetsaw or drysaw, work gloves, safety goggles, dust mask

The opening in this detached patio is for a center fire ring, but openings in patios can serve a number of functions and can be placed wherever you choose to put them. Consider adding flower boxes or low shrubbery in the corners or enclosing a tree to make it part of the patio space.

You'll need to know some special techniques for creating openings. Patio construction with a central opening such as this one starts at the opening and is laid out toward the edges. Edge restraints at the opening help keep the pavers in a straight line, but no restraints are in place along the edge of the patio at this point. They will be added when the patio is finished and trimmed. Ensuring that the pavers come out in the right spots and in straight lines requires special attention to layout. If it seems as if you are forever adjusting layout lines, taking them out, and then putting them back, it's because you are. However, if you aren't systematic about your layout, you may make a mistake—often one that can be fixed only by starting over. Working methodically, measuring carefully, and putting in accurate layout lines pay off.

No matter how you plan it, when you put down the last paver, the edges of the patio will be ragged. Trim them with a drysaw, then put in the edge restraints. (See "Laying a paver patio," beginning on page 48, for more information.)

▲ **Detached patios offer secluded spots for quiet moments** and can take advantage of views that may be different from the house. The addition of a fire ring makes this detached soft-set paver patio at least a three-season gathering place. Plantings around the edges could be added to create an opening, and a paver or gravel path could create access to the space from the house or other area.

Including a fire pit or decorative opening (continued)

1 Lay out the edges of the patio. Lay out the edges of the patio with batterboards and mason's line as you ordinarily would. Double-check that opposite sides are parallel and that the corners meet at 90 degrees. This will probably mean adjusting and moving lines several times until the opening is square. (For more information, see pages 34-39.)

2 Transfer the lines to the ground. Sprinkle powdered chalk, lime, flour, or sand along the lines marking the edges of the patio. Lay out the opening, too, if it doesn't already exist. Excavate for the patio, digging an opening extending about a foot past the layout lines in each direction. Remove soil right up to the opening. Compact the soil with a power tamper and put down landscape fabric. Build up a 4-inch compacted gravel bed.

3 Put in a sand bed and screed it level. Put a 1½- to 2-inch sand bed on top of the gravel. Temporarily put a couple of boards under the layout lines. Measure down at several points and shim as needed until they are the same distance below the line. Guide a notched board, or screed, across them to smooth the sand. (See "Laying a paver patio," beginning on page 48, for more information.)

4 Stretch a line along one side of the opening in the center of the patio. Determine the edges of the opening. If the patio is against a house or other structure, make the distance between the opening and house a multiple of the paver length to minimize cutting. The length and width of the opening also should be a multiple of the paver length. Set batterboards beyond the edges of the patio and stretch a line between them along one edge of the interior opening.

5 Stretch a perpendicular line. Put in a second set of batterboards. Stretch a line between them that is perpendicular to the first and runs along the edge of the opening.

6 Check for square. If the opening isn't square, you'll have odd-shape spaces that a paver won't fill. Check the layout with a 3-4-5 triangle: Put a piece of tape 3 feet from where the lines cross along one line and another piece of tape 4 feet from where the lines cross on the other line. The layout is square if the distance between the pieces of tape is 5 feet. If not, slide the appropriate line along the batterboards until it is.

7 Stretch parallel lines. Stretch lines over the remaining sides of the opening. Check that each is parallel with the line on the opposite side and double-check that they are square.

8 Mark the corners. Drop a plumb bob from the point where the lines meet at one corner of the patio. Mark the spot on the ground with a nail through a piece of paper for visibility. Repeat in each corner. Then drop a plumb bob from the lines marking the edge of the opening and mark where the lines meet the edges of the patio.

9 Snap lines. Snap a chalkline between nails on opposite corners of the patio. (Dry sand won't mark well, so you may want to mist the entire patio with a hose before you start your layout. If you still can't see the lines, stretch mason's line between the nails as a guide.) Snap lines marking all four edges of the patio and the opening. Remove the layout lines.

10 Put edge restraints for the interior opening, following the lines you snapped. The upright face of the edging should be closest to the outside of the patio. Anchor the edging as directed by the manufacturer. For now don't put any edge restraints along the edge of the patio.

11 Set up a guideline. Laying the pavers begins in the middle of this patio, where only a short edge restraint is in place to guide you. Stretch a line to keep the first row straight. Run it along the edge of the opening to the nails at the edge of the patio and stake it in place.

12 Start laying at the opening. Lay pavers along the edge of the opening, aligning the ends of the pavers with the ends of the opening. Continue laying a row of pavers, following the line in one direction. When you reach the line marking the edge of the patio, lay the paver so that it either just meets the line or goes past it, as the pattern dictates. Repeat in the other direction.

13 **Lay from the opening to the edge of the patio.**
Once the first row is in place, lay one next to it. Lay row by row until you reach the outer edge of the patio. Knee pads make the job more comfortable.

14 **Lay the other side.** Go to the opposite side of the opening. Start laying pavers at the opening, aligning the ends of the pavers with the ends of the opening. Lay pavers in this section of the patio the same way you did on the opposite side of the patio.

15 **Fill in the sides.** Starting at the edge restraints, fill in each gap on the remaining sides of the opening. A little adjustment may be necessary here, but if your layout lines were accurate, the pavers will fit.

16 **Cut the edges.** Snap lines to mark the edges of the patio. Spray the lines with clear lacquer so they stay put as you work. Cut along the lines with a drysaw.

17 **Install the edging.** Put the edging tight against the pavers and fasten it as directed by the edging manufacturer.

18 **Bed the pavers.** Sweep sand over the patio and compact it into the joints, repeating until the joints are full.

Building a concrete patio

Skill level:	Time to complete:	Materials: ¾-inch gravel, 2× lumber, ½-inch plywood, 10d (3-inch) duplex nails, ½-inch expansion joint, 6×6-10/10 wire mesh, tie wire, concrete, plastic sheeting, form-release agent	Tools: Mattock, spade, shovel, rake, tape measure, power tamper, hammer, 3-pound sledgehammer, mason's line, brick chisel, wheelbarrow, bull float, darby, edger, control jointer, pointing trowel, magnesium float, broom, safety goggles, work gloves, paintbrush
★★★☆☆	Experienced 14 hrs. Handy 17 hrs. Novice 20 hrs.		

The foundation of rigid patios—mortared brick, mortared flagstone, tile, or concrete—is a concrete pad. Concrete provides a solid base beneath these materials. It also prevents them from cracking as the ground shifts from temperature changes.

In most areas, a concrete patio begins with 4 inches of compacted stone. Areas with excellent drainage don't require a stone base—check with your local building inspector's office to see what's required. A 4-inch concrete slab is laid on the stone.

The following instructions are for building a concrete patio on grade. The steps are the same if you build a base for a rigid patio.

The difference is the depth you dig before you pour. If you install a concrete patio, dig out a space 8 inches deep—4 inches for the stone and another 4 inches for the concrete. If you install a brick patio, the base will need to be about 10+ inches deep—4 inches for the stone, 4 inches for the concrete, and another 2+ inches to allow for mortar and brick. If you build in brick, stone, or tile, simply read how the pad is poured. You'll find information on setting the pad at the right depth in later projects.

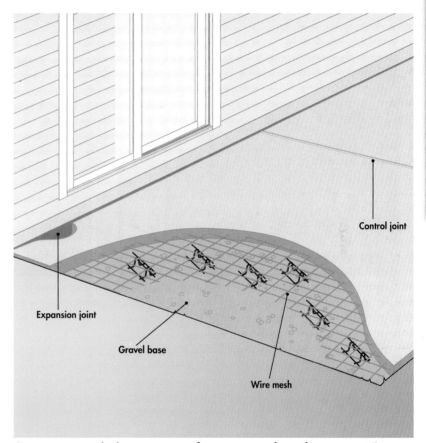

Control joint

Expansion joint

Gravel base

Wire mesh

A concrete patio is a system of stone, metal, and concrete. The top 4 inches is a concrete slab. A wire mesh running through the middle of the pad ties the patio together. Beneath the concrete is a gravel bed, which improves drainage and is easier to level than soil. An expansion joint between the patio and any structure allows the two to move independently when the ground shifts. Forms hold the concrete in place when you pour it. They also act as guides—immediately after you pour the concrete, you drag a board across the forms to level the surface. The forms usually are removed after the concrete cures, but you can leave them in place as decorative trim.

 ## Get along, little dobie

You'll find a number of specialty products designed to keep concrete wire mesh centered in a poured slab. Wire supports, or "chairs" are inexpensive and will do the job, but can prove cumbersome to work with, especially if you have to tie several hundred to the mesh on a large site. Precast concrete dobies are another alternative, and some come with wire "pigtails" already embedded in their surface. Newer polypropylene "chairs" have large circular bases that won't tip readily and feature crossed plastic sockets on top into which the wire or rebar intersection simply snaps. No matter which you choose, specify their height at half the thickness of your slab. Do not use brick dobies. They will pull moisture from the concrete.

 DESIGN TIP
FINISHING TOUCHES

A broomed surface is skid resistant and easy to apply.

Other surfaces, such as exposed aggregate, are more attractive and also skid resistant. For more on surface treatments, see "Special Surface Finishes," page 346.

Building a concrete patio (continued)

Assembling forms

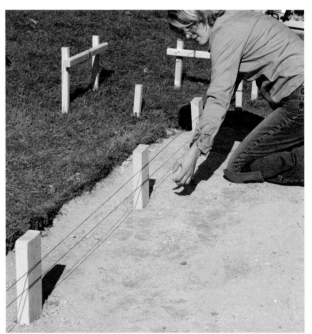

1 Lay out and excavate the patio. Lay out the patio with batterboards and mason's line. Remove the sod, dig out 8 inches of soil, and compact the exposed surface. Spread gravel on the surface in 2-inch layers, compacting each layer and adding gravel for a bed 4 inches deep.

2 Lay out the outside edge of the forms. Install a second set of layout lines on stakes. Position the stakes outside the first set of lines, offset from the first set by the width of the forms you'll use. Level the lines with a line level or water level.

3 Drive stakes along the new layout lines. Drive stakes along the layout lines, putting them at the corners of the patio and every 2 feet in between. Drive the stakes straight up and down, firmly embedding them in the ground. Trim them to height later.

4 Mark the stakes. The patio must slope away from the house at a rate of 1/8 to 1/4 inch per foot—check local code for the proper rate. Measure down from the batterboards and mark the two end stakes at the finished height of the patio. Hold a chalk line tight at the marks you made and snap it to mark the rest of the stakes.

5 **Nail the first form in place.** Align a 2×4 with the marks on the stakes and nail it in place with two duplex (double-headed) nails. Brace the form board with a 3-pound sledgehammer while you pound in the nails. Nail the rest of the stakes to the form board the same way.

6 **Cut off the stakes.** Cut the stakes flush with or slightly below the tops of the forms. You will use the tops of the forms as a guide to level the surface of the concrete, and any stake sticking above the surface will keep you from getting a smooth surface.

BUYER'S GUIDE
$ A MATTER OF FORM

As most do-it-yourselfers discover sooner or later, 2×4s are not 2×4. In the process for the lumberyard, they lose ½ inch in each direction to the planer. Not a problem in most cases, but what if you use 2×4s as forms to pour a 4-inch slab?

Not a problem here either. When you nail the forms to the stakes, just make sure the top of the 2× is at what will be the top of the pad. You'll have a ½-inch space between the 2× and the gravel, and the concrete will flow out through the cracks a bit. This doesn't affect the quality of the job, however, and in the end, the ooze gets buried, and no one sees it.

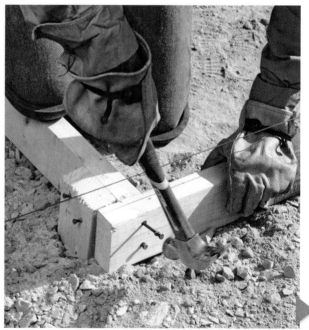

7 **Install the remaining forms.** Cut a 2×4 long enough to span each of the remaining sides. Put each board in place so the top is level with the marks you made earlier on the stakes. Attach stakes to forms with duplex nails. Nail in the remaining forms.

Building a concrete patio (continued)

8 Splice boards together, if necessary. On sides too long for a single board, butt two boards together. Cut a strip of 1/2-inch plywood and nail it across the joint. Drive a 2×4 stake at each end of the plywood strip and nail it to the form with duplex nails.

9 Install the expansion joint. Place a 1/2×4-inch expansion joint against the foundation of the house and any other existing concrete that meets the patio. This will prevent the pad and foundation from bonding and then cracking if they settle at different rates.

10 Coat the forms with release agent. Coat the form boards with a coat of commercial release agent or vegetable oil to prevent the concrete from sticking to the form boards. Motor oil—an early substitute for the release agent—doesn't work as well and contaminates the ground.

DESIGN TIP
MIXED MEDIA

Break up the bland look of a concrete patio with a grid of permanent form boards. Install the boards just like temporary forms but pound the stakes below the top of the forms so the poured concrete will conceal them. If you want to stain the wood, soak the boards in the finish first, then cover the wood with masking tape when you make the pour.

11 Place the mesh. Reinforce the concrete with 6×6-10/10 wire mesh (6-inch squares of 10-gauge metal). Put the mesh on wire supports, sold separately, so it sits roughly in the middle of the slab's thickness. Leave a few inches of space between the mesh and the edges of the forms to prevent rust. Overlap sections by 4 inches and tie them together with wire. Wire the mesh to the supports.

Pouring concrete

1 Pour the concrete into the forms. If you're using a wheelbarrow, build a temporary ramp over the forms so that the wheelbarrow won't knock them out of place. Start in a corner and dump the loads of concrete against each other. Have a helper with a shovel spread the concrete into corners and against the forms and expansion joints.

2 Remove trapped air. Lay a wide board across the forms so you can reach the interior of the pour. If the concrete causes the wire mesh to sink, pull it up with a rake so that it's in the middle of the slab. Work a shovel or rake up and down to remove air pockets, especially alongside the forms.

3 Flatten the surface. With a helper pull a screed (a long, straight 2×4) across the forms to level the concrete. Tilt the screed forward and slide it from side to side as you push it forward. Shovel off excess concrete in front of the screed and fill in low spots. Make a second pass with the screed tilted the opposite direction.

4 Float the concrete. Work a bull float back and forth with the blade flat against the surface to smooth and compact the concrete. For small surfaces use a darby instead of a bull float. Work the concrete until water forms on the surface.

 Scratching the surface

If you're going to lay bricks or pavers on top of a concrete patio, make sure it's flat but don't spend a lot of time getting a smooth finish. Instead you'll need to scratch the surface to help the mortar bond to the concrete. Begin by building a homemade scarifier. Drive 10d (3-inch) nails 1 inch apart into a piece of scrap wood. Then drag the scarifier over the concrete before it sets fully, cutting grooves into the surface.

 WORK SMART
POURING CONCRETE

Pour concrete into the forms as close as possible to its final position and dump each wheelbarrow load against the previous load. If you don't, the cement and sand will ooze away from the gravel in the mix, and you'll get rough and smooth spots in the surface.

Start by pouring the concrete into a corner, and then work your way along the form, as shown in Step 1. Once you've dumped concrete along the entire edge, move your ramp to the other side of the patio. Extend the ramp across the patio so that you can get as close as possible to the concrete you've already poured, and start pouring new concrete against it.

Running the ramp, or the wheelbarrow, along the reinforcing mesh will cause the mesh to bend, but don't worry. It's unavoidable. Pull bent mesh back up in place with a rake just before you pour concrete over it.

Building a concrete patio (continued)

Finishing concrete

1 Round the edges. When you've finished floating, separate the concrete from the forms by running the tip of a pointing trowel between the two. Then slide the cutting edge of an edger along the forms to round over the patio edge, making it less likely to chip. Lift the leading edge of the tool to avoid marring the concrete.

2 Cut control joints. Cut shallow grooves, called control joints, in the wet cement pad. These weaken the spots a little so that if the ground shifts, the resulting crack should form along the control joint. You need a joint every 8 feet, so make marks every 8 feet along the forms. Place a jointer at each mark. Guide the jointer against a board that spans the patio. Control joints can also be cut after the concrete has cured using a circular saw with a cement or masonry blade. (See inset.) Snap a chalkline to follow while cutting.

3 Float the surface again. After cutting the control joints, and when any water sheen has left the surface, run a wood or magnesium hand float over the surface to provide a final smoothing. Raise the leading edge of the float slightly as you work to avoid making lines on the surface of the concrete.

4 Brush the surface. For improved traction, pull a stiff-bristle broom across the surface. Draw the broom in either straight or wavy lines. If you don't like the pattern or if it is too coarse, trowel, wait, and broom again. The longer the concrete dries, the finer the broomed surface. Make another pass along the perimeter with the edger.

5 Let the concrete cure. Lay plastic sheeting over the finished surface. The moisture trapped inside eliminates the need for watering during the curing stage. Let the concrete cure at least 48 hours, then remove the form boards.

DESIGN TIP
FINISH OPTIONS

Function often dictates how a patio should be finished. For a smoother finish, use a magnesium float instead of a wooden one. Avoid finishing concrete with a steel trowel because it will create a finish so smooth that it becomes slick and dangerous when wet. A skid-free, broomed finish is an especially good idea around pools.

Preparing an existing slab for a mortar bed

Skill level:
★☆☆☆

Time to complete:
Experienced 2 hrs.
Handy 3 hrs.
Novice 4 hrs.

Materials: Muriatic acid, foam rods, silicone rubber caulk, mortar mix, bonding agent

Tools: Bucket, putty knife, caulk gun, paintbrush, steel trowel, safety goggles, rubber gloves, work gloves

A new patio doesn't necessarily mean you need to pour a new slab. In many cases you can apply brick, stone, or tile over an existing slab. You'll need to patch and clean it, but it's considerably less work than starting from scratch.

Control joints in the concrete can cause cracking in the surface above them, so tile and brick work best on an old surface. Lay out the brick or tile so a mortar joint is directly above the control joint, and fill the joint with caulk instead of mortar or grout.

First make sure the existing slab is sound. Cracks and irregularities can be repaired, as can a few small areas that have broken away. Make sure the area is flat—if a crack has created a step in the surface, it will crack again after you patch it, and the crack will eventually work its way through the brick, stone, or tile.

Crumbling areas spell big trouble: Either the concrete was poorly mixed or multiple freeze/thaw cycles have broken the surface. If the slab surface is crumbling, talk to a mason about whether the pad can be repaired.

Check that the surface of the slab slopes away from the house at a rate of at least $1/8$ inch per foot. If it doesn't you can correct the problem by sloping the forms when you apply the mortar.

Etch the concrete surface with a mixture of muriatic acid and water to clean it and create a surface to which mortar will stick. Make sure you add the acid to the water—not the water to the acid—to avoid dangerous splashes.

Ensure a good bond for the mortar and brick, stone, or tile by applying a bonding agent.

Cracks and shifting occur naturally in concrete slabs. Even the best-laid slabs will eventually be affected by years of seasonal changes and freeze/thaw cycles. Repairing cracks and covering an existing slab with mortared bricks or pavers adds a design element to your yard and saves you the labor of removing damaged concrete.

1 Clean the surface. Scrape off gum, wax, and dirt. Carefully mix five parts water and one part muriatic acid, adding the acid to the water to avoid dangerous splashes. Carefully pour the solution on the slab. Rinse the slab thoroughly with fresh water. **Wear rubber gloves and safety goggles when working with muriatic acid.**

2 Fill in the control joints. Patch broken or wide control joints by pushing foam backing rods below the surface with a putty knife. Seal the crack with a silicone rubber caulk. If you are laying brick or tile on top of the concrete, put the mortar joint directly above the control joint to avoid cracking.

Preparing an existing slab for a mortar bed (continued)

3 Fill in cracks. Brush a concrete bonding agent on an area 6 inches wider and longer than the crack. Then fill the crack with mortar and level it with a steel trowel.

4 Apply a bonding agent. Just before you apply mortar, brush on a coat of concrete bonding adhesive to the entire surface, following the directions on the package.

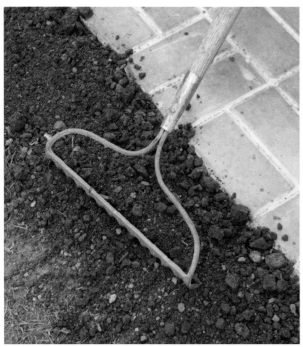

5 Regrade the area around the pad. Once you install the brick, stone, or tile, the surface of the patio will be above the adjacent ground surface. Regrade the area, adding soil and raking it smooth until it is flush with the patio surface.

Shifty surfaces

Steps are cracks that have shifted so much that one surface is higher than the other. Steps can cause problems because they are likely to appear again and may mean that the pad has to be removed and repoured. Consult a professional landscape or concrete contractor to make sure the steps won't reappear, this time through your new patio.

WORK SMART
CORRECTING THE SLOPE

You can add a bed of mortar up to 4 inches thick to a patio without compromising the strength. Take advantage of this method to correct any problems with the existing patio's slope. First build forms around the patio the way you would if you were pouring a new patio, keeping the surface as low as possible while making sure the forms have the correct slope. Fill the forms with mortar and pull a screed across it to flatten it. Let the mortar cure, then lay the stone, brick, or tile, following the directions beginning on page 69.

Laying a mortared brick patio

Skill level:
★★★☆☆

Time to complete:
Experienced 10 hrs.
Handy 14 hrs.
Novice 18 hrs.

Materials: 2× lumber, 10d (3-inch) duplex nails, mortar, bricks

Tools: Mason's line, 3-pound sledgehammer, hammer, mixing tub, mason's trowel, rubber mallet, circular saw and masonry blade, brick chisel, mortar bag, jointer, concave jointer, safety glasses, work gloves, dust mask

Bricks can be laid directly on a sand-and-gravel base (page 52), but for a long-lasting patio, lay the bricks on a concrete base. The glue that holds bricks to concrete—and bricks to bricks—is mortar, a mix of Portland cement, lime, sand, and water. Use Type M mortar—it's designed for outdoor use.

A word about bricks: A 4×8-inch brick is narrower by the width of the intended joint between bricks. Rounding up makes calculating brick amounts easier, but if you use the wrong joint size, laying some patterns becomes impossible. As a rule, if the brick is shy of its named size by ½ inch, use ½-inch joints; if shy by ⅜ inch, use ⅜-inch joints. If it measures a full 4×8 inches, get another brick.

Expansion joint
Mortar joint
Brick
Mortar bed
Concrete base

A mortared brick patio is essentially a series of layers. A concrete foundation supports the bricks and establishes the slope that directs water away from the house. The exact depth of the foundation varies, but it's positioned so the patio is about 2 inches above ground. A ½-inch layer of mortar applied to the top of the concrete holds the bricks in place. Once the bricks are laid, you apply more mortar between them and shape, or "strike," the joints with a jointer.

Mortaring bricks

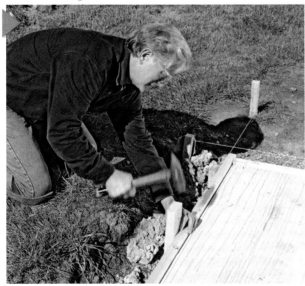

1 Set mason's lines at the finished height and slope of the patio. Set form boards so the tops are ½ inch above the slab surface. Add corner stakes to support the forms and drive them in until they are flush with the form boards. Nail stakes every 2 feet against the boards.

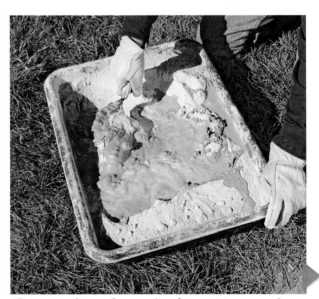

2 Pour a bag of pre-mixed Type M mortar into a mixing tub or wheelbarrow. Make a small well in the middle and pour in water, a bit at a time. (The instructions give you the approximate amount.) Mix with a trowel. The mortar is the right consistency when it is firm enough to cling to a trowel turned on edge.

3 **Divide the patio into sections** 4 feet wide with a temporary pipe or board the same height as the top of the forms. Throw mortar into an area roughly 4×4 feet. Make a screed from a straight 2×4 that spans the width of the forms. Draw the screed over the mortar to level and smooth it into a ½-inch bed.

4 **For a basket-weave pattern,** lay the first pair of bricks in a corner even with the inside edge of the forms. Space the bricks with a spacer. Tap the bricks firmly into the mortar with a rubber mallet.

5 **If you work on a large patio,** run a mason's line across it, flush with the top of the first two courses, to keep the bricks properly aligned. Lay a pair of bricks perpendicular to the first two. Continue laying the bricks, alternating their direction.

 Laying dry-mortar joints

As its name suggests, dry mortar contains no water. You simply sweep it into the joints. Mix four parts sand and one part dry portland cement and sweep the mixture into the joints with a stiff brush. Then spray the patio—and especially the joints—with water. While the joints are still damp, shape each one with a concave jointer. Once the mortar has hardened for a few hours, scrub the patio surface to remove any excess mortar.

6 **Check for high and low spots** as you proceed by placing a 2×4 across the bricks. Put mortar under low bricks; seat high ones by tapping them with the mallet. Lay another 4×4-foot patch of mortar and bricks, repeating until the patio is finished.

7 **When a brick has to be cut,** score it ⅛ inch deep with a circular saw with a masonry blade. Once the brick is scored, cut it with a solid blow from a brick chisel and a 3-pound sledgehammer. **Wear a dust mask and safety glasses when cutting bricks.**

8 **When all the bricks are set in the mortar bed,** fill the joints between bricks with mortar from a grout bag, also called a blow bag. Working back and forth, squeeze the mortar carefully into the joints until they are filled. Shape the joints with a concave jointer.

9 **Clean the brick**. Be careful not to get mortar on the brick. Remove any mortar that does get on the brick by rubbing it with a piece of wet burlap. Let the mortar cure for three days before using the patio. If you missed any mortar spots, you can usually remove them by sweeping wet sand over them.

Selecting a brick pattern

A running bond is the easiest to lay. Every second row begins with a half brick to stagger the joints. (For directions on laying running bond, see page 42.)

Herringbone requires a little more planning than running bond. It can be laid either diagonally or parallel to the sides of the patio. (For directions on laying herringbone, see pages 44–45.)

DESIGN TIP
PATTERN POSSIBILITIES

You aren't limited to just one pattern when you lay bricks. You can create interesting effects by combining two patterns on the same patio. Start with a basket-weave pattern, for example, then lay a couple of rows of running bond before resuming the basket-weave pattern. Experiment on paper first to make sure the overall pattern looks good.

Laying a mortared stone patio

Skill level:	Time to complete:	Materials: 2× lumber, 10d (3-inch) duplex nails, mortar, stones	Tools: Hammer, 3-pound sledgehammer, brick chisel, carpenter's pencil, pointing trowel, mason's trowel, grout bag, rubber mallet, concave jointer, sponge, shovel, safety glasses, work gloves, dust mask, mixing tub
★★★★★	Experienced 12 hrs. Handy 16 hrs. Novice 20 hrs.		

Stone for patios is sold under various names, such as flagstone, flat stone, and bluestone. Whatever the name, choose a natural, sedimentary, layered rock. Although you can buy stones precut, the patio shown here uses natural stone laid with gaps of ½ or ¾ inch between stones. This patio slopes for drainage and is supported by a concrete foundation.

Because of the uneven nature of stone, a stone patio sits in a relatively thick 1-inch bed of mortar. Temporary forms hold the wet mortar in place. You'll drag a board across the forms to smooth the bed, so set the forms to follow the desired slope of the patio. The concrete pad under the patio supports it and keeps it from cracking when the ground underneath it shifts. To help the stones adhere to the mortar, coat them with slurry, a mixture of cement and water that has the consistency of cream.

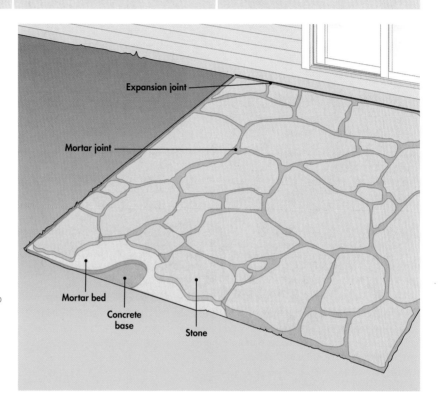

Expansion joint

Mortar joint

Mortar bed

Concrete base

Stone

1 Build forms for the mortar. Put 2× forms around the concrete slab to hold the mortar bed. The forms should sit 1 inch above the slab and follow its slope. Hold the forms in place with stakes driven every 2 feet.

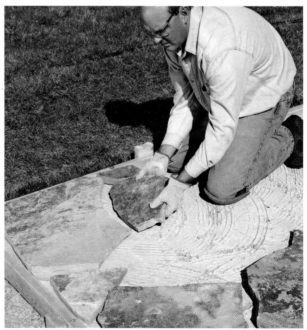

2 Lay out the stones. Lay a dry run of stones on the patio. The best way to do this is to randomly spread the large stones across the patio and then fill in with smaller ones. Group the stones so there is as little space as possible between them. Inevitable empty spots are OK.

3 Fill in the voids. Place large stones over the voids. Use a pencil to sketch the shape required to fill the void. A carpenter's pencil makes a more visible line than a regular pencil.

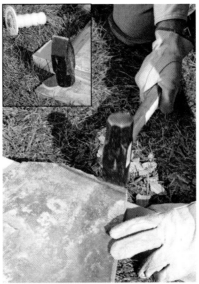

4 Cut the stone. Chip away at the stones with the pointed end of a mason's hammer to cut the shape. To cut a straight line, score the line with a 3-pound sledgehammer and a brick chisel. Place the scored line over the edge of a piece of 1×2 or a pipe. Sever with a solid blow from the sledgehammer.

5 Number the stones. Once the stones fit, number the bottoms and lay them out in order next to the patio.

6 Mix mortar. Pour a bag of pre-mixed Type M mortar into a mixing tub. Make a small well in the middle. Pour water into the well, a little at a time, and mix with the trowel. The mix may take slightly more or less water than called for by the manufacturer. It is the right consistency when it is firm enough to cling to a trowel turned on edge.

7 Spread a small amount of mortar. Using a mason's trowel, lay a 1-inch mortar bed for two or three stones at a time. Use the forms to help lay the right amount of mortar. Screed it with a straight 2×4 that spans the width of the forms. (If laid stones obstruct screeding, guide the screed along two 1-inch O.D. [outside diameter] pipes temporarily set on the slab.)

8 Lay the stones. Place the first stone in the mortar and embed it firmly in place by tapping it with a rubber mallet. Lay adjoining stones, referring to the numbers on the bottom to help reposition them in the proper order. Check for high and low spots as you proceed by laying a 2×4 on top of the stones.

9 Level and coat with slurry. Add mortar to raise stones that are too low; tap harder to set any that are too high. After laying stones in about a 4×4-foot section, tip the stones up one at a time and paint the bottom with a cream-textured cement-water slurry. Lay the stones back and recheck their level.

10 Lay the rest of the patio. Continue laying the patio in 4×4-foot sections. Make a dry run for each section, number the stones, then set them in mortar. When you finish, let the mortar cure for one or two days. Then remove the temporary forms around the patio.

11 Mortar between the stones. Mix another batch of Type M mortar. Pack it between the stones with a pointing trowel.

12 Tool the joints. Compress and smooth the mortar joints with a ¾-inch concave jointer. Remove any mortar crumbs from the joint edges.

13 Remove mortar from the stones. After a few hours clean up any mortar on the stones with a damp sponge or a rough burlap rag and water.

14 Cover the patio with plastic. Wait 24 hours for the mortar to cure. Remove the plastic and backfill the edges around the patio with soil. Tamp the soil and reseed or plant.

Laying a tile patio

Skill level:
★★★☆☆

Time to complete:	
Experienced	3.5 hrs.
Handy	4.5 hrs.
Novice	5.5 hrs.

Materials: Tile, tile spacers, mortar, grout, tile sealer

Tools: Tape measure, chalkline, 5-gallon bucket, ½-inch drill, mortar paddle, notched trowel, rubber gloves, sponge, rags, sponge mop, bead blaster, tile saw or snap cutter, grout float

Ceramic tile patios are popular in the southern United States, where they're used along with indoor tile to bridge the gap between indoors and out. But ceramic tile makers say there's no reason not to build tile patios in the north too.

The first step—no matter where you live—is to purchase the right tile. You can find out what you need to know by reading a series of icons and labels on the tile cartons. For all floor uses, get tile rated Grade 1, which is designed for floors. Grade 2 has imperfections; Grade 3 tiles are wall tiles and will crack on floors.

Look for tile that has :
■ PEI (Porcelain Enamel Institute) Wear Rating 3, meaning it's for residential use.
■ WA (water absorption) rating of 5 percent or less. This keeps the inside of the tile dry enough to prevent freezing.
■ COF (coefficient of friction) rating of .60 or less, meaning it has some texture for traction. Double-check by running your hand across the surface.
■ Frost resistance. Look for a snowflake icon that indicates the tile will survive the freeze/thaw cycle.

The next step is to get the latex-modified mortar; the latex helps keep water from working its way into the mortar, where it can freeze and loosen the tile. The farther north you live, the more latex needed. Ask at the store about what's right for the job in your area.

Set tile on concrete. If you pour a new pad, give it a broomed finish that the mortar can grab on to. If you tile an existing pad, it probably has a smooth steel trowel finish and probably was coated with a curing compound after it was poured. Either will keep the mortar from forming a firm bond with the concrete, causing the tile to come loose. To solve the problem, rent a bead blaster to rough up the surface.

▲ **Adding a tile to a concrete pad** will create a distinctive addition to your outdoor living space. Be sure to choose a tile rated to survive freeze/thaw cycles in northern climates.

Preparing the site

1 Prepare the concrete. Rough up the surface of the concrete and remove any sealer or curing compound with a bead blaster. Slowly push the blaster across the floor as it shoots metal balls at the floor and vacuums them up. The impact will wear off any coatings and create a rough surface for the mortar.

2 Snap layout lines. Snap chalk lines at the middle of opposite sides. Measure 3 feet from the intersection along one line and 4 feet along the other line. If the distance between the points is 5 feet, the lines are square. If not, reposition one of the lines until it is square with the other. (See page 35.)

3 **Test-fit the tiles.** When you buy tiles, buy spacers the size of the mortar joint. Starting where the lines cross, put tiles along each line with plastic spacers between them. Insert the spacers on edge between the tiles for easy removal. If any of the tiles along the edges are less than half a tile wide, snap a new line to solve the problem.

4 **Mix the mortar.** Add about half the water called for on the mortar box or bag. Slowly add the rest while mixing at slow speed with a paddle designed for mortar (not paint). After mixing let the mortar rest for 10 minutes, then mix again before use.

Laying the tile

1 **Spread the mortar.** Start at the intersection of the chalklines and spread mortar over an 8- to 10-square-foot area. Press the mortar into the slab with a trowel held at a shallow angle.

2 **Comb the mortar.** Comb the mortar in straight lines, holding the trowel at a 45-degree angle to the slab and forcing the teeth of the trowel against the concrete. This ensures you have the right amount of mortar on the concrete. The size of the notch should equal the thickness of the tile.

3 **Lay the first tile.** Start at the intersection of the lines, put the tile in the mortar, and twist it slightly to embed it in the mortar. Leave a space the size of a grout joint between the tile and any structures.

4 Check the back. Pull up the tile and look at the back. Parallel mortar lines mean the bed isn't thick enough; dry areas mean the mortar is too old. In either event scrape up the mortar and reapply. If the bed was too thin, hold the trowel at a greater angle when you comb out the mortar.

5 Work your way across the mortar. When the mortar bed is right, lay the first two tiles and a couple of spacers placed on end between them. Lay all the tiles in the mortared area. Lay a short 2×4 on top of the tiles and lightly tap with a rubber mallet to level the tiles.

Using a snap cutter

6 Lay the rest of the site. Lay mortar over an area the same size as the first and set tiles in it. Check the back of a tile occasionally to make sure you're laying enough mortar. Work area by area until you tile the entire patio.

7 Cut tiles to fit along the edge of the patio. At the edge of the patio, you'll probably need to cut tiles to fit. Mark where you need to make cuts and cut with either a tile saw or a snap cutter.

To use a snap cutter, place the tile with the cutting wheel on top of the layout line, then move the wheel back toward the far edge of the tile. Pull the wheel toward you, putting light pressure on the handle. Lower the foot of the cutter onto the tile and strike the handle quickly to snap along the scored line.

Laying a tile patio (continued)

Applying grout

1 Mix and apply grout. Remove the spacers. Mix the grout at slow speed in a 5-gallon bucket with a mortar paddle and a 1/2-inch drill. Let the grout rest for 10 to 15 minutes, then remix.

2 Spread the grout. Apply the grout with a rubber grout float held at a shallow angle. Press the grout into the joints to fill them. For joints wider than 3/8 inch, use a grout bag. Fill the joints between the patio and any structures with caulk instead of grout.

3 Remove excess grout. Hold the grout float at a steep angle. Diagonally sweep the float across the tiles so the float doesn't dip into the joints.

4 Rinse, rinse, and rinse again. Immediately wash off the haze left by the grout before it dries. Rinse repeatedly and keep the water clean in order to remove the haze.

5 Mist the grout. Let the grout damp cure by spraying it with a mist (don't drench it) several times a day for three days. If the patio receives direct sunlight, cover it with plastic sheeting between mistings.

6 Apply sealer. Check the directions that come with the sealer to see how long you should wait before applying it. Apply the sealer with a sponge mop and wipe up the excess before it dries. Follow the manufacturer's directions for the number of applications.

Maintaining patios

Skill level:
★ ☆ ☆ ☆ ☆

Time to complete:
Experienced 30 min.
Handy 1 hr.
Novice 2 hrs.

Materials: Mortar, mason's sand, grout, thinset, 2×4, bonding agent, concrete, duplex nails, gravel, expansion joint, wire mesh, burlap

Tools: Stiff-bristle brush, putty knife, rubber mallet, hose, point punch, cold chisel, brick chisel, plugging chisel, pointing trowel, jointer, 3-pound and 7-pound sledgehammers, mixing tub, mortar bag, carbide scoring tool, straightedge, grout float, metal or wooden float, work gloves, safety glasses, dust mask, knee pads

Whether you use your patio every day of the year or only during the summer, it's exposed to the elements year-round. Eventually it needs maintenance. Both traffic and weather affect patios. Freezing, thawing, and rain attack the most vulnerable spot—the joints. Watch for small problems with the sand between pavers or the mortar along stones, and you'll avoid larger problems later.

Cleaning pavers

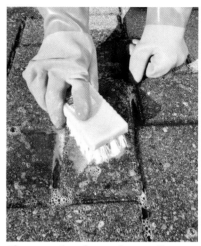

Pull weeds out of the joints by sliding a putty knife along the gaps between the bricks. (If you place landscaping fabric under your patio when building it, you will rarely encounter this problem.)

Clean stains from the walk with a stiff-bristle brush and warm, soapy water. For tough stains use diluted (1:9) muriatic acid or a trisodium phosphate (TSP) solution. Don't use acid on stone surfaces—it may stain. A stubborn stain on stone or brick often can be removed by rubbing it with a piece of similar stone or brick.

Repairing sand-bed pavers

1 Remove the paver. Sometimes part of a patio will sink a little, creating a low spot. To correct the problem remove the lowest paver by prying it loose with a cold chisel or screwdriver.

2 Add and level sand. After you remove all the low bricks, add sand. Level the area to the height of the surrounding bed and screed the sand bed with a notched 2×4 resting the ends of the 2×4 on the nearby bricks or pavers.

3 Replace the pavers. Tap the pavers back into place with a rubber mallet. Check their position relative to their neighbors with a straight 2×4. If one or more pavers are uneven, add or remove sand beneath them until they are even with the surrounding pavers.

4 Fill in with sand. Sprinkle mason's sand over the restored area. Sweep the sand into the joints with a stiff-bristle brush. Spray the repair with water to settle the sand firmly into the joints. Add more sand and respray, if necessary.

Cleaning concrete

Commercial cleaning agents, when used with rented power washers, are good for general cleaning. Some stains, such as the chalky, salty residue after a rainfall, can be brushed off with a stiff-bristle brush. For oil and grease stains, scrub the stain with mineral spirits, sprinkle it with kitty litter or sand, then sweep it up. Stains that have penetrated can be dissolved with commercial cleaners. Remove rust stains with bleach and a stiff-bristle scrub brush.

DESIGN TIP
MAKING NEW BRICK LOOK OLD

When adding new bricks to an older pattern, the color and texture may not match. Soak new bricks in sandy or muddy water to give them the color of older bricks. Rubbing sand against the bricks gives the surface a worn look and prevents the coloring from rubbing away easily. Also try rubbing a few of the newer bricks against one another to age them.

Repairing mortar joints

1 Chisel out the old mortar. Remove damaged mortar from around bricks with a 3-pound sledgehammer and a cold chisel. Work carefully, removing only as much mortar as necessary. **When chipping mortar, wear work gloves and safety glasses.**

2 Clean the surface. After you chisel away the mortar, sweep away loose particles with a stiff-bristle brush or whisk.

BUILDING PATIOS

3 **Mix mortar.** In a mixing tub mix one part portland cement and three parts mason's sand. Add water, blending the materials together until the mortar is workable yet stiff. For small jobs use premixed mortar.

4 **Fill with mortar.** Fill the joints with a grout bag, also known as a blow bag. Squeeze the bag gently and evenly so you don't use too much mortar; excess mortar is hard to clean up.

5 **Tool the joints.** Strike the joints with a jointer that matches the profile of the original joint. Start the strike on an old joint and follow through into the new mortar so the new joint looks like the old ones.

Replacing a brick, stone, or tile

1 **Remove the mortar or grout.** Replacing brick, stone, and tile are much the same. Chisel out the mortar around brick or stone with a plugging chisel. Remove the grout around tile with a grout saw. **Wear safety glasses when breaking up pavers, mortar, or concrete.**

2 **Break up the paver.** Remove a damaged brick or stone by breaking it into smaller pieces with a hammer and cold chisel. Score a tile repeatedly on the diagonals with a carbide scoring tool and straightedge until the line is 1/16 inch deep. Strike in the middle with a point punch and hammer. Break up the rest of it with a cold chisel.

3 **Remove the mortar.** Chip away the mortar or thinset with a brick chisel. The resulting surface doesn't need to be perfect; remove enough to make room for a new bed of mortar or thinset.

Maintaining patios (continued)

4 Replace the mortar or thinset. Apply a ½-inch layer of mortar for use under brick or stone. Apply thinset under tile, combing it out with a trowel that has notches the same size as the tile's thickness.

5 Set the paver. Put the brick, stone, or tile in place. Use a straightedge to make sure it is the same height as the surrounding pavers. Tap with a rubber mallet to set it deeper; add mortar or thinset, if necessary, to raise it.

6 Apply mortar or grout. Fill in around bricks or stone with mortar and tool it to match the surrounding mortar. When replacing a tile, remove the thinset around the tile while it is still wet. Once the thinset under the tile has dried, apply grout with a grout float. After 15 minutes clean the tile with a scrub pad and water to remove excess grout.

Repairing small cracks in concrete

1 Prepare the cracks. Fill cracks less than ⅛ inch wide with latex or epoxy patching compound, following the manufacturer's instructions. Larger cracks need to be undercut with a cold chisel angled slightly outward. Rap it with a 3-pound sledgehammer, widening the crack at the bottom. **Wear gloves and safety glasses when chiseling concrete.**

2 Apply mortar. Sweep the crack clean with a stiff-bristle brush, dampen it, then brush the surface with a concrete bonding agent. Wait 15 minutes before adding mortar to the crack. Prepare mortar by mixing one part portland cement and three parts mason's sand. Add enough water to make a thick paste. For small jobs use premixed mortar.

3 Smooth the surface. Trowel on the mortar and smooth the surface with either a metal or wooden float.

Replacing concrete

1 Remove the concrete. Break the damaged section of concrete with a 12-pound sledgehammer. If the area is more than a few square feet, you may want to rent a jackhammer. Break up the concrete into small pieces.

2 Install forms. Replace the existing gravel and tamp the surface. Install form boards against the existing concrete, holding it in place with 2×4 stakes. Nail the forms to the stakes with duplex nails.

3 Install reinforcing mesh. Place wire mesh on wire supports in the repair area at about the midpoint of the concrete's depth. If the concrete abuts a solid structure, such as a house foundation, place an expansion joint along the edge.

4 Pour the concrete. Empty bagged premixed concrete into a wheelbarrow, add water, and mix until the consistency is firm yet workable. Put a bonding agent on the broken edges of the concrete and pour concrete into the damaged area.

5 Screed, finish, and cure. Screed the surface of the repaired area with a 2×4 so it is smooth and level with surrounding concrete. Float and finish the surface to match the old concrete. Cover the repaired area with a sheet of plastic and allow the concrete to cure for at least one day.

TOOL TIP
CURING COMPOUNDS

Curing is the process by which concrete hardens. During this process you must take steps to make sure the concrete does not lose moisture too quickly. Curing products are available at home centers to ensure smooth, even curing of concrete walks and patios. Wax- and resin-based compounds are the most popular. Apply the curing compound with a paintbrush or roller while the concrete is still damp. For larger areas, use a sprayer. Apply a second coat, brushing or spraying perpendicular to the first coat.

CHAPTER 3

Building landscape steps

Steps are connectors that provide transitions from one level to another while adding a strong design element. Ramps do this too, and they offer an easy means of moving from one level to another, especially important for physically challenged people.

Choose the materials for your steps to complement the installation. Bricks or pavers offer color and a sense of order, while rough stone creates a free-form look and blends with the surrounding landscape.

Combining timbers and brick to make steps adds texture and a dynamic architectural element to any setting.

Practically speaking, be sure that risers and treads are balanced in height and width so they are comfortable to walk up and down at a normal pace. Steps that are too narrow and too short encourage slips and falls. Ensure that edges are clearly visible. Not being able to discern where a step ends is a prime cause of accidents.

Contents

It's about the look, but it's also about the terrain.

Choosing the right materials for your landscape steps and connecting walkways certainly involves decisions about how the design and materials will complement your landscape. It also involves questions about the ease of installation and where the steps fall in the existing terrain. For example, a hard-set walkway that climbs straight up a steep hill needs terracing or connecting steps. But such an installation may also require extensive excavation for the multiple step foundations. Conversely, soft-set walkways can be more easily adapted to slopes, meandering over the landscape and following natural pathways, reducing the number of steps.

The choice of style and materials also depends on how the steps and walkway will be used. Soft-set stones may have high aesthetic appeal but might not hold up effectively in areas of heavy traffic, such as a driveway or a section where drainage is a constant problem. If all you're looking for is easy access to a utility area, such as a garage or storage shed, a poured concrete sidewalk might be the best choice.

As you make your decisions, consider the amount of labor required to install the materials, as well as the ongoing maintenance requirements of the material. Be objective and willing to consider other solutions.

Building landscape steps tool kit

3-pound sledgehammer

Circular saw

Darby

Hand tamper

Power tamper

Sponge

Bead blaster

Cold chisel

Drysaw

Handsaw

Putty knives

Straightedge

Brick chisel

Concave jointer

Dust mask

Levels

Rubber gloves

Trowels

Broom

Concrete edger

Framing square

Mattock

Rubber mallet

Wet saw

Caulk gun

Concrete float

Garden rake

Paintbrush

Safety glasses

Wheelbarrow

Chalk line

Control jointer

Grout bag

Plumb bob

Shovel and spade

Work gloves

Materials

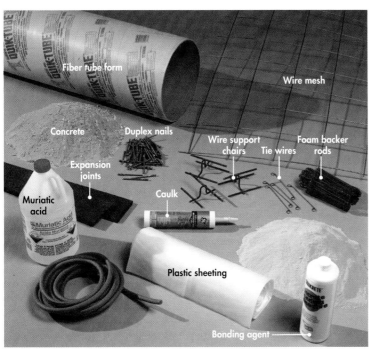

◄ **Concrete** comes in a bag, or ready-mixed from a truck. Pour the concrete into either 2×4 or **fiber tube forms.** If you make the forms from 2×4s, use **duplex nails,** which are relatively easy to remove. Before you pour, put in **wire mesh** to help tie the pad together; support it on small **wire support chairs,** and fasten it with **tie wires.** Put a **expansion joint** between the new concrete and existing concrete so the two can move independently if the ground shifts. If you're putting bricks, stone, or tile on top of an existing pad, wash it carefully with **muriatic acid,** and fill the cracks and control joints with **foam backer rods,** followed by **caulk.** On brick, stone, and tile patios, brush on a **bonding agent** to help the mortar stick to the concrete. Cover the patio with **plastic sheeting** while the concrete dries.

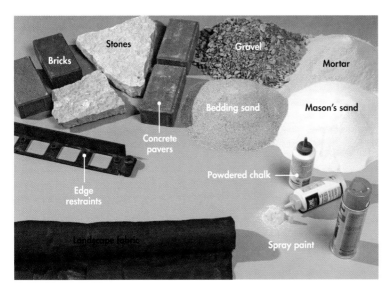

◄ Paving materials such as **bricks, stones,** and **concrete pavers,** can sit either on a bed of **gravel** and **bedding sand** or on **mortar** supported by a concrete pad. On gravel and sand beds, a finer sand, called **mason's sand,** is swept into the joints to keep the pavers from moving. **Edge restraints** help lock the whole thing in place. **Landscape fabric** is often used in a sand and gravel bed to keep the layers separate. Layout for a patio is done with mason's line and stakes or batterboards, but you can use **spray paint** or **powdered chalk** to transfer the lines to the ground.

◄ A wheelchair ramp is supported on **4×4 posts;** with **2×6 beams** and held together with **½"×8" bolts, washers,** and **nuts.** The surface is **⁵⁄₄ (five-quarter) decking.** Code also requires **handrails.**

Laying out steps

Skill level:	Time to complete:	Materials: 2×4s, 2×2s, galvanized 10d (3-inch) nails, masking tape	Tools: Tape measure, 3-pound sledgehammer, mason's line, line level, plumb bob, powdered chalk, framing square, spade, level, tamper
★★★☆☆	Experienced 1 hr.		
	Handy 1.5 hr.		
	Novice 2 hrs.		

How much room does your foot need for each step? And how high should you have to raise your foot to get to the next step?

Here's a formula for the ideal relationship between the height of the step (the rise) and the depth (the run). Twice the rise plus the run should equal 25 to 27 inches. This formula results in steps that are less steep than steps indoors but more comfortable to climb. You'll appreciate lower individual steps when trudging through snow or hauling firewood up the slope.

When you design your steps, plan the top step so it will be level with the grade. That way, people can see it easily as they approach.

Calculating riser/tread ratios

Standard treads

Double treads

Riser height:	Tread range:
Standard Treads	
7"	11"-13"
6½"	12"-14"
6"	13"-15"
5½"	14"-16"
5"	15"-17"
Double Treads	
7"	22"-26"
6½"	24"-28"
6"	26"-30"
5½"	28"-32"
5"	30"-34"

Changing the number of steps on a hill changes both the size of the tread and the rise between treads.
Some combinations make for more comfortable climbing than others. The chart above shows you the most comfortable combinations of tread and rise for both single- and double-tread stairs. The step-by-step directions guide you through the decisionmaking process.

 Planning stairs with a 16-inch total rise and a 60-inch run

1) Calculate the number of risers. Divide the total rise (16 inches) by the riser height you've chosen (use 6 inches as an example) to find the number of risers (2⅔). Round up to the nearest whole number (3), if necessary.

2) Calculate the actual size of the riser. If you had to round up to get the actual number of steps, you'll have to recalculate the rise they require. Divide the total rise by the number of risers to get the actual rise. In this case the actual rise is 5⅓ inches.

3) Calculate the depth of the tread. Steps have an equal number of risers and treads—three of each in the example. Divide the total run by the number of steps to get the distance from the front to the back of each step. In this case the steps will be 20 inches deep making a run of 60 inches.

4) Sketch out your stairs. Make a rough drawing of your stairs to use while you work. Draw in the rise, run, riser height, and size of the treads. Double-check your math by adding the numbers. The combined height of the risers should equal the total rise. The combined size of the treads should equal the total run.

Laying out and excavating

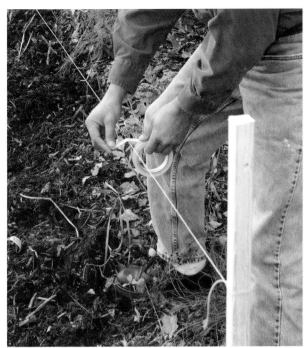

1 Set up stakes and line. Drive 2×2 stakes into the ground at the top and bottom of the slope a little beyond the ends of the steps. Drive a tall stake at the bottom of the slope. Run a mason's line from the base of the top stake to the bottom stake along what will be one edge of the steps and level it with a line level.

2 Lay out the length of the stairs. Choose the points on the ground where you want the run of the stairway to start and stop. Mark them on the mason's line with masking tape.

3 Measure the rise. Stand at the bottom of the slope and measure the distance from the line to the ground in inches. The distance is the total rise of the stairway.

4 Measure the run. Have a helper stand at the top of the hill holding one end of a tape measure at the bottom piece of tape while you stand at the bottom, holding the other end at the top tape. Measure the distance to find out the run of the stairs.

Laying out steps (continued)

5 Lay out the steps on the ground. Once you calculate the number and size of the risers and treads, make any required adjustments to your layout stakes and mason's line. Then measure along the mason's line and tape where each tread will begin. Transfer the marks to the ground with a plumb bob and powdered chalk.

6 Lay out the walk. Lower the mason's line to just above the ground, then mark the opposite edge of the steps with a parallel line. Lay out the front of each tread with stakes and line, intersecting the lines at the marks on the ground. Use a framing square to make sure corners are perfectly square.

7 Double-check for square. Double-check for square by measuring the diagonals of the overall layout—they will be equal if the layout is square. Check that the individual steps are square, too, and make any necessary adjustments.

WORK SMART
IF THE SHOE WON'T FIT

If the risers and treads don't meet the standards for comfort (see page 88), recalculate using a different riser height. If you still can't get what you want, make the stairway longer or shorter. A longer stairway results in shorter rises. A shorter stairway results in higher rises.

If you build steps on a short, steep slope, finding an acceptable riser/tread ratio sometimes can be challenging. One solution is to construct the steps at an angle to the slope rather than build them straight up and down the slope, building—in effect—a longer stairway.

8 Dig out the first step. Remove the sod and dig a rough step in the soil. At the back of the step, dig down the thickness of the paving material. Dig far enough past the back of each tread to allow room for a riser—typically 6 to 8 inches, depending on the material you use to build the steps.

9 Dig out the remaining steps. Continue to excavate the other steps the same way, measuring up the riser height and using your layout lines as guides. Level the ground roughly from front to back and side to side on each tread, using a level on a straight 2×4.

Building timber-and-paver steps

Skill level:	Time to complete:		Materials: Pressure-treated 6×6s, No. 4 (1/2-inch) rebar, 12-inch spikes, 3/4-inch gravel, landscape fabric, sand, pavers	Tools: Spade, circular saw, level, 3/8-inch drill and 1/2-inch extension bit, 3-pound sledgehammer, hand tamper, rubber mallet, work gloves, safety glasses
★★★☆☆	Experienced	4 hrs.		
	Handy	7 hrs.		
	Novice	9 hrs.		

The rise of a timber step is a Goldilocks story: Steps made from 4×4s are too low, steps made from 8×8s are too high, but steps made from 6×6s are just right. Given that, few choices are available for the depth of the treads. Those shown in the chart below are the best choices. (The depth is measured from the riser to the front edge of the stair.)

When possible, choose a double tread. Double treads are easy to climb because you take a step on one tread before stepping up to the next one. Depending on the total length of the steps, however, double treads may not be possible. If your steps have a run of 48 inches, for example, no combination of 32-inch steps will work. Instead use a single tread: three 16-inch treads fit just right.

You can adjust the size of the tread a little. The narrowest it can be is 5½ inches (the true width of a 6×6) plus the length of a paver. If you want to make it wider, make it wider by the full size— width or length—of the paver you're using. If necessary you can make the stairs a bit longer or shorter. Exactly where you start or stop on a hill is usually a matter of choice.

Building timber-and-paver steps doesn't require specialized skills, but it is labor intensive.

Make the frames of .40 pressure-treated 6×6s, nailing the corners together with 12-inch spikes. Anchor the timbers to the ground with 24-inch lengths of No. 4 (½-inch) rebar. The pavers call for a standard installation: Lay down landscape fabric, add and compact gravel, and prepare the sand base so the pavers are flush with the top of the timbers.

Tread depth for timber steps	
Single tread	Double tread
14"-16"	28"-32"

These steps are built with 5½-inch risers—the actual size of a 6×6 timber. A tread depth of 29½ inches accommodates three 8-inch-long pavers plus the thickness of a riser, so there's no need to cut pavers. The 2-inch-thick pavers sit flush with the top of the timber frames, resting on a gravel-and-sand bed. Each frame consists of a front piece the width of the step, two side pieces the depth of the tread, and a back piece cut to fit between the sides. The frames are assembled with spikes and anchored into the ground with No. 4 (½-inch) rebar.

1 Lay out steps. Design the steps with a riser height of 5½ inches and with a tread length from the chart (left). Lay out each step with stakes or batterboards and mason's line. Excavate rough steps in the hill. Dig the first tread 6 inches longer than the actual tread measurement (front to back). Dig the others the length of the tread.

2 Build the frames. Assemble a 6×6 timber frame for each step, making it 5½ inches longer than the actual tread size. To make sure the frame is the right size, build a corner of the frame and square it with a framing square. Dry-lay your paver pattern against it and position the remaining parts of the frame about 1/16 inch from the pavers.

Building timber-and-paver steps (continued)

3 **Drill holes and finish assembly.** Drill holes slightly narrower and shorter than 12-inch spikes, then spike the corners together. Drill 1/2-inch holes through the top and out the bottom of the timbers for the No. 4 (1/2-inch) rebar that you'll drive in later.

4 **Position the frames.** Put the first frame in place at the bottom of the stairs. Level it from side to side. Slope it down toward the front by 1/4 inch per foot. Test the slope with a 2-foot level that has a 1/2-inch spacer under one end. The slope is correct when the bubble is centered.

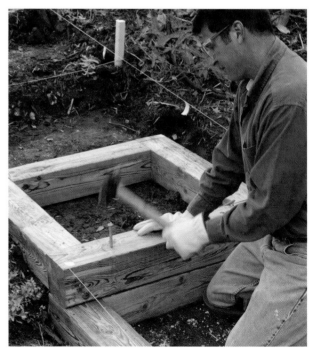

5 **Stake the frame to the ground.** Drive 24-inch lengths of No. 4 rebar through the timbers and into the ground. Mark the positions of the rebars in chalk on the back of the timbers so you don't hit the rebars with spikes when nailing in the next frame.

6 **Install the second step.** Set the front timber of the next step on the back of the first. Fasten them together by drilling pilot holes and then driving a pair of 12-inch spikes through the front of the tread. Anchor the back piece with rebar.

7 **Install the rest of the steps.** Put the steps in place one at a time. Check that each is level from side to side. Slope each step for drainage.

8 **Fill with gravel and sand.** Tamp the soil with a hand tamper to compact any loose soil. Shovel a 1½-inch layer of gravel into the frames, and level and tamp it. Put a layer of landscape fabric on the gravel. Add about 2 inches of sand over the fabric.

9 **Smooth out the sand.** Build a screed by nailing a 1×4 to a 2×4 so the 1×4 extends below the 2×4 by the thickness of a paver. Screed the sand level.

10 **Lay the pavers.** Lay the pavers in the desired pattern. (See pages 50-51.) Bed them in the sand with a rubber mallet.

11 **Fill the joints with sand.** Sweep mason's sand onto the pavers. Spray the steps with water to wash sand into the joints and to compact it. Sweep away the excess sand when it is dry and repeat the process, if necessary.

DESIGN TIP
SOLID TIMBER STEPS

Full timbers make excellent steps that are easy to install. Excavate rough steps in the ground and add a 4-inch base of tamped gravel. Lay the timbers and fasten them together with spikes. Anchor the timbers by driving 24-inch lengths of No. 4 (½-inch) rebar through predrilled holes into the ground.

Pouring concrete steps

Skill level:	Time to complete:	Materials: 2×12s, 2×8s, duplex nails, bagged concrete, form-release agent, curing compound	Tools: Mason's line, level, combination square, framing square, circular saw, hammer, wheelbarrow, mason's hoe, shovel, edger, mason's trowel, stiff-bristle broom, garden sprayer
★★★★★	Experienced 8 hrs. Handy 12 hrs. Novice 18 hrs.		

The steps shown here are garden steps designed to go up a hillside but not to be attached to any structures. Steps attached to structures require footings and sidewalls. Local codes govern installation. Attached steps are best left to the pros.

Garden steps are typically 48 inches wide so they can accommodate two people walking side by side.

Steps are made of treads and risers. The tread is what you walk on; the riser is the wall at the back of the step. The total height of the stairs is the rise; the length, or run, is measured horizontally rather than along the ground.

For steps with a total rise of fewer than 30 inches, a combination of an 11-inch tread and a 7½-inch riser is the most comfortable to climb. Steps with a total rise of more than 30 inches are more work to climb. The ideal riser height is 6 inches; the ideal tread is 12 inches. For more on treads and risers, see page 88.

The forms needed for concrete steps are similar to the risers made for wood steps. They're laid out the same way, then the lines are adjusted so the tread slopes forward and the riser slopes slightly backward. This creates a tread that won't puddle in the rain, while moving the riser back to prevent stubbing your toes.

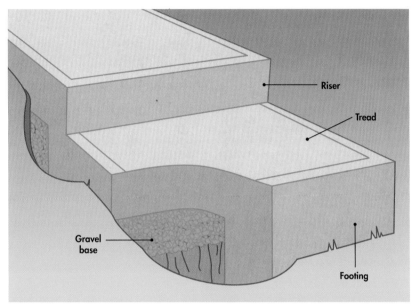

Riser

Tread

Gravel base

Footing

The forms built to pour steps are similar to the stringers made for wooden steps. Wet concrete is heavy, and bracing the forms, as shown, is essential. Remove the forms while the concrete is still wet to trowel and broom the surface.

The total volume of a stairway is huge, but the concrete is only 4 inches thick. Masons partially fill the form with stones to save time, labor, and concrete.

As you'll discover, the forms get in the way of troweling the concrete. Trowel the surface as best you can, wait a while, then remove the forms when the concrete can support its own weight. The rest of the finishing, including a nonskid broomed surface, takes place after the forms are removed.

 OOPS
NOT WIDE ENOUGH

Steps are usually designed to be wide enough for two people to walk comfortably side-by-side. If your steps are too narrow, you can fix them while you're installing the forms. Once the concrete is poured, however, you'll be walking single file. Review the details before you do the installation. Doing the job once correctly is far more satisfying than doing it twice to fix a mistake.

1 Set up stakes and line. Lay out the sides of the stairs with mason's line and 2×2 stakes set in the ground about 6 inches past the top and bottom of the slope. Position the mason's line so that it runs level from the base of the top stakes to the bottom stakes.

2 Lay out the length of the stairs. Drive landscape spikes in the ground to mark the top and bottom of one side of the stairs. Transfer the mark to layout lines with a plumb bob and mark them with tape.

3 Measure the rise. At the bottom of the stairs, measure the distance from the tape to the ground in inches. The distance is the total rise of the stairway.

4 Measure the run. Have a helper stand at the top of the hill holding one end of a tape measure while you stand at the bottom holding the other end. Measure between the pieces of tape (in inches) to figure the total run of the stairs.

5 Sprinkle sand on the ground about 6 inches outside the layout lines. Remove the grass and at least 6 inches of soil, letting the bottom of the excavation follow the slope of the ground.

6 Build a gravel bed. Fill the excavation with gravel in 2-inch layers, compacting between layers, until the gravel is at grade level.

7 Calculate the size of the risers. Divide the total rise by 7½ inches (the ideal riser height). Round up to get the number of risers. Then divide the total rise by the number of risers to get the height of each riser. Mark the height on the narrow arm of a framing square using a stair gauge. (Divide by 6 if the total rise is more than 30 inches.)

Pouring concrete steps (continued)

7 Determine the tread depth. Divide the total run by 11 inches (the ideal tread depth) and round up to get the number of steps. Divide the total run by the number of steps to get the depth of a tread. Mark the depth on the wide arm of a framing square using a stair gauge. (Divide by 12 if the rise is more than 30 inches.)

8 Lay out the bottom of each form. You will need two stepped forms; lay out and cut one as directed here, then repeat to build the other. Start by putting the square against the edge of a 2×12, as shown, and draw a line marking the bottom of the form. Extend the line across the board as shown in Step 9.

9 Lay out the first step. Slide the square along the edge of the form until the gauge on the wide arm meets the line you drew. Trace along the wide arm to lay out the tread. Trace along the narrow arm to lay out the riser.

10 Lay out the next step. Move the square farther up the form. Slide the framing square until the gauge on the wide arm meets the line marking the riser of the first step. Trace along the square, outlining the rise and the run. Repeat the process for each step.

11 Lay out the top of the form. Once you've drawn the line for the last riser, extend it across the form to mark the top end of the form.

12 Draw in the slope. The back of the treads should be $1/4$ inch higher than the front so water will run off. Measure up this amount at the back of each tread and draw a new tread. Slope the riser in 1 inch at the bottom for extra foot room.

13 **Cut out the top and bottom of the form.** Set your circular saw to cut through the form. Cut along the layout line that marks the top of the form. Move to the other end of the form and cut along the line marking the bottom of the form.

14 **Cut out the risers.** Cut along the layout lines that mark the risers. Stop when the blade reaches the layout line for the tread. Repeat to cut out the treads, stopping when the saw cut reaches the layout line marking the riser.

15 **Finish the cuts by hand.** Because of the shape of the blade, the saw will leave an uncut section of wood on the back of the form. Finish the cut with a handsaw.

16 **Cut riser forms.** The forms need boards nailed across the front of the risers to hold back the wet concrete. Cut 2×8s to the length and height of the risers. Bevel an edge so the boards don't cover the step below.

17 **Install the sides.** Put the side forms in place. Nail a riser across the front and back of the forms. Square the assembly with a framing square and level the forms side to side.

18 **Install the risers.** Stake the sides every 4 feet on center and nail the stakes to them with duplex nails, which remove easily. Nail the risers in place starting at the top so you won't stand on risers you just installed. Coat the forms with a form-release agent or vegetable oil so they will be easy to remove from the dried concrete.

Pouring concrete steps (continued)

Filling the forms

1 **Put stone in the forms.** Save on the concrete you'll need by partially filling the forms with 1- to 2-inch stones. Keep the stones at least 4 inches from the sides and tops of the forms. Wet the stones just before putting in the concrete to keep them from sucking water from the concrete.

2 **Fill the bottom step with concrete.** Mix enough concrete to fill the entire form, following the directions on the bag. Fill the bottom step first, overfilling it slightly. Work a shovel up and down to remove trapped air.

3 **Trowel the surface smooth.** Strike the concrete level with the top of the step with a trowel. Fill the steps, one at a time, the way you filled the first.

4 **Trowel the risers.** After about one hour, remove the form on the front riser. If the concrete sags, put the riser back, and test again later. When the concrete can support its own weight, remove the forms entirely, and smooth the concrete with a mason's trowel until water forms on the surface.

5 **Broom the surface.** Wait until the sheen is gone from the surface. Round over all edges of each step with an edger. Pull a damp stiff-bristled broom across the treads perpendicular to traffic to give them a non-skid surface.

6 **Apply curing compound.** Pour a curing compound into a garden sprayer and spray it onto the steps while the concrete is still wet. The compound keeps moisture in the concrete so that it won't crack as it hardens. Allow to cure 5 days in warm weather and 7 days in cold weather before walking on the steps.

Laying mortared brick or stone steps

Skill level:	Time to complete:		Materials: 1¼-inch screws, duplex nails, 2×4, plywood, Type M mortar, bricks, flat stones, cement slurry	Tools: Hammer, mixing tub, mason's trowel, screed, level, rubber mallet, 3-pound sledgehammer, brick chisel, mortar bag, paintbrush, jointer, work gloves, safety glasses, burlap rag, carpenter's pencil
★★★☆☆	Experienced	8 hrs.		
	Handy	12 hrs.		
	Novice	15 hrs.		

Mortared brick or stone steps are laid on concrete. Construct concrete steps as shown on pages 94-99. For brick steps, try to plan for a riser height of 6½ inches and a tread depth of about 12½ inches. Don't finish the concrete; the mortar will adhere better to a rough concrete surface.

Excavate 6 inches around the steps to install forms, setting them ½ inch above the concrete for bricks and 1 inch above for stones. Apply a bed of mortar, screed it, and lay the bricks or stones. Use face bricks rather than paver bricks, which are too smooth for stairs. Use bricks rated SW or SX in climates that have severe weather conditions; MW or MX bricks are acceptable in moderate climates where there is no freezing. If you apply stone, choose bluestone or slate.

Mortar joint · Tread brick · Concrete · Mortar bed · Riser brick

Concrete provides the foundation for the steps and prevents the mortar from cracking due to ground shifts from freezing and thawing. Mortar holds the bricks or stones to the concrete and fills the spaces between them. A rowlock pattern—bricks placed on edge—is strong, durable, and the most common way to lay bricks on steps. If using stones, choose large, flat stones at least 1 inch thick. Lay a ½-inch-thick mortar bed for bricks, a 1-inch-thick bed for stones. Bricks or stones on treads can overlap risers by 1 to 2 inches as long as the overlap is equal on each step.

Laying mortared brick steps

1 Build forms for the mortar. Put form boards against the sides of the concrete steps with the tops of the forms ½ inch—the thickness of the mortar bed—above the steps. Hold the boards in place with 2×4 stakes driven into the ground. Attach the stakes to the forms with 1¼-inch screws or duplex nails.

2 Mix mortar. Pour a bag of premixed Type M mortar into a mixing tub or wheelbarrow. Make a small well in the middle of the mix and gradually add water, stirring with a trowel or mason's hoe. The instructions on the bag will indicate how much water to add. When the mortar clings to a trowel set on edge, it is the right consistency.

Laying mortared brick or stone steps (continued)

3 Apply bricks to the first riser. Lay the mortar and bricks for one riser and tread at a time. Spread about ½ inch of mortar along the face of the first riser. Then spread the same amount of mortar on the bottom and ends of individual bricks and put them against the riser.

4 Apply mortar to the first tread. Spread ½ inch of mortar on the first tread. Pull a screed across the forms to level the mortar. Trowel mortar on the top of the riser bricks you just laid, up to the height of the tread.

5 Lay bricks across the first tread. Space them ³⁄₈ inch to ½ inch apart with plywood spacers, positioning them as shown. Tap the bricks in place with a rubber mallet to level them with each other and to embed them in the mortar.

DESIGN TIP
BRICK PATTERNS

You can create variety on your steps by laying the bricks in different patterns. Do a dry run first to make sure the bricks align properly.

6 Build more steps and fill mortar between the bricks. Put a 2×4 across the tread to check for high and low spots. To fix a low spot, add mortar. For a high spot, tap the brick with the rubber mallet. Continue to lay bricks this way until the steps are complete, then remove the form boards and spacers. Using a grout bag, fill the joints between bricks with mortar.

7 Tool the joints. Smooth and compress the joints with a convex jointer, working from back to front. Before the mortar dries, wipe any excess mortar from the bricks with a dry burlap rag. Cover with a sheet of plastic and let the mortar harden for three to four days. Wait one week before using the steps.

Laying mortared stone steps

1 Fit the stones. Install forms that extend one inch above the height of the mortar bed and test-fit the stones on both treads and risers. Mark where stones need to be cut using a carpenter's pencil. Stones on the treads can overhang those on the risers by 1 to 2 inches. Number the stones so you can reposition them correctly.

2 Cut the stones. Score cut lines along the pencil marks by striking them with a cold chisel and a 3-pound sledgehammer. Then prop the scored section over a scrap piece of wood or pipe and break it off with a sharp blow from the sledgehammer. (For more on cutting stone, see page 31.)

3 Apply mortar. Mix Type M mortar in a tub and spread about 1 inch on the first riser and tread. Draw a screed across the forms to level the mortar. Brush the bottom of each stone with a cream-textured slurry made of portland cement and water to help the stones stick to the mortar.

4 Lay the first step. Put the first stones against the riser. Tap them gently with a rubber mallet to help embed them evenly with each other in the mortar. Place stones on the tread the same way.

5 Apply mortar between the stones. Working one riser and tread at a time, continue setting stones as in Step 4 until the steps are laid. Remove the form boards, then use a trowel to pack the joints between the stones with mortar.

6 Tool the joints. Smooth and compress the joints with a concave jointer. Wipe off excess mortar with a damp rag. Cover with a sheet of plastic and let dry for three to four days. Keep foot traffic off the steps for one week.

Building a wheelchair ramp

Skill level:
★★★★★

Time to complete:
Experienced	6 days
Handy	10 days
Novice	12 days

Materials: ¾-inch gravel, landscape fabric, fiber tube forms, premixed concrete, pressure-treated 1×s, 2×s, 4×4s, and 5/4×6 decking, galvanized 10d (3-inch) nails, 8d (2½-inch) nails or No. 8 2-inch deck screws, seismic anchors/hurricane ties, ⅜×7-inch hex-head bolts, washers and nuts, joist hangers, 1½-inch handrail, handrail brackets

Tools: Tape measure, mason's line, line level, plumb bob, 3-pound sledgehammer, mattock, spade or shovel, garden rake, posthole digger, wheelbarrow, circular saw, handsaw, framing square, combination square, 4-foot level, ⅜-inch electric drill and bits, speed square, hammer, ratchet and socket wrenches, safety glasses, work gloves, dust mask, mason's hoe, darby, wood float, concrete broom, concrete edger

Ramps, usually constructed for wheelchairs, are also ideal for strollers, and they can add resale value to your home. The Americans with Disabilities Act (ADA) sets strict standards for ramps. The slope, for example, must be no more than 1 inch per foot. Ramps, therefore, tend to be long. You'll need a ramp at least 20 feet long to reach a deck 20 inches high. Construct the ramp with pressure-treated lumber, using posts rated for ground contact. Before you start building, be sure to check your local codes for requirements.

This 43-inch-wide wheelchair ramp provides access from ground level to a deck 20 inches high. A level 5×5-foot landing at the top accommodates turning. Pairs of pressure-treated 4×4 posts set in concrete every 5 feet on center hold 2×6 crosspieces that support a framework of 2×6 joists. The posts are cut tall enough to hold 2×4 side rails and 2×6 cap rails, as well as handrails 36 inches above the decking.

 Meeting design requirements

The following requirements are required by the Americans with Disabilities Act (ADA). Design your ramp accordingly.

- **Rise:** A maximum of 1 inch rise for every 12 inches of run. A rise of 1 inch for every 20 inches is ideal.
- **Width:** A minimum clearance of 36 inches between handrails or curbs.
- **Landings:** A minimum level area of 60×60 inches for every 30 inches of rise and for every change of direction.
- **Surfaces:** Slip-resistant and flush with adjacent surfaces at top and bottom.
- **Handrails:** Continuous, 1¼ to 1½ inches in diameter, round or oval, 34 to 38 inches high on both sides and extending 12 inches beyond end points.

 Ramp specs

- **Width:** 43 inches.
- **Length:** Measure up from the ground to the porch or deck to find how many inches the ramp must rise. A 1:20-inch slope requires 20 inches of run for every inch of height.
- **Posts:** 4×4s, spaced 5 feet on center along the length of the ramp and 39½ inches across the width.
- **Crosspieces:** Two 2×6s bolted to opposite sides of the posts with tops beveled to follow the slope of the walk.
- **Joists:** Four 2×6 joists, running the length of the ramp.
- **Decking:** 5/4 deck boards.

Installing posts

1 Determine the length. Measure up from the ground to determine how many inches the ramp must rise. For every inch of rise, you'll need at least a foot of run. A 20-inch-high deck, for example, requires a 20-foot-long ramp.

2 Lay out the landing. To accommodate turning at the top of the ramp, lay out a 5-foot-square landing with batterboards and mason's lines. Level each line and use a 3-4-5 triangle to square the lines with the house. Slide the lines along the batterboards until the distance between two points 3 feet and 4 feet from the corner is 5 feet. (See page 35.)

3 Lay out the outside edges of the ramp with batterboards and mason's lines. Level the lines and square them using a 3-4-5 triangle. Remove the sod from the site and dig out 2 to 3 inches of soil. Dig a few inches deeper at the bottom of the ramp so you can build as close to ground level as possible.

4 Lay out the posts. Plant posts against the house, porch, or deck that the ramp will lead to, at the corners of the landing, and every 5 feet on center along the length of the ramp. Lay out the posts with mason's lines, marking their positions with masking tape. Transfer the taped marks to the ground with a plumb bob and powdered chalk.

5 Dig the footings. Mark the position of the mason's lines on the batterboards and untie them. Dig holes for posts at least 6 inches below the frost line, tapering them from 12 inches wide at the top to 18 inches wide at the bottom. Reattach the lines and move the tape 1¾ inches so it marks the location of the outside face of the posts.

6 Pour footings. Cut fiber tube forms 6 inches shorter than the holes are deep. Nail 2×4s to opposite sides of the forms and suspend the forms in the holes so they sit about 8 inches from the bottom. Put posts in the holes, and plumb and brace them. Fill the tubes with bagged concrete, mixed according to the directions on the bag. Remove the forms after 48 hours and fill in the holes.

Building a wheelchair ramp (continued)

Building a frame and adding decking

1 Build the landing. Code requires a landing at the top of the ramp so wheelchair users can open doors easily. Run crosspieces from post to post across the ramp and bolt them to the posts. Install joists on top with joist hangers. Position the landing so the decking will be flush with the door threshold.

2 Lay out the crosspieces and joists. Snap a chalkline from the top of the crosspiece at the landing to the ground at the bottom of the ramp to show where the crosspieces and joists will meet each post. Snap a chalkline 5½ inches higher to show the top of the joists.

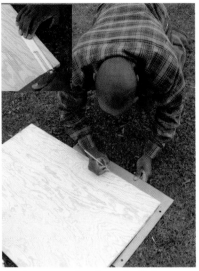

3 Lay out the bevel of the crosspieces. The crosspieces are beveled so the joists rest on the entire top surface of the crosspiece. Lay out the bevel with a framing square and plywood. Mark 1 inch along the side of the plywood and 12 inches (or the appropriate slope ratio) along the other side. Connect the points with a straight line and set a bevel gauge to the angle.

4 Cut the crosspieces. Measure across the ramp from outside the post to outside the opposite post. Cut the crosspieces to this length. Set the blade on a tablesaw to match the slope of the bevel gauge, and cut the top edge of each board to the angle.

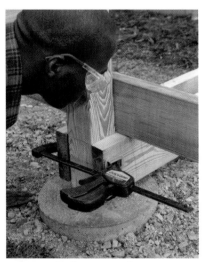

5 Install the crosspieces. Temporarily clamp the crosspieces along the chalklines that mark the bottom of the joists. Clamp them to several posts, then check their position by resting a joist on them. Reposition any crosspieces that are too high or too low. Clamp them firmly in place; drill ½-inch-diameter holes through the crosspiece, into the post, and out the other side of the second crosspiece. Bolt them in place with ½-inch bolts, nuts, and washers. Install all the crosspieces.

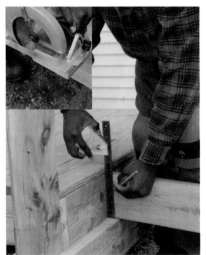

6 Cut the upper ends of the joists. Rest a joist on the crosspieces and butt it up to the landing. Lay out the angle on the end by tracing along a scrap of wood or the arm of a framing square held against the landing. Cut along the line. Repeat for the other joists.

7 **Lay out a splice on the outer joist.** If the outer joist isn't long enough, you'll have to splice two joists together. Mark the center of the post and transfer the mark to the joist. Make a square cut at the joist to cut it to length. Do the same on the opposite side.

8 **Lay out the second half of the splice.** Temporarily put the next joist in place. Trace along the joist you just cut to lay out the angle you need on the mating joist. Nail or screw reinforcement along the seam as shown in the inset.

9 **Install inner joists.** If you need to splice joists, cut the spliced end to extend beyond the crosspiece by at least 8 inches. Position the next joist so it overlaps the crosspiece by an equal amount. Nail or screw the two together. Attach joists to crosspieces with seismic anchors/hurricane ties.

10 **Cut the ends of the joists.** Trace along the posts to lay out the end of the outside joists. Temporarily position the inner joist against the post, too, and trace along it to lay out the cut. Cut the joists to length with a circular saw. Attach all the joists to the crosspieces with seismic anchors/hurricane ties.

11 **Cut and install an end joist.** Cut a piece to fit across the end of the ramp. Nail or screw it to the ends of the joists.

12 **Attach the decking.** Nail or screw the deck boards to the joists with galvanized 8d (2½-inch) nails or No. 8 2-inch deck screws. Butt the boards together; because they're pressure-treated, they will shrink as they dry, leaving about an 1/8-inch gap for drainage.

Building a wheelchair ramp (continued)

Adding railings

1 **Snap a chalkline to mark the top of the posts.** Measure 40 inches up from the decking and mark the top post. Repeat for the post at the bottom of the ramp. Snap a chalkline between the marks. Repeat on the other side of the posts and on the other set of posts.

2 **Cut the posts.** To cut each post clamp a speed square in place to follow the slope of the chalk line and to support your circular saw with the blade at the cut line. Saw across the face of the post. The cut won't go all the way through, so repeat on the other side of the post.

3 **Install the rails.** Install 2×4 side rails along the inner faces of the posts with galvanized 10d (3-inch) nails. Put one rail at the top, another at the bottom no higher than 4 inches above the decking, and the other two evenly spaced between the top and bottom.

4 **Attach the handrail.** Cut a piece of 2×4 to fit between the upper two rails on each post. Screw the 2×4s in place, then screw brackets for a 1½-inch handrail to them, positioning the rail 34 to 38 inches above the decking. Screw a handrail to each side of the ramp.

5 **Attach the cap rails.** Nail 2×6 cap rails to the tops of the posts with galvanized 10d (3-inch) nails. Set them flush with the inner faces of the posts, and miter the corners. Toenail the mitered corners together with galvanized 8d (2½-inch) nails.

6 **Pour a concrete ramp.** Dig for and install a 4-inch gravel bed, then build forms and pour concrete for a 4-inch-thick ramp that runs from the end of the wooden ramp to ground level. Screed the concrete and give it a broom finish. (For more on concrete, see pages 330–338.)

Maintaining ramps

Skill level:
★☆☆☆

Time to complete:
Experienced 1 hr.
Handy 2 hrs.
Novice 3 hrs.

Materials: Brightener, finish, pressure-treated lumber, baking soda, wood putty, premixed concrete, galvanized 10d (3-inch) nails, hex-head bolts, J-bolt, post anchor

Tools: Broom, putty knife, pressure sprayer, scrub brush, bucket, awl, paintbrush, keyhole saw, handsaw, circular saw, hammer, screw jack, level, 3/8-inch drill and bits, wood chisel, trowel, plumb bob, ratchet and socket wrenches, safety glasses, rubber gloves, work gloves, dust mask

Build a wheelchair ramp well, and it will provide years of service. But don't expect it to be maintenance free. Rain, wind, snow, and sun eventually exact their toll.

Inspect your structure once or twice a year and make repairs as soon as damage is evident. The old saying holds true: An ounce of prevention applies here too.

Sweep surfaces regularly, paying particular attention to the decking, stairs, corners, and out-of-the-way spots. To remove dirt and stains, scrub the deck with a solution of mild household detergent and water.

Remove debris from between boards with a putty knife. Debris caught between boards allows water to pool, causing wood to rot.

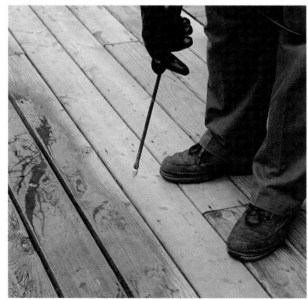

Brighten weathered wood by applying a commercial deck brightener with a pressure sprayer. Spray, wait 10 minutes, scrub the deck with a stiff-bristle brush, then rinse with cold water. Let the deck dry thoroughly before applying a finish.

Apply a finish either by spray or brush. Use a paintbrush to eliminate drips and to apply the finish in cracks and hard-to-reach areas.

CHAPTER 4

Fences & gates

Before you build a fence, first consider why you want one. Then find a few fences that meet those needs. Look at the back of these fences, not just the front. They're almost always different. Any fence that is beautiful from your yard but unattractive from the neighbor's is probably a poor choice.

Once you've decided on a type of fence, choose the material—chain link, vinyl, redwood, cedar, ornamental iron, or pressure-treated wood. While chain link wins no awards for beauty, it will keep the kids in the backyard, it doesn't block your view of the neighborhood, and it is maintenance-free. Many vinyl fences come in white, but it's a white that stays maintenance-free for years.

You can build almost any kind of fence with wood, then paint it, stain it, or simply admire the grain. Wood, however, needs

periodic maintenance. Fortunately, pressure-treated wood pretty much solves the problem. Once you get above ground, the resistance to decay is considerably less troublesome. Here, cedar, redwood, and pressure-treated wood will give you similar results. (Use pressure-treated timber rated "above ground" for everything except posts.)

Whether you're building from scratch or prefab panels, if you go with pressure-treated wood, stain it rather than paint it. Even the best paint will eventually chip. Cedar and redwood can both do with or without a finish. Both exterior-grade clear finish (other than varnish) and finishes made to match the wood apply easily. Both will also darken the wood somewhat, as will time and weather. Time and weather, however, won't lengthen the life of the fence. A good finish will.

Contents

Good fences make good neighbors

Fences are simple to install, but they do require time and a certain amount of muscle. In the lower half of the United States, a simple guideline keeps fence builders out of most trouble: Put your fence posts in holes that are at least half as deep as the fence is tall. A fence 4 feet high belongs in a hole that's 2 feet deep. A 6-foot fence belongs in a 3-foot hole, and an 8-foot fence belongs in a 4-foot hole. Looked at another way, this formula means that at least one-third of the total length of the fence pole is underground, more than enough to anchor the fence against high winds and backyard disasters.

As you go farther north, however, freezing and thawing causes the ground—and anything in it—to shift. To protect the posts, their holes must be dug at least 6 inches below the frost line, as well as at least half the height of the exposed fence. The map on page 180 will help you find the frost line in your area, but it's always a good idea to check with your municipality for local requirements. To further anchor the posts, set the end and gateposts in concrete. If you expect the fence to face real abuse, you can set all the other posts in concrete too. Think twice about putting concrete around anything but end and gateposts, however. If you ever have to remove the fence, you'll also have to remove the concrete.

Fences & gates tool kit

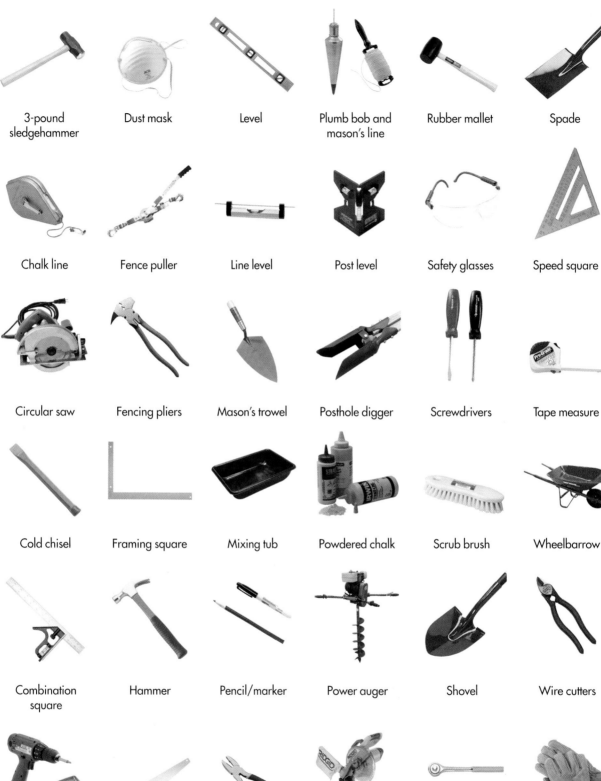

3-pound sledgehammer	Dust mask	Level	Plumb bob and mason's line	Rubber mallet	Spade
Chalk line	Fence puller	Line level	Post level	Safety glasses	Speed square
Circular saw	Fencing pliers	Mason's trowel	Posthole digger	Screwdrivers	Tape measure
Cold chisel	Framing square	Mixing tub	Powdered chalk	Scrub brush	Wheelbarrow
Combination square	Hammer	Pencil/marker	Power auger	Shovel	Wire cutters
Drill and bits	Handsaw	Pliers	Power miter saw	Socket wrenches	Work gloves

Materials

Post cap

Pressure-treated 2×4 rail

Pressure-treated 4×4

Prefab fencing panel

1×6

1×4

Cedar

Precut mortised posts and rails

Wire fencing

Redwood

▲ Basic materials for constructing a wood fence include ***pressure-treated 4×4s*** for posts; a stamp indicates that they are suitable for below ground level. Protect the tops of posts from exposure to water with ***post caps. Prefab fencing panels*** go up quickly and come in a variety of styles. If you want to build a fence from scratch, nail ***pressure-treated 2×4 rails*** to the posts to build a frame for the fencing. Fence boards made from ***1×6s*** apply to fencing styles such as the alternate board, louver, or basket weave. You can also make your own pickets by cutting shapes from ***1×4s. Cedar*** and ***redwood*** fence boards resist rot naturally and are virtually maintenance-free. ***Wire fencing*** is yet another option. Build a rustic fence without the old-time work, using ***precut mortised posts and rails,*** or nail rails to a 6-inch post.

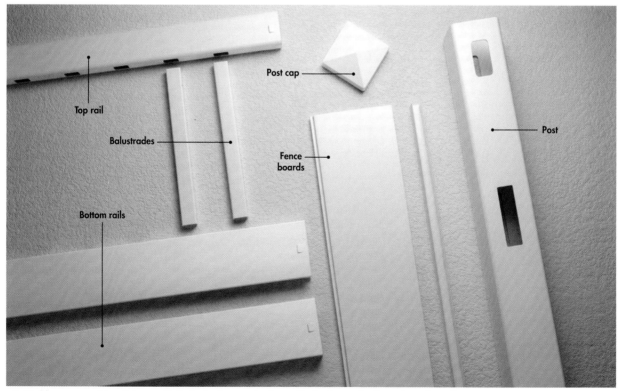

Top rail

Balustrades

Bottom rails

Post cap

Fence boards

Post

▲ Vinyl fences come with ready-to-assemble ***balustrades, posts, top rails, bottom rails, fence boards, and post caps.***

Materials (continued)

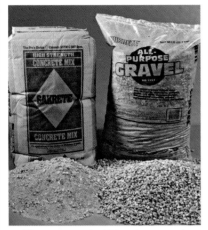

▲ Mix **concrete** and put it in end, corner, and gatepost holes to anchor the posts in the ground. Put **gravel** underneath the other posts to help drain away water.

Tension band

Tension wire

Brace bands

Tension bars

Rail

1³⁄₈-inch-diameter rail and cap

1⁵⁄₈-inch-diameter line post and cap

Tie wires

Hog rings

2¹⁄₂-inch-diameter end post and cap

Chain link fencing

▲ A chain-link fence is easy to put up—don't be scared off by its large number of parts. For the basic frame you'll need **2¹⁄₂-inch-diameter end posts and caps, 1⁵⁄₈-inch-diameter line posts and caps, and 1³⁄₈-inch-diameter rails and caps. Attach rail caps to posts with brace bands.** Assemble a gate with **top, bottom, and side rails** or buy all the parts together in a kit. Install **chain-link fencing** with **tension bands, tension bars, tension wires, tie wires,** and **hog rings.**

Hanger and galvanized hanger nails

Deck screws

Galvanized nails

Self-closing butt hinge

Strap hinge

Staples

T hinge

Strike latch

Lag-and-strap latch

Slide-bolt latches

Drop latch

Barrel bolt

Hasp latch

Spring closure

Thumb latches

Antisag kit

◄ Choose fasteners and hardware suited to the type of fence and gate you're building. Fit rails edge up between posts with **hangers and galvanized hanger nails.** Fasten fence boards with **deck screws** or **galvanized nails.** Attach wire fencing to wood posts and rails with **staples.** Hang a gate with **self-closing butt hinges, strap hinges, T hinges,** or **lag-and-strap hinges. Strike latches** automaticaly latch a gate when it swings shut. Other types of latches include a **drop latch,** a **slide-bolt latch,** a **thumb latch,** and a **hasp latch.** For a double gate, install a **barrel bolt. A spring closure** swings a gate shut automatically. Correct a sagging gate with a turnbuckle-style **antisag kit.**

Choosing lumber

Most, if not all, lumber used outdoors comes from evergreens. Evergreens and other trees which keep their foliage during winter are called softwoods. Trees that lose their leaves in winter are called deciduous or hardwood. Hardwood and softwood, however, are only generalizations: Balsa, for example, is technically a hardwood.

The softwoods used in outdoor construction include cedar, redwood, cypress, and pressure-treated pine. Like all trees, these trees have both heartwood and sapwood. The sapwood is the narrow, lighter-color wood near the bark that completely encases the heartwood. Sapwood is never as strong or rot resistant as the heartwood. Avoid lumber that has lighter strips running along the edges.

Rot-resistance, however, has been standardized. All pressure-treated wood carries a stamp from the American Wood Preserver's Association (AWPA) that indicates the best use for the board based on the amount of preservative in it. Boards for above ground use—such as decking— are stamped "above ground." Boards for use as posts are stamped "ground contact."

As of January 1, 2004, chromium copper arsenate (CCA) is no longer used. The new treatments require the same care when handling the wood, however: Wear a dust mask and safety glasses when cutting the wood, shower when you finish working, and wash the clothes you wore separately from other clothes. Do not burn pressure-treated wood. Put it in the trash or bury it.

Cedar is found on both the East and West Coasts. Red cedar is dull to bright red with white sapwood. White cedar is light brown with white sapwood. Eastern white cedar is aromatic and is also used in blanket chests and closets. All cedars are rotresistant and stable and shrink little with changes in weather and humidity levels.

Pressure-treated wood has been pressure-impregnated with a liquid preservative. Studies show that once it's in the wood, the preservative stays there, and experience shows the wood lasts longer. Results vary, depending on the wood and the type and amount of the preservative. The best guide comes from manufacturers, who say that pressure-treated wood will last at least eight times longer than untreated wood. Pressure-treated wood is made from softwoods because softwoods readily absorb the preservatives. Some Western woods are perforated slightly to help the preservative soak in, but most of the wood is Southern pine, which requires no perforation. Because Southern pine includes several types of trees (longleaf pine, shortleaf pine, loblolly pine, and slash pine), the density and strength of pressure-treated wood varies.

Redwood grows along the coast of California and produces a wood that is light red to dark brown. It's more easily obtained on the West Coast than on the East, where it is quite expensive. The wood is lightweight, works easily, and is stable. It expands and contracts very little, making it ideal for outdoor use. Heartwood from old-growth trees is highly decay-resistant; second-growth lumber is slightly less so.

Cypress is a Southern wood that comes from the bald cypress, one of two needle-leafed trees that lose their leaves in the winter (the other is the larch). Old-growth cypress is among the most decay-resistant trees and is a favorite for windows, boats, and even caskets. Second-growth cypress is slightly less rot resistant but still a reliable wood for outdoor use. The heartwood is from light yellowish brown to chocolate color. The wood is moderately strong, moderately heavy, and moderately hard.

Checking for level and plumb

Using an electronic water level

1 Fill the tube with water. Attach one end of the tube to the measuring unit. Measure the amount of water recommended by the manufacturer into a container. Put the free end of the tube in the water (dyed red in the photo to make it easier to see). Keep the end attached to the measuring unit at a point somewhere below the container. Suck on the tube attached to the unit to fill the tube. Tighten the clamps to trap the water in the tube.

2 Put the measuring unit at the desired height. Once it's in place, loosen the clamps. Take the free end of the tube to the object you want to check, temporarily keeping the free end below the end attached to the unit.

3 Lift the free end until the unit beeps. When the unit beeps, the water at the free end of the tube is at the same height as the water in the measuring unit. Points that are even with the water at each end are level with each other.

Using a line level

A line level hooks onto a mason's line and is used to level a layout line. The line is level when the bubble is centered in the vial. Raise or lower an end, as needed, to bring the line into alignment.

Plumbing a post

A post should be plumb in all directions. Check it with a post level, which slips over a corner of the post and gives readings from both faces.

⛫ Using a level

Put the level flat against a vertical surface. The surface is plumb if the bubbles in the vials in the end of the level are centered between the lines. The object shown here is out of plumb. To see how far it's out, lift one end away from the surface until the bubble centers between the lines. The amount of gap between the edge of the level and the surface is the amount the surface is out of plumb.

Laying out fences and gates

Skill level:
★☆☆☆☆

Time to complete:
Experienced 1 hrs.
Handy 1.5 hrs.
Novice 2 hrs

Materials: 2×2s, 2×4s, 12-inch landscape spike, 10d (3-inch) nails, masking tape

Tools: Tape measure, mason's line, hammer, 3-pound sledgehammer, circular saw, line level, plumb bob, powdered chalk

The best way to lay out a fence is with batterboards, which allow you to reposition your layout lines without moving the batterboards themselves. For layout lines, use mason's line—it won't sag like regular string does.

If the fence has two or more sides, they need to be at right angles to each other. It's not the sort of thing you can easily check with a framing square, so you'll have to measure the diagonal between two points near the corner.

Once you've run the lines, you can put tape on them to mark where the posts will go. Depending on the fencing you're using, the posts will be either 6 or 8 feet apart.

1 Build batterboards. Build a pair of batterboards for each run of fencing. Start by cutting points into the ends of two 2-foot 2×4s. Nail a 2×4 crosspiece to them about 2 inches from the top.

2 Drive the batterboards into the ground about 18 inches beyond the planned end points of the fence. Tie mason's line to one of the crosspieces, stretch the line to the other crosspiece, and tie the line in place so it's taut.

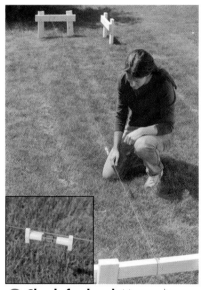

3 Check for level. Hang a line level on the middle of the line. Drive one of the batterboards farther into the ground to level the line, if necessary. Measure from a fixed object, such as the house or patio, and slide the line along the crosspiece until it's the same distance from the fixed object along its entire length.

4 Lay out adjoining sides of the fence. Drive more batterboards and stretch line to lay out adjoining sides of the fence. Level the line by driving one of the batterboards farther into the ground, then adjust so the line replicates the path of the fence.

5 Check for square. Start at the corner where the lines cross; measure 3 feet along one line and mark the spot with tape. Put a piece of tape 4 feet from the intersection on the other piece of line. The lines are square if the distance between the pieces of tape is 5 feet. If they're not square, slide one of the lines along the batterboard until they are.

Laying out fences and gates (continued)

6 **Mark the corners and ends of the fence.** Drop a plumb bob from the intersection of the mason's lines. Mark the spot below the plumb bob with chalk. If the fence ends without forming a corner, measure along the line to a distance equal to the length of your fence. Mark this end point on the line with tape, drop a plumb bob, then mark the ground with chalk.

7 **Lay out the posts.** Measure along the mason's line, and put tape on the line to indicate the position of the line posts (the posts between the end posts). Drop a plumb bob from the tape and mark each spot with chalk or a piece of paper and a nail.

Laying out a curved fence

1 **Find a center point that's the same distance from each end of the curve** and make a "compass" from mason's line and a chalk bottle.

2 **To lay out the posts on a curve,** measure in a straight line between points on the curve.

Installing fence posts

Skill level:
★☆☆☆

Time to complete:
Experienced	8 hrs.
Handy	10 hrs.
Novice	12 hrs.

Materials: Gravel; pressure-treated 4×4s, 2×4s, and 2×2s rated for ground burial; duplex nails; bagged concrete

Tools: Power auger, tape measure, post level, wheelbarrow, shovel, hammer, clamps, level, mason's trowel, line level, drill and bits, chalk line, speed or combination square, circular saw, stepladder, clamps, safety glasses, dust mask, work gloves

If you want your fence to outlast its first summer, you need to set the posts deep enough in the ground to withstand wind, rain, and frost. With that in mind, there is only one hard-and-fast rule when you're digging a fence posthole: Dig a hole for the post that is half as deep as the fence is high. In areas with frost, dig the hole at least that deep or 6 inches below the frost line, whichever is deeper. Other than that, there are some variables:

- You can set the post in concrete or fill the hole with the soil that came out of it and tamp the soil in place.
- You can dig the hole a bit deeper and put 4 inches of gravel on the bottom for drainage.
- Generally speaking the hole should be 4 inches wider than the widest dimension of the post, but the size of the hole depends on the height of the fence and quality of the soil. (See "Sizing Footings" on page 118.)

On the following pages, you'll see how to set posts two different ways—in concrete or in tamped soil. For the best results, set the end, corner, and gateposts in concrete. You can set the other posts, called line posts, in concrete, too, but it isn't strictly necessary. The tamped soil is usually enough.

As a rule, a posthole should be about 4 inches wider than the post. If no frost is present, dig a hole for the post that is as deep as half the height of the fence. In areas with frost, the holes should be the same depth and at least 6 inches below the frost line. Add 4 inches to the depths of the holes if you're putting in a gravel drainage bed. Ideally, set end and gateposts in concrete: Widen the bottom of the hole a few inches, pour in the concrete, and set the post so that it's 6 inches from the bottom of the hole. **Locate underground utilities before you start to dig postholes.**

 Regional variation

Gas-powered augers are a good way to dig fence postholes in loose or sandy soil but can catch and turn into a merry-go-round in rocky ground. If you have rocky or hard ground, consider hiring a fencing contractor whose auger is mounted on a truck or tractor. You'll save yourself time—and possible injury. Lay out the holes in advance so you don't pay the contractor to wait while you get ready.

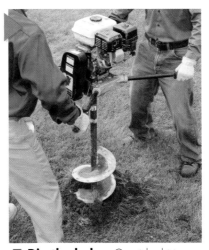

1 Dig the holes. Consider hiring a contractor to dig the holes in rocky soil. Rent a power auger for holes that aren't in rocky soil. Work with a helper and follow the manufacturer's instructions. Raise the auger after every few inches of digging to clear out soil. Dig to the depth required for the posts, plus 4 inches for a gravel base.

2 Pour footings for end, corner, and gateposts. You'll set corner posts, end posts, and gateposts in concrete. The others are set in tamped soil. Start by lining the bottom of all the holes with 4 inches of gravel. Then mix concrete in a wheelbarrow and fill the end, corner, and gatepost holes with 6 inches of concrete. (If you're setting more than two posts in concrete, pour and set one hole at a time.)

3 Put in end, corner, and gateposts. Restring the layout lines and use them as guides to set the end, corner, and gateposts. (You'll set the line posts later.) While the concrete is still wet, put the posts in their holes. Plumb each post with a level and hold it in place with braces and stakes.

4 Put concrete on top of the footings. Mix more concrete in the wheelbarrow. Fill the hole about one-third of the way.

5 Tamp to remove trapped air. Air trapped in the concrete will weaken it. Work a 2x4 up and down in the concrete to release the air.

Sizing frost-free footings			
Fence height	Footing diameter x depth (inches)		
	Loose soil	Medium soil	Hard soil
4'	9x24	8x24	7x24
5'	9x24	8x24	7x24
6'	10x30	8x30	7x30
7'	11x36	9x36	7x36
8'	12x42	10x42	8x42
9'	13x48	11x48	9x48
10'	14x48	12x48	10x48
11'	15x48	14x48	12x48
12'	16x48	14x48	12x48

If you live in a frost-free area, the table above gives you the diameter and depth of footings for fence posts 4 inches in diameter. For fences with 10-foot sections, add 25 percent to either the diameter or depth. If you're putting in a 4-inch layer of gravel, dig postholes that much deeper.

☑ WORK SMART
VARIATIONS

It's usually a good idea to dig postholes a few at a time rather than all at once so you can account for variations in panel widths and contours in the terrain as you go. This ensures that all the holes will be in the right place.

☑ WORK SMART
SETTING POSTS WITH DECORATIVE TOPS

Cutting posts to height after they've been set in the ground isn't something you'll want to do if the posts have a decorative top already in place. If this is the case, set the end posts at the desired height, then run a level mason's line between them. Double-check the height of each post against the mason's line. Working one post at a time, dig a hole until it holds the post at the right height. Plumb and brace the post and backfill around it before digging the next hole.

6 Fill the holes. Continue filling the holes with concrete up to about 2 inches above ground level. Smooth the surface of the concrete with a mason's trowel, sloping it away from the post so rain will drain off. Let the concrete harden at least 48 hours before trimming the post and removing the braces.

7 Set the line posts in their holes using the mason's line as guides. Align and plumb each post, then backfill around it and tamp the soil. Slope the soil at the top of the holes away from the posts for drainage.

Trimming posts

1 Mark a level line on all the posts. Start by marking one of the end posts at the desired height. Hold chalk line against the mark and stretch it to the other end post. Level the line with a line level and snap it against the line posts. If the fence is long, work no more than three or four posts at a time to avoid problems caused by sag in the line. Extend the chalkline across all four faces of each post with a combination square.

2 Clamp a speed square to the post. Position the square so when you rest the saw on it, it will make a cut along the line, marking the top of the post.

3 Cut the post to length. Guide the saw along the top of the square to cut off the top of the post. If your saw won't cut deep enough to cut through a fence post (most saws won't), remove the square and screw it to the opposite side of the post. Cut as before to cut through the post.

Installing prefab fence panels

Skill level:	**Time to complete:**	**Materials:** Prefab wood panels, rail hangers, hanger nails, post caps, galvanized 8d (2½-inch) nails, construction adhesive	**Tools:** Tape measure, mason's line, line level, framing square, speed or combination square, level hammer, circular saw, safety glasses, work gloves
★★★☆☆	Experienced 5 hrs. Handy 10 hrs. Novice 12 hrs.		

Prefab fence panels are one of the fastest ways to build an attractive fence. Panels come in a variety of designs, from picket fences to board fences topped with lattice. It pays to shop around for the panels that best suit your house, your pocketbook, and your tastes.

Compared to other fencing styles, for which a lot of cutting and nailing is required, prefab fencing is both fast and easy. You dig holes for the fence posts and put the posts in place. But before you plumb the posts and fill the holes, you attach the fence section to each post so the fence fits perfectly between the poles. Doing so also makes it easier to plumb the posts: Plumb the panel, and the posts are automatically plumb too.

Space the posts to match the panels. 6- and 8-foot lengths are standard. Add ¼ to ½ inch at each end. Attach the panels so they clear the ground by 3 or 4 inches. Because you may need to install the panels at different heights due to changes in the ground level, wait until you've installed the entire fence before trimming the posts to length.

Hanging panels

1 Install an end post. Plumb the end post, brace it, then fill in the hole with concrete. Measure and mark layout lines where the top and bottom of a panel will meet the post. Brace the next post temporarily in place, then transfer the layout lines with a mason's line and line level.

2 Install hangers. Extend the layout marks to the inner faces of the posts using a square. Measure from the top of the fence to the rails and nail hangers this distance from the mark you made. Bend down the flange on the top bracket, as shown above. Don't bend the flange on the bottom bracket.

3 **Put the panel in place.** Put the first panel between the end post and the next post, sliding it into place until the bottom rail sits on the hangers. Check the panel for level and adjust the braces, if necessary. Plumb the loose post and fill the holes with soil, tamping the soil as you go.

4 **Nail the fence in place.** Nail the sides of the brackets to the panels. Once the first panel is installed, work your way down the fence, installing one panel at a time. Set any gateposts, corner posts, or end posts in concrete.

5 **Cut off the posts.** Draw a line where you want to cut the posts. Because most circular saws don't cut deep enough to cut through a fence post, use a combination or speed square to extend the line all the way around. Clamp a speed square to the post to guide the saw, cut through the post, then move the saw to the opposite side of the post and cut again.

6 **Install caps on the posts to protect them from water.** Spread construction adhesive on the top of the post, center the cap, and drive in two 8d (2½-inch) nails at an angle.

☑ WORK SMART
ATTACHING PANELS TO POSTS

There are three options for attaching fence panels to the posts. First, nails (which are inexpensive and available everywhere), second, with metal hangers, and third with grooved wooden U-channels. (Hangers and U-channels may only be available in certain regions.) Screw the channel to the fence, then slide the panel into the groove. The channels provide support along the full height of the panel. Spacing is as critical as for hangers, so follow the same technique: Set both posts in the ground but don't fill the holes until you've attached the panel.

🎨 DESIGN TIP
AN ALTERNATIVE APPROACH TO PREFAB

No rule prevents you from installing prefabricated fence panels across the face of the posts instead of between them. You might even hang alternate panels on alternate sides of the posts. A benefit of this approach is that spacing between posts doesn't have to be as exact, and small differences go unnoticed. For a strong fence, fasten the panels to the posts with No. 8 2½-inch deck screws.

Installing wood fence rails

Skill level:	Time to complete:	Materials: Pressure-treated or rot-resistant rails	Tools: Tape measure, pencil, mason's line, line level,
★ ☆ ☆ ☆	Experienced 2 hrs.	(2×4, 2×2, or 1×2 depending on the fence), rail	combination square, hammer, ³⁄₈-inch drill and bits, safety
	Handy 3 hrs.	hangers, No. 8 2¹⁄₂-inch deck screws, galvanized 10d	glasses, work gloves
	Novice 4 hrs.	(3-inch) nails	

Even in the age of prefab panels, it's possible to build a fence from scratch. The job starts with posts. You dig the holes, align the posts, and fill in the holes. The rails come next, followed by the fencing (pickets, basket weave, or countless other possibilities). You can attach a rail several ways; none is necessarily better than the others. If your fence will be taller than 4 feet or particularly heavy, however, you'll need to install a third rail midway between the other two.

You can install rails between posts or across them, and you can fasten them with hangers, nails, or screws. Rails placed wide side up resist side-to-side pressure. Rails placed narrow side up sag the least and are recommended for heavy fences and those whose posts are 6 feet or more apart. When attaching rails to the sides of posts, use 16-foot rails and stagger them so there is only one joint per post.

Installing rails on posts

1 Lay out rails on the first post. Start at an end post and measure up from the ground to draw layout lines marking the location of each rail.

2 Transfer the lines to other posts. Transfer the layout lines to the other posts using a line level and mason's line. If you're hanging the rails between posts, use a square to transfer the lines to the inside faces of the posts.

Hanging rails between posts

Narrow edge up. Nail rail hangers to the posts. Slide the ends of each rail into the hangers, then nail the side flanges of each hanger to the rail.

Face up on cleats. Fasten 2x cleats to the fence with No. 8 2½-inch deck screws. Place the rails on the cleats and drive two screws at an angle through the ends of the rails into the cleats.

Attaching rails to the side of posts

Narrow edge up. Cut the rails so joints fall at the center of posts and the ends butt together tightly. Fasten the rail to the posts with No. 8 2½-inch deck screws.

Cap rails. Cut rails so the joints fall at the center of the posts and the ends butt together tightly. Cut a 45-degree miter on rails that meet over corner posts. Fasten with 10d (3-inch) nails or No. 8 2½-inch deck screws.

Hanging rails for curved fencing

Cut rails so the joints fall at the center of the posts. Put the rails on the posts, butting the ends tightly. Fasten the rails to the posts with No. 8 2½-inch deck screws.

Hillside fencing

If you're installing a fence on a hill, you'll need to take the slope into account. You have two choices: You can follow the contour or you can build a stepped fence. This page covers contoured fencing; stepped fences are discussed on the next page.

To lay out a contoured fence, first drive 2×2 stakes at the top and the bottom of the slope. Run a level mason's line between the stakes, measure along it, and mark locations for line posts with tape. Transfer the taped marks to the ground with a plumb bob, and mark each spot with powdered chalk.

Dig holes for the posts and install them before trimming them to the uniform height.

The rails on a contour fence follow the slope of the ground. Lay out the posts as described below. Once they're in place, measure up from the ground to lay out the bottom rails. Measure up from the bottom rails to lay out the top rails. Cut the rails so the ends fall at the middle of the posts and fasten them with No. 8 2½-inch deck screws.

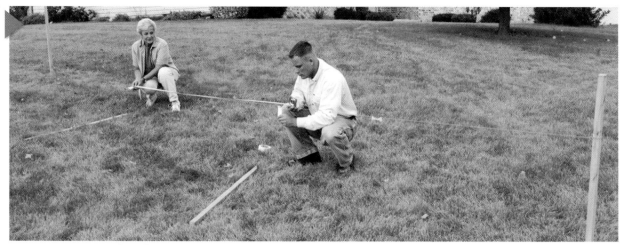

1 Run a mason's line between the end stakes. Drive a stake at the top and bottom of the slope. Tie a line to each stake and level it with a line level. Measure along the line to lay out the locations of the posts, and mark the locations with tape.

2 Transfer the marks to the ground. Drop a plumb bob from the tape to transfer the marks to the ground. Mark the spot with powdered chalk, then with stakes. Dig holes and install the stakes so that each is a little more than finished height above the ground.

Stepped hillside fencing

Some fences, such as alternate-board fences, work best when they step down a hillside. To lay out a stepped hillside fence, drive a 2×2 stake into the ground at the top and bottom of the slope. Run a level mason's line from the base of the top stake to the bottom stake. The distance between the ground and the line at the bottom post is the drop in elevation between stakes. Divide the drop by the number of fencing sections (not posts) to find the drop per section. In the example below, the overall drop is 24 inches over three sections of fence. Divide 24 inches by the three sections to come up with the drop per section: 8 inches.

When installing the posts, set each one slightly higher than the desired height. Measure to find the top of the upper post, and transfer the drop per section to the other posts with the help of a line level. Once the posts are laid out, trim the posts to height.

As its name implies, stepped hillside fencing goes down the hill in a series of steps. First lay out the top of the upper post. Measure down by the amount of drop, and transfer this height to the next post with the help of a line level. Continue measuring and transferring until you reach the bottom of the hill.

1 Lay out the posts. Drive a stake at the top and bottom of the fence run. Run a mason's line from the base of the top stake to the bottom stake, then level the line with a line level. Measure the distance between the line and the ground at the bottom stake to find out how much the fence drops along the run. Measure along the line and mark the location of the posts with masking tape. Count the sections of fence you'll need, then divide the overall drop of the fence by the number of sections to find the drop per section.

2 Lay out the top of the posts. Dig holes and install the posts so each one is slightly taller than the finished height of the fence. Measure to find where the top of the upper post will be and draw a line to mark where you'll cut it. Measure down by the drop per section—which you figured out in Step 1—and tie a line at that point. Tie the other end to the next post, and level the line. The point at which it crosses the second post will be the top of that post. Mark the top, move the line down by the drop per section, then stretch it to the third post and level it. Mark as before. Continue down the hill, marking the top, measuring down, and stretching a level line until you reach the bottom of the hill. Cut off the tops of the posts at the layout lines.

Building your own fence sections

| Skill level:
★★★☆☆ | Time to complete:
Experienced 8 hrs.
Handy 12 hrs.
Novice 16 hrs. | **Materials:** 1× fence boards, pressure- treated 1×2s, 2×2s, 2×4s, No. 8 2-inch and 2½-inch deck screws | **Tools:** Tape measure, mason's line, line level, level, circular saw, jigsaw, power miter saw, clamps, ⅜-inch drill and screwdriver bit, hammer, safety glasses |

Y ou can nail almost anything to a standard post-and-rail skeleton. The most popular fence types are picket, alternate board, solid board, louver, and basket weave.

Building any of these fences is a three-step process: install the posts, install the rails, and screw on the fencing. Intervals of 4, 6, and 8 feet between posts are typical. Choose one (such as picket) and adjust the spacing of the fence boards so they are spaced evenly. Factor in the type of fence style, too, when you put up rails. The rails of some styles, such as louvered fencing, must be installed with the wide face up. Others such as the basket weave require the addition of a cap rail. Fences 48 inches or taller require a middle rail.

Check local codes for restrictions on fence height. Install the fence at least 2 inches above the ground to prevent the boards from rotting.

Traditional pickets are 4 feet high. They are typically 1×3s with the space between them equal to the width of each picket. Rails to hold the pickets are installed at the top and bottom; taller pickets need the support of a middle rail. No matter what size or shape you install, space pickets at intervals less than 4 inches or greater than 6 inches to minimize the risk of children or pets getting stuck between them. Check local codes.

WORK SMART
CONTOUR PICKET FENCING

To lay out pickets that follow the contour of the ground, hold them upside down next to the spacer. Draw a line where the picket meets the top of the spacer; which if it's built correctly, aligns with the top of the pickets. Cut at the line and install the picket right side up.

1 Lay out and cut the pickets. Many pickets are flattop, but you can also lay out your own custom shapes. For customized pickets, make a pattern, trace the shape onto the boards, and cut outside curves with a jigsaw. Start inside curves with a hole saw, if possible. (See inset.) To speed up the job, clamp a couple of boards together and cut them at the same time.

2 Make a spacer. Make a spacer that is as wide as the space between pickets. Screw a 2×2 block to the top of the spacer so when you hang it from the rail, the top of the spacer is level with the top of the pickets. Screw a small torpedo level to the spacer to tell if the pickets are plumb (see step 3).

3 Attach the first picket. Butt the spacer against the post and butt a picket against the spacer. Make sure the picket is plumb, then screw the picket to the rails with No. 8 2-inch deck screws.

4 Attach the remaining pickets. Butt the spacer against the first picket, position the next picket against it, and screw the picket to the rails. Continue installing pickets the same way, checking for plumb as you go and making any necessary adjustments.

Building and installing curved-top panels

1 Build a frame for the pickets. You can dress up ordinary pickets by cutting a curve along the top of each section. First assemble a frame of 2x4s that fits snugly between the posts. Fasten the frame parts together with No. 8 2½-inch deck screws, then screw or nail the pickets to the frame.

2 Lay out and cut the curve. Drive a nail into the pickets, marking each end of the curve. Drive a third nail into the center picket, marking the center point of the curve. With a helper, flex a thin piece of wood—roughly ¼ inch thick—between the end and center nail while you use it as a guide to trace along the panel. (Lattice or doorstop molding also works well.) Repeat, flexing the wood between the center nail and other end. Cut the curve with a saber saw.

3 Install the completed panel. Put the completed panel between the posts, propping it on blocks at the desired height above the ground and level along its length. Fasten the panel to the posts with No. 8 2½-inch deck screws.

Installing wood fencing

Skill level:
★★★☆☆

Time to complete:
Experienced 8 hrs.
Handy 12 hrs.
Novice 16 hrs.

Materials: 1× fence boards, 1×2s, 2×2s, 2×4s, galvanized 6d (2-inch) nails, No. 8 2-inch and 2½-inch deck screws

Tools: Tape measure, mason's line, line level, level, circular saw, saber saw, power miter saw, clamps, ⅜-inch drill and screwdriver bit, hammer, safety glasses

FENCES & GATES

A standard post-and-rail skeleton supports many styles of fencing. You'll find the most popular types on the following pages. Most styles have posts that are mounted at intervals of 4, 6, or 8 feet, and the space between face-boards is usually uniform. Choose a fence style and face board, then cut rails to fit between the posts.

Factor in the fencing style, too, when you put up rails. The rails for some styles, such as the louver, are installed face up. Others such as the basket weave require a cap rail after the fencing is installed. Fences more than 48 inches high need a third rail in the middle.

Check local codes for restrictions on height. Install fencing so the bottom of each board is at least 2 inches above the ground to prevent premature decay.

Alternate-board fencing

Post cap   Top rail

Bottom rail   Fence board   Post

An alternate-board fence is made of boards—usually 1×6s—that alternate between opposite sides of the fence. The space between boards on either side of the fence is usually equal to the width of the boards, but you can increase privacy by making the space slightly narrower so that the boards overlap. Opt for 1×4s instead of 1×6s to create a taller, narrower look. Stay away from 1×8s; they tend to warp.

1 Space the posts to match the width of the fence boards.
Space the posts so that you can attach the fence boards without having to cut them to width. If necessary you can make small adjustments as you install the boards so that they'll fit on a standard 6- or 8-foot rail. Once the posts are in, attach the rails. (See "Installing wood fence rails," page 122.)

2 Make a spacer. Make a spacer that is as wide as the space between boards. Screw a 2×2 block to the top of the spacer so that when you hang it from the rail, the top of the spacer is level with the top of the boards. Screw a small torpedo level to the spacer so you can tell if the boards are plumb.

For the want of a nail
Fastening fence boards in place with nails applies enough force to knock the fence down before it's finished. Instead of looking for tricks or workarounds to modify your nailing technique, fasten the boards to the rails with deck screws. These screws are designed to penetrate the wood without pilot holes and will hold the boards more securely than nails. They drive easily with a cordless drill. Get No. 8 deck screws. They're coated to prevent rust.

3 **Lay out the bottom of the fence boards.** Run a mason's line between posts and level it at the desired height above the ground. The location of the line will affect the length of the vertical boards. Measure up from the mason's line to the top of the post to determine the proper length of the fence boards.

4 **Cut the boards to length.** Clamp two or three boards together and cut them at the same time to speed up the job.

5 **Put in the first board.** Align a fence board with the mason's line and butt it against the first post. Check that it is plumb and screw it to the rails with No. 8 2-inch deck screws.

◉ DESIGN TIP
KICKBOARDS

To close the gap under the fence, install kickboards before putting in the fence boards. Make the kickboard from rot-resistant lumber such as cedar, redwood, cypress, or .60 pressure-treated wood. You can either screw the kickboard to the face of the rail and the post (below left) or center it beneath the rail and secure it with a screw through the top of the rail (below right). A kickboard attached to the face of the rail adds strength to the rail itself, but the centering option is a little more attractive. If you're attaching it to the face, keep the top edge level so that you can rest the fence boards on it as you install them.

Keep burrowing animals out of the yard by extending the kickboard into a 4- to 6-inch trench dug between the posts.

☑ WORK SMART
LEVELING THE PLAYING FIELD

Sometimes it's impossible to remove rocks and other obstructions on the ground. If you have an obstruction you can't get rid of, cut the fence board to follow the shape of the obstruction. To lay out the cut, clamp the full-length board plumb and in position. Scribe the shape of the ground onto the board with a scrap 2×4 and a pencil. Make the cut with a saber saw, then trim the board to length and install it.

Installing wood fencing (continued)

6 **Install boards on one side of the fence.** Hang the spacer on the top rail and butt it against the first fence board. Butt a fence board against the spacer. Check to make sure it's plumb, and screw the board to the rails with No. 8 2-inch deck screws. Work your way along the fence, positioning the spacer and screwing the boards in place.

7 **Install boards on the other side of the fence.** Go to the other side of the fence. Fasten the first fence board at the offset you've planned. Put the spacer against the first board, and install the second board against the spacer. Install boards along the entire side, spacing them as you go.

Fences and trees

Incorporate a tree into the fence rather than build around it or cut it down. Set posts within 4 feet of the tree and install the rails as you normally would. Continue the fence rails from the post to within 4 inches of each side of the tree. Connect the rails with a rail that follows the slope of the tree, and create a frame that's rigid enough to hold fence boards. Support the frame with a short post if necessary.

1 **Install top and bottom rails to within a few inches of the tree.** Prop the bottom rail in position on a block. Nail a 2×4 brace to the top rail to temporarily support it. Hold a third rail in place at the end of these rails and trace along them to draw a line on the third rail. Cut along the line, then screw the third rail between the top and bottom rails using No. 8 2½-inch deck screws.

2 **Install full-length fence boards until the tree prevents you from doing so,** then remove the temporary brace. Lay out the rest of the fence boards, one at a time, tracing along the sloped rail to get the proper shape.

Installing solid-board fencing

A solid-board fence is made of posts and rails like any other fence. A few differences, however, make it both more durable and more attractive. Most important is the cap rail that runs across the top. The cap rail protects the tops of the posts, which absorb water more readily and are more likely to rot than any other surface of the post. The fence is also designed to be attractive from both sides—something your neighbor is likely to appreciate.

1 Build the structure. Install 4x4 posts and 2x4 top and bottom rails, then nail a 1x4 cap rail over the top rail. Rip supports from 2x stock so the combined width of two supports and the fence boards won't be wider than the rails. Screw the supports along the outside edge of the bottom rail on one side of the fence, fastening them every 6 to 8 inches with No. 8 2-inch deck screws. Repeat on the top rail.

2 Install the fence boards. Put the first board in place next to a post, make sure it's plumb, and screw it to the supports with No. 8 1⅝-inch deck screws. Work your way down the fence, using a nail as a spacer between boards so they have room to expand in humid weather. Then screw a second set of supports tightly against the fence boards.

Installing board-and-batten fencing

Board-and-batten fencing mimics the siding once applied to farm sheds, barns, and similar outbuildings. An important part of this fence is the cap rail. Without it, the end grain of every board would be exposed to the weather, shortening the life of the fence.

1 Build the structure. Install the posts, top and bottom rails, and a cap rail that overhangs the side of the rail on which you'll hang the fence boards. Cut the boards to length and tuck them under the cap rail, spacing them with the narrow edges of a batten. Plumb the boards with a level and fasten them with 1⅝-inch deck screws.

2 Install the battens. Cut the battens to length with a circular saw or power mitersaw. Center each batten over the space between boards and screw it to the top rail. Plumb with a level, then screw to the lower rail.

Putting up louver fencing

Louver fencing is a fancy version of standard board fencing. The boards are mounted at an angle to the face of the fence, and because of the angle, they provide nearly as much privacy as a board fence, along with ventilation. The trick to getting a uniform angle from board to board is to put angled spacers between the boards. Ideally use a power miter saw to cut spacers.

This louvered fence is made of 1×6s mounted at an angle on the rails. The boards are sandwiched between 1×4 spacers that are cut at an angle to hold the boards in place.

1 Build the structure. Install posts and rails. The top rails overlap the posts and are fastened to them. The bottom rails butt into the posts and are supported by small blocks fastened to the posts. Once the rails are installed, measure the exact distance between them and cut fence boards to this length.

2 Make spacers. Set the blade of a power miter saw to 45 degrees. Cut a 45-degree angle on a piece of scrap and clamp it to the saw so it's 2 inches from the blade. (See inset.) Using the board as a stop, butt a 1×4 gently against it and cut the 1×4 to length. Continue cutting: Each section of fence has a triangular spacer at each end and parallelogram-shape spacers between all other boards.

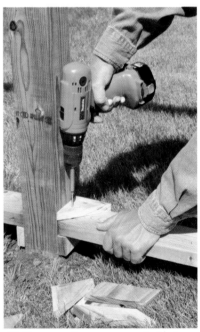

3 Fasten the spacers. Drill pilot holes into the spacers to reduce the potential for splitting. Fasten an end spacer to the top and bottom rails with No. 8 2-inch deck screws. Don't drive the screws all the way in until you have plumbed the first fence board.

4 **Put in the first board.** Butt a board against the end spacers so one edge is flush with the post. Plumb the board with a level and move a spacer, if necessary, to support the board firmly. Fasten the board to the spacer with #8 2-inch deck screws.

5 **Put in the remaining boards.** Put a parallelogram-shape spacer against the top and bottom of the first picket. Screw the spacers to the rails, then screw the next fence board to the spacers. Continue installing spacers and boards until you reach the next post.

6 **Put in the final spacer.** Screw the last picket of the section in place. Put two triangular spacers between the post and board (top and bottom), then screw the spacers to the rails. Screw the cap rail to the top rail, ensuring that joints are staggered from the 2×4 top rail.

Making a basket-weave fence

A simple trick to achieve a fancier fence is to weave spacers between fence boards. Start by installing the bottom rail, then nail supports to the posts. Screw one end of the fence boards to a support, and insert a spacer. Put in a second spacer a bit farther down the section, then screw the free end of the boards to their support. Add a cap rail to protect the tops of the posts from weather.

ANOTHER BOARD BITES THE DUST

Because of the spacers, each fence board needs to be longer than the distance between posts. Be sure to allow for that when you're ordering your lumber.

To make a basket-weave fence, weave 2×2 spacers between 1×6 fence boards. Hold the ends of the boards in place by sandwiching them between two 1×2 supports nailed to each post. Fasten a 2×4 cap rail to the tops of the rails and posts to protect them from rain, snow, and hot sun.

Installing wood fencing (continued)

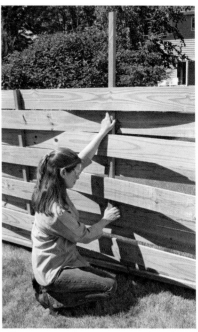

1 Build the structure. Install posts and rails. Cut two 1×2 supports that fit between the rails and fasten them to the post flush with the edge with No. 8 2½-inch deck screws. Cut two 2×2 spacers to weave between the fence boards and mark their locations on the bottom rail.

2 Cut the fence boards to fit. Cut three fence boards 2 inches or so longer than the distance between two posts. Tack one end of each board to one of the supports and insert the spacers between them. Draw a line on the board showing where the free end meets the other support. Cut the boards at the line, then fasten one end of each to the supports.

3 Weave the spacers. If the first three boards fit properly, cut the remaining boards to length. Screw one end of each to a support and weave the 2×2 spacers into place. Use a level to plumb the spacers.

4 Fasten the loose ends of the boards. Working up from the bottom, fasten the loose ends of the fence boards. Level each board as you screw it in place.

5 Install a second set of supports. Cut a second set of 1×2 supports and screw them to the posts on the side opposite the first set of supports.

6 Work your way down the fence. Install supports, fence boards, and spacers one section at a time. Once all the pieces are in place, nail a cap rail across the top of the fence with 10d (3-inch) nails.

Making and hanging a wood gate

Skill level:	Time to complete:	Materials: 2×4s, fence boards, No. 8 2-inch and 2½-inch deck screws, hinges, latch assembly, barrel bolt assembly	Tools: Tape measure, pencil, framing square, circular saw, jigsaw, ⅜-inch drill and bits, screwdriver, level, safety glasses
★★★☆☆	Experienced 3 hrs.		
	Handy 5 hrs.		
	Novice 6 hrs.		

Good fences make good neighbors, and good gates make good fences. Unfortunately a gate that isn't wide enough is no good at all. It must be 3 feet wide to handle equipment such as lawn mowers, wheelbarrows, and even larger machinery. Measure your garden equipment, add 6 to 12 inches for clearance to the widest piece, and make the opening at least that wide. A single gate handles an opening up to 4 feet wide. Make it wider, and you'll need a double gate.

Make sure the gate swings in the right direction, which is usually into your yard. Across a slope, however, hang the gate so it opens downhill. If there are steps on either side of the gate, it's best for the gate to swing away from them. (You don't want to knock anyone down the steps.)

Fence board

Latch assembly

Top rail

Bottom rail

Post

Crossbrace

Hinge

When you build a gate, make sure the posts that support it are plumb. If not, the gate won't swing properly, and depending on how far the posts are out of plumb, the gap at one edge could vary by as much as an inch from top to bottom. To help ensure plumb gateposts, lay out and install the gateposts first, then build the rest of the fence around them. When it comes time to build the gate, build the frame first. Then run a crossbrace from the bottom hinge to the top of the latch to keep the gate square. Last apply the boards that make the surface of the gate.

Building the gate

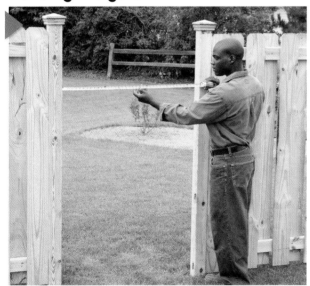

1 Cut parts for the frame. Measure between posts to double-check the width of the opening. Subtract the space required by the hardware and cut 2×4 top and bottom rails to this length. For this gate, measure from the bottom of the lower fence rail to the bottom of the upper rail and cut two gate side rails to this length. If you redesign the gate, cut the pieces to allow for joinery.

2 Cut joints and assemble the frame. The top and bottom rails are notched to house the side rails. Cut the notches with a jigsaw—each notch is as wide as a side rail and half as deep as the top rail. Hold the pieces together and drill pilot and countersink holes for No. 8 2-inch deck screws with a combination bit. Screw the frame together.

Making and hanging a wood gate (continued)

3 **Cut the crossbrace.** Check the gate for square by measuring its diagonals. The measurements will be the same if the gate is square. If not, push gently on the corners of the long diagonal until they are. Lay the frame over a 2×4 crossbrace and trace along the frame to lay out the ends of the brace. Cut along the lines with a jigsaw or circular saw.

4 **Attach the crossbrace.** Put the crossbrace into place between the rails, trimming it to fit, if necessary. Drill pilot holes at an angle and drive No. 8 2-inch deck screws through the crossbrace into the rails.

5 **Attach the first fence board.** Cut fence boards to length and make a spacer as long as the fence boards and as wide as the space you want between them. To help position the fence boards, screw a cleat to the top of the spacer so when the spacer sits on the top rail, you can position the fence boards by aligning them with the spacer. Fasten the first board to the top and bottom rails with No. 8 2-inch deck screws.

 Framing a heavy gate

Tall, wide gates not only need strong hinges, they need extra reinforcement. Build them with side rails and top, bottom, and center rails. Run two diagonal crossbraces: one from the bottom rail on the hinge side to the latch side of the center rail and the other from the hinge side of the center rail to the latch side of the top rail. Hang the latch on the center rail.

6 **Attach the rest of the boards.** Align subsequent fence boards one at a time with the spacer and screw them to the rails. If the fence has boards on both sides, turn the gate over and attach boards that match.

Hanging the gate

1 Screw the hinges to the gate. Put the hinges on the gate so the hinge barrels edge the gate, as shown. Center the hinges on the rails, mark the screw holes, then bore pilot holes slightly narrower than the screw shank. Screw the hinges to the gate.

2 Put the gate temporarily in place between the posts. Prop it on a block of wood so it's at the desired height.

3 Screw the hinges in place. Mark the screw holes on the post. Drill pilot holes slightly smaller than the screw's diameter, then screw the hinges to the post.

For a stronger gate, install the hinges with screws a bit longer than the ones with which they're packed.

4 Screw the latch to the post. Hold the latch—the part that you grab to lock and unlock the gate—on the post and align it with the center of the top rail. Eyeball the latch, making sure it looks level. Mark the screw holes on the post with a pencil, then bore pilot holes for them. Screw the latch to the post.

5 Screw the strike bar to the gate. Put the strike in the latch and hold it against the gate, aligning it so it looks level. Mark screw holes on the gate with a pencil, and bore pilot holes. Screw the strike bar to the gate. Test the latch and make any necessary adjustments.

6 Attach a latch string, if necessary. On tall fences, it's difficult to reach over the gate to unfasten the latch. To make the latch easy to open from both sides, bore a ³⁄₈-inch-diameter hole through the post a few inches above the latch. Tie one end of a string to the latch, thread it through the hole, and tie the other end to a pull ring. Pull on the ring to open the latch.

Installing lag-and-strap hangers

1 Screw holes for the lags. To make a drill guide, drill a hole into a 2×4, then make two 45-degree cuts, centered on the hole to create a 90-degree notch. Make marks on the post to show where you want the center of the lags to be. Put the drill guide over one mark and drill a ½-inch-deep hole for the lag into the post. Repeat at the other mark, then screw the lags in place so the pins are plumb.

2 Attach the straps. Prop the gate in place at the proper height. Put the straps on the lag pins, then place the straps against the gate. Mark the holes. Drill bolt holes or pilot holes for screwss, depending on the hardware, then fasten the straps to the gate.

Building and hanging a double gate

If your gate crosses a driveway, you'll need an opening that's at least 8 feet wide. The only way to achieve such an opening is with a double gate. Each side should be the same size and hang the same way on the posts.

Hinge Latch assembly Top rail

Crossbrace PVC pipe Bottom rail

When covering a large opening, build two single gates, each one half the distance between the posts minus 1½ to 2 inches clearance for hardware. Install crossbraces on the gates at diagonals so each one fits between the bottom rail on the hinge side and the top rail on the latch side. Install the latch on the top rail and a barrel bolt along the bottom rail to keep the gates in position when latched. Drill a hole in the driveway and insert a piece of PVC pipe so you can slide the barrel bolt into the driveway. A 2×4 block above the bolt will keep it in place when it's in the raised position. (See inset.)

**☑ WORK SMART
...AND CLOSE THE
GATE BEHIND YOU**

Install a spring closer so the gate closes on its own. Screw one end of the closer to the hinge side of the gate and the other end to the post. Tighten or loosen the adjustment nut to control the speed at which the gate closes.

 Bottoms up

Hanging two gates isn't that much harder than hanging one, and the same rules apply. The gates need crossbraces that run diagonally from the lower hinge to the latch. If you wonder why your gate is sagging, it's usually because the braces run in the wrong direction. When you install the gate, make sure you do it right side up.

Building a post-and-rail fence

Skill level:	Time to complete:	Materials: 4×4 posts; premix concrete in bags; 1×6, 2×6, or precut tapered rails; 10d (3-inch) deck screws, roofing cement, wire, masking tape	Tools: Tape measure, pencil/marker, mason's line, hammer, line level, 3-pound sledgehammer, posthole digger, shovel, drill and screwdriver bit, circular saw, wood chisel, rubber mallet, level, framing square, wheelbarrow, safety glasses, work gloves
★★★☆☆	Experienced 8 hrs.		
	Handy 12 hrs.		
	Novice 16 hrs.		

The simplest wood fences are post-and-rail fences, three of which are shown on the following pages. The fence and the way you install it depends on whether the posts are square, round, or premortised. Set square posts in the ground, trim them to height, and install rails. Before setting round posts into the ground, cut notches for the rails. Set and plumb mortised posts as you install the rails.

Begin building a basic post-and-rail fence by setting the posts in the ground at regular 6- to 8-foot intervals. Trim the posts to height and screw on the rails. Fasten the bottom rail 3 to 4 inches above ground level and the top rail so it's flush with the top of the posts. Cut cross rails and fasten them so the joints fall in the center of each post.

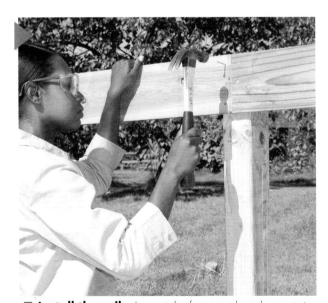

1 Install the rails. Lay out the fence and set the posts in the ground. Mark the posts for bottom rails that are 3 to 4 inches above the ground and top rails flush with the top of the posts. Install top and bottom 1×6 rails long enough to span three posts. The joints should fall at the center of the posts so two joints never fall on the same post. Level each rail and nail in place with galvanized 10d (3-inch) nails or screw it in place with 3-inch deck screws.

2 Install the cross rails. Tack cross rails to the posts and mark them for cutting with a framing square. Remove the cross rails, make the cuts with a circular saw, then fasten the cross rails to the posts with galvanized 10d (3-inch) nails or screw them in place with 3-inch deck screws.

Installing mortised posts and rails

A mortised post-and-rail fence is laid out much like the post-and-rail fences discussed on earlier pages. The parts are prefabricated, and because of the rail lengths, the posts are usually spaced 6 feet apart and no taller than 5 feet. Both round and square posts are available; round posts tend to give the fence a more rustic feel.

The rails have tapered ends that fit into mortises in the posts. The mortise runs completely through the post: One rail comes in from one side, the other from the other side. Corner posts are mortised on adjacent sides. Mortises for corners aren't as deep as they are for line posts, so you may have to shorten a rail in order to fit it snugly in the post.

Start a post-and-rail fence by digging holes for all the posts. Put a corner or end post in its hole, plumb it, brace it, and fill the hole with concrete. Put the neighboring post in its hole and run the rails from mortise to mortise. Plumb and brace the post, and backfill the hole. Work your way along the fence, installing rails and posts one section at a time.

Rail

Corner post

Line post

The mortised post-and-rail fence has fewer components than most fences, which makes it easier to install. Line posts usually have mortises at 10 and 24 inches from the top. Corner posts have mortises at the same height but are mortised so the rails meet at 90 degrees. The rails are identical and tapered to fit in the mortises.

1 Lay out the posts. Lay out the fence with batterboards or stakes and string. Assemble the posts and fence rails on the ground along the string. Put a piece of tape on the string to mark the center of each post.

2 Dig the postholes. Dig postholes below each piece of tape using a posthole digger. Make sure you dig deep enough so the post is at least 6 inches below the frost line or so one-third of the overall length of the post is buried (whichever is deeper).

3 Put in a corner or end post.
Coat the bottom of a corner or end post with roofing cement and plumb and brace it in its hole with scrap 1×4s or 2×4s. Verify that the post is plumb and screw the braces into place.

4 Fill the hole with concrete.
Mix fast-setting concrete in a wheelbarrow and pour it in the hole. Work a board up and down in the concrete to remove trapped air bubbles. Slope the top of the concrete with a trowel to direct water away from the post.

5 Put in a line post. Coat the bottom of a line post with roofing cement and place it in its hole. Put one end of a rail in the end or corner post, then put the other end in the line post, wiggling as needed to get it to fit. Repeat with the second rail. Plumb the line post and check the rails for level. Fill the hole with concrete as before (see inset). If the concrete won't hold the post in place, brace it as before.

6 Put in more line posts. Once you've set the first line post, continue working down the run one section at a time. Plumb and brace each line post and level the rails before filling the hole with concrete and moving on to the next. Finish each run of fence with either an end post or corner post.

Closing the door after the horse is gone

Many home center retail outlets experience a big demand for horse fencing. Post-and-rail fences are a popular choice, but many a horse lover has had to chase a horse that escaped the fence. If you're fencing in horses, build a fence that has a top rail that is at least 5 feet above the ground. Make sure you buy posts with mortises for a third rail to keep curious colts from squeezing through.

Building a wire fence

Skill level:	Time to complete:	Materials: Wire mesh, fence staples, galvanized 10d (3-inch) nails, 2×4s, 4×4s, 1×6s	Tools: Hammer, level, fencing pliers, safety glasses, work gloves
★★★☆☆	Experienced 8 hrs. Handy 12 hrs. Novice 16 hrs.		

A wire fence may not be a thing of beauty, but it isn't meant to be. It's meant to be a good, strong utilitarian fence that goes up quickly. The quickest are made with metal posts simply driven into the ground. A sturdier version features regular wood posts set in holes. To build the wood version, set the posts every 8 feet on center, then nail a 2×4 top rail across two sections. Install bottom rails between every set of posts, then staple the wire in place. Finish the fence off with a 1×6 cap rail.

Whether you opt for metal posts or wood posts, the height of the fence depends on the mesh you buy. It usually comes in rolls that are 4 or 5 feet wide.

A wire fence is built on a wood frame or on metal posts. A wood-framed fence has 4×4 posts with 2×4 top and bottom rails to which the mesh is stapled. A 1×6 cap rail dresses up the fence and further strengthens it.

1 Build the fence frame. Install the posts and cut the top rails long enough to span three posts. Nail the rails in place on top of the posts so their ends are on the center of the posts. Then cut the bottom rails to fit and toenail them into place between the posts.

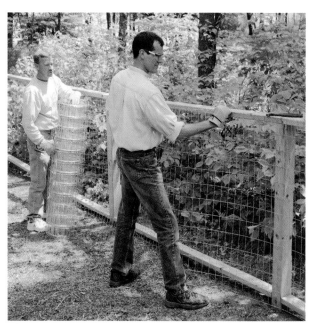

2 Staple mesh to the post and to the top rail. With a helper, unroll enough mesh to reach from end post to end post. Align the end of the mesh with the edge of the post and attach it to the post with fence staples. To prevent sagging, staple the mesh to the top rail every 3 inches, temporarily leaving the bottom unattached. Work your way to the next post.

3 Staple mesh to the post and bottom rail. When you reach the post, pull the mesh taut. Starting at the top, staple the mesh to the post every 6 inches with ½-inch or larger staples. When you reach the bottom of the post, work your way back along the bottom rail, stapling the mesh to it as you go.

4 Trim excess mesh. Work your way along the fence, attaching mesh in the same order as before: along the top rail, down the post, then back along the bottom rail. When you reach the end of the roll, use fencing pliers to trim any mesh that extends beyond the post.

5 Splice in a new roll, if necessary. If you need more than one roll of fencing, cut the first roll even with the edge of the post, as described in the previous step. Begin the new roll on the same post, positioning it so at least one row of rectangles overlaps those already on the post.

7 Add a cap rail. Once you have attached the mesh to the posts and rails, center a 1×6 cap rail on the 2×4 top rail, positioning the 1×6 so the seams between boards never fall above those in the 2×4s. Nail the cap rail in place with 10d (3-inch) nails.

 Faster fencing

Metal posts are a quick alternative to wooden posts. Space metal posts—also known as T stakes—8 feet apart and drive them into firm ground. You can use a 3-pound sledgehammer, but you're better off using a post driver made specially for the job. A post driver is a hollow 2½-foot-long metal tube with handles and a cap at the top. Fit it over the post, lift the tube, and ram the top down on the posts. Once all the posts are set, hook the mesh over the hooks on one end post. Pull the mesh taut, then attach it to the next post, working your way from post to post until the fence is complete.

Installing a vinyl fence

Skill level:	Time to complete:		Materials: Vinyl posts, rails, fence sections, and	Tools: Tape measure, mason's line, level, plumb bob,
★★★☆☆	Experienced	8 hrs.	gate; hinges; latch assembly; premix bags of concrete; duct	powdered chalk, posthole digger, post level, screwdriver,
	Handy	12 hrs.	tape; CPVC or PVC primer and cement	shovel, garden trowel, adjustable wrench, drill and bits,
	Novice	16 hrs.		power miter saw, safety glasses, work gloves

Installing a vinyl fence is much like installing a prefab wood fence (see "Installing Prefab Fence Panels," page 120). You put a post in a posthole, attach a fence section, and attach the section to a second post. Don't fill in the holes until you've attached all the sections to all the posts so that you can space the posts to match the fence sections exactly.

Some manufacturers diverge from the general rule that says one-third of the overall length of a post should be in the ground. Almost all of them, however, recommend that you set the post in concrete. Follow the directions that come with the fence.

Vinyl fences look much like wood fences but require virtually no maintenance. They come in a variety of colors, sizes, and styles and, if necessary, can be cut just like wood to fit any size yard. Sections come 6 and 8 feet long and are generally available in 3-, 4-, 5-, 6-, and 7-foot heights.

Because vinyl fences are manufactured, the exact installation technique depends on the maker. Most manufacturers call for an 8- to 12-inch-diameter posthole lined with gravel for drainage and filled with concrete for strength. The fence sections won't fit if the posts are too close together or too far apart, so attach the fencing to the posts as you go. Don't fill in the holes until you've attached all the fencing and verified that it's level and plumb.

Laying out the fence

1 Lay out the fence with mason's line and batterboards. Mark all the post positions on the lines with pieces of masking tape. Drop a plumb bob from the tape, and mark the ground with powdered chalk.

2 Dig the postholes. With a posthole digger, dig holes 12 inches in diameter and 6 inches below the frost line or as directed by the manufacturer. Add another 6 inches of depth for a gravel bed to provide drainage. Pour in the gravel and tamp it with the end of a 2×4.

Installing the gate

1 Attach the gate hinges.
Installation begins with the gate. Work on a flat surface and place a spacer between each gatepost and the gate (sizes vary depending on the manufacturer). Insert a metal support, if provided, into the post for the hinges, and screw the hinges to the post and gate. If necessary, drill your own holes.

2 Attach the latch. Screw the latch assembly to the gate, then put the strike bar in the latch and screw it to the post.

3 Temporarily tape the gate assembly together. Tape the two posts and gate together with strips of duct tape. Leave the tape in place until all of the posts have been set and the concrete around them has hardened.

4 Set the gate on blocks. Place 4x4 blocks, bricks, or other spacers between the postholes. Pick up the gate with a helper, place the posts in the holes, and rest the gate on the blocks or bricks.

5 Plumb the gate and set it in concrete. The posts must be straight up and down in two directions: left to right and front to back. Put a post level on the post so you can check both directions at the same time. Have a helper put tapered shims (sold at hardware stores and home centers) between the gate and blocks until the gate is plumb in both directions. Fill the posthole with concrete and let it dry.

WORK SMART
☑ ASSUME NOTHING

Study manufacturer recommendations for installation before you begin assembly. Test-fit pieces and double-check measurements before you begin digging holes and making cuts. It's easier to make adjustments before the concrete is poured and posts are set.

  Don't stop yet

What turns out to be a mistake often starts as a good idea. For example, suppose you consider pre-assembling the gate, posts, and hinges, and decided to screw the gate stop in place, too. Once you set everything in concrete, however, the world might not seem quite as perfect as it was when you attached the stop. Posts can settle a bit, and if so, the stop will no longer be in the right place. This will be easy enough to fix: simply remount the stop. But as timesavers go, however, this one could turn out to be a loser.

Installing fencing panels

1 Reinforce the bottom rail. Many fences have a metal bar that slides inside the bottom rail to strengthen it. If yours does, slide the bar into each of the bottom rails. Rails longer than 8 feet will have metal inserts while rails shorter than 8 feet usually do not.

2 Assemble the fence panels. Fence panels come either assembled or disassembled. To assemble, slide the fence boards or pickets into the bottom rails, then slide the pickets or boards into the top rail. Assemble all the panels you'll be using.

3 Put the panels in the first post. This section has been cut to fit the yard, but you can install a full section in the same way. Fit the rails of the assembled panels into the holes of the first post, put the next post in place, and slip the rails into it too. Plumb the post and support the rails on blocks.

4 Put the rails in the next post. Move to the next posthole. Put the next post in its hole and insert the fence rails into the post. Prop the rails on blocks and leave them until you fill the postholes with concrete.

5 Work your way down the fence one section at a time. Put a fence section into the last post you installed and put a post in the neighboring hole. Slide the rails into the holes in the posts as you go.

6 Plumb, level, and brace the posts. Plumb all the posts in both directions and level the panels. If a post is out of alignment, correct the problem with wooden shims: Use the same technique you used for the gate.

7 Shovel concrete in the holes.
Mix enough concrete to fill
a posthole, leaving the mixture
somewhat stiff so it will hold the posts in
place as it dries. Verify that the post is
plumb, pour the concrete into the hole,
and let the concrete harden. Work your
way along the fence, filling the
postholes with concrete.

8 Install the gate stop. Once the
concrete has hardened, return to
the gate. Close it and mark where the
stop goes. Open the gate, put the stop
in place, and mark where the holes for
it go. Drill them and then screw the stop
to the post with the screws provided.

9 Install post caps. Put a post
cap on the top of each post with
the primer and cement recommended
by the manufacturer. Once the concrete
dries, remove the blocks that support
the fence.

Cutting vinyl fencing

**Not all yards evenly divide into
6- and 8-foot sections.** If your yard is one
of them, you can cut fence sections to size with
a handsaw, circular saw, jigsaw, or power miter
box. A power miter box makes the cleanest,
truest, and squarest cut. Measure and make the
cut on the rail so that you remove full pickets or
boards. (They're hollow and look pretty silly if
you try to cut one to width.) Cut the rails before
you put in the pickets or fence boards. If your
fence has lattice across the top, it's probably at
least partially pre-assembled, and the lattice may
have a piece of trim on each end. If so, cut
enough off each side to remove the trim.

▶ *You can cut vinyl with standard
woodworking tools. A power miter box
(sometimes called a chop saw) will give you the
best results.*

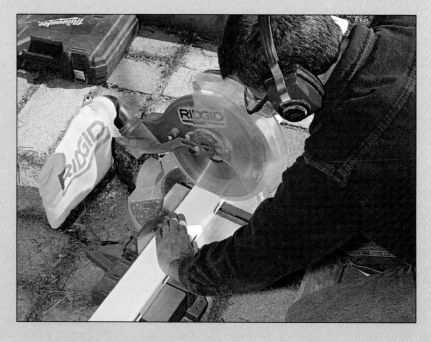

Installing chain-link fences

Skill level:	Time to complete:	Materials: Chain link mesh, rails, posts,	Tools: Posthole digger, pipe cutter or hacksaw, shovel,
★★★☆☆	Experienced 8 hrs.	caps, hinges, latch, tension bars and bands, brace bands, tie	trowel, mason's line, line level, plumb bob, level, rubber
	Handy 12 hrs.	wires, tension wires or hog rings, gravel, premix concrete	mallet, socket wrenches, fence puller, pull bar, pliers, safety
	Novice 16 hrs.		glasses, work gloves

Chain-link fences have a language all their own: brace band, rail cap, tension band, and tension bars. A chain-link fence has a skeleton made of posts and rails. The pieces holding the framework together are called caps. The chain-link itself is stretched tightly across the skeleton after the skeleton is installed. A metal bar called a tension bar is woven into the end of the mesh and attached to the end posts with tension bands.

Mesh is usually sold in rolls 4, 5, or 6 feet tall. Steel is the strongest mesh. Aluminum is lighter. As for the posts, they come in two diameters. The wider diameter, 2⅜ inches, is for corner and end posts. The smaller diameter is 1⅜ inches and is for the other posts in the fence, or line posts. When laying out the gateposts, leave an extra 3¾ inches (or as directed by the manufacturer) between them to make room for the hinges and latch.

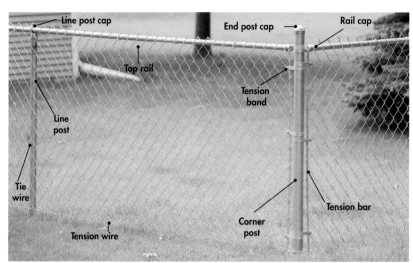

Post and rails provide the basic structure for a chain-link fence.
The rails fit through looped caps on the line posts and are attached to corner and end posts by rail caps. The chain-link mesh is stretched across the posts, and tension bands slip around the end post to hold what's called a tension bar. Fasten the top of the mesh to the rails and the line posts, and run a tension wire through the bottom of the mesh to hold it in place.

Assembling posts and rails

1 Dig the postholes. Dig postholes three times wider than the post diameter: 6 to 8 inches for end and corner posts, 4 to 6 inches for line posts. Depth should be ⅓ of the length of the pole plus 4 inches for gravel. Fill all the holes with 4 inches of gravel and tamp. Add 6 inches of concrete to the corner, gate, and end postholes only. Put posts in the wet concrete and plumb them with a level.

2 Fill end, gate, and corner postholes with concrete. Finish filling in the corner, gate, and end postholes with concrete. Check the posts for plumb after every few shovelfuls and adjust as needed. Slope the top of the concrete so water drains away from the posts. Let the concrete cure for two to three days. Do not fill the holes for the line posts with concrete, and don't put the line posts in place.

3 Attach tension bands and gate hardware. Slide tension bands onto each corner, gate, and end post. (The bands will help hold the mesh in place once it's installed. You will use 3 for a 4-foot fence, 4 for a 5-foot fence, and 5 for a 6-foot fence.) Put hinges and latch hardware onto the gateposts at roughly their final positions—they're hard to install later. Use a rubber mallet to drive end post caps onto the gate, corner, and end posts and slip a brace band over each installed post.

4 Install line post caps, end post caps, and rail caps. Drive line post caps onto the line posts with the mallet and put the posts in their holes, but don't fill the holes. Bolt a rail cap to each brace band, tightening just enough to hold the cap in place. Feed the rails through the line post caps. Cut rails with a pipe cutter or hacksaw, if needed. If you need longer rails, join them together using rails with a slightly smaller swaged end that fits into a standard rail end.

5 Attach the rails. Fit the rails into the rail caps and raise or lower each cap to the final height of the mesh, including 2 inches clearance at the bottom. Tighten the brace bands, fill the holes around the line posts with dirt, and tamp until firm.

Installing the chain-link

1 Unroll the mesh and install a tension bar. Lay the chain-link mesh on the ground outside the fence. Run a tension bar through the links at the end of the mesh. The bar makes the end of the fence rigid and provides something to attach to the posts.

2 Attach the tension bar to the posts. With a helper, stand the mesh up and use a socket wrench to bolt the tension bar into the tension bands on one of the end posts. Align the mesh so it overlaps the rail by 1 to 2 inches and sits about 2 inches above the ground.

3 Stretch the mesh. Chain link mesh must be pulled taut or it will sag. Stretching is done with a tool called a fence puller. Insert a pull bar through the unattached mesh a few feet from the final post. Attach the yoke to the pull bar.

4 Attach the other end of the fence puller to the final post. Crank the fence puller until the loops of mesh move no more than 1/4 inch when you squeeze them together. If the mesh changed height or became distorted during tightening, pull on it to reshape it.

5 Insert a tension bar. Without releasing the fence puller, insert a tension bar in the mesh, close enough so it can be fastened to the tension bands on the end post nearest the fence puller. To remove the excess mesh between the tension bar and end post, open a loop at the top and bottom, then twist and pull the strand free.

6 Attach the tension bar. Pull the tension bar into the tension bands on the end post by hand, insert a bolt through the tension band and tighten the nut. Release the fence puller and remove the pull bar to which it was attached. Repeat the entire hanging and stretching process along the remaining sides of the fence.

**DESIGN TIP
PRIVACY SLATS**

A chain link fence serves well to keep the dog in the yard, but it won't give you much privacy. Privacy slats, available at most home centers, let you keep the dog in (or out) and give you some privacy. Privacy slats are available in a variety of colors. The easiest to work with are thin and flexible, much like the slats of venetian blinds. Weave the slats on a diagonal through the mesh.

7 Tie the fence to the rails. Bend one end of an aluminum tie wire into a hook and grab the bottom strand of the opening above the rail. Loop the tie wire around the top rail, pull it firmly, and tie it back onto the mesh. Space the tie wires every 12 to 16 inches along the rail, then attach them to the line posts.

8 Run wire through the bottom loops of mesh. Thread a tension wire through the bottom loops of the mesh and tighten it around the end posts. Wrap the wire around itself several times to fasten it. An alternative to threading the wire is to attach it to the mesh every 2 feet or so with hog rings.

Assembling and hanging a chain-link gate

Skill level:
★★★☆☆

Time to complete:
Experienced   1 hr.
Handy   1.5 hrs.
Novice   2 hrs.

Materials: Top, bottom, and side rails; chain-link mesh; tension bars; tension bands; tie wires; hinges; latch assembly

Tools: Socket wrenches, pliers, wire cutters

Most of the time, the best way to buy a chain-link gate is to buy one that's pre-assembled. Sometimes, however, you may want a custom gate—one large enough to accommodate a big landscaping tractor, for example. Building a gate is a lot like building a short section of fence, except you won't need a fence puller. When building your own gate, first fit the frame together, then attach the mesh by slipping tension bars into the tension bands. You also can buy special corner brackets that let you customize the width of your gate.

Top rail

Latch

Hinge

Side rail

Tension band

Tension bar

Bottom rail

A chain link gate is amazingly strong. Unlike its wooden counterparts, a chain-link gate isn't likely to sag over time. The mesh is stretched across a frame of metal tubing and held by tension bars, which are anchored to tension bands. Standard tie wires hold the mesh at the top and bottom. Metal hinge pins hold the gate in place, while an adjustable metal latch keeps the gate securely closed.

Assembling the gate

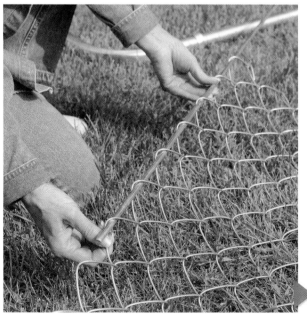

1 Assemble the frame. Slip tension bands onto the pieces of tubing that make up the frame. You'll need at least three tension bands for each tension bar—four if the gate is more than 4 feet high. Assemble the frame by sliding the pieces of tubing together.

2 Put a tension bar in the mesh. Insert a tension bar into the chain-link mesh by sliding it through the end loops of the mesh.

3 **Attach the tension bar to the frame.** Attach the tension bar to the tension bands on one side rail. Thread a second tension bar into the mesh close enough to the other side rail to hold the mesh taut once it's attached to the tension bands. Unhook the strand of mesh near the outside of the second tension bar and pull it out to remove the excess mesh.

4 **Attach the second tension bar to the frame.** Pull the mesh and the second tension bar tightly and slip the tension bar into the tension bands. If the mesh isn't tight enough, unhook the tension bar and slip it into the next set of loops, then unravel the excess mesh and hook the bar back into the tension bands.

5 **Tie the mesh in place.** Once the chain-link mesh is firmly in place, attach tie wires to the top and bottom rails. Hook the tie wires around the mesh intersections, pull the mesh so it is slightly above the gate frame, and wrap the free end of the tie wire around the mesh.

Hanging the gate

1 **Hang the hinge straps.** Install the hinge straps on the gate, spacing them evenly from the top and bottom. Position the gate and support it on wood blocks. Mark the gatepost to show where the hinge straps will meet it.

2 **Hang the hinges.** Set the gate aside, then slide the hinge pins onto the post at the marks and tighten them with the top pin pointing down and the bottom pin pointing up. Install the gate on the post, lowering the bottom strap onto the lower pin, Lift the upper hinge strap onto the top pin.

3 **Hang the gate.** Tighten the hinges. Then position the latch catch on the gatepost opposite the hinges and tighten it. Slide the latch pin onto the side rail of the gate, line it up with the catch, and tighten it with a socket wrench.

Installing a pet fence

Skill level: ★★★☆☆

Time to complete:
Experienced 2 hrs.
Handy 4 hrs.
Novice 5 hrs.

Materials: Transmitter, wire, marking flags, collar receiver

Tools: Wire cutter, spade, screwdriver

An underground pet fence isn't a fence in the traditional sense: It's more like a remote control system for your dog. You bury a wire antenna around the part of the yard in which you want to keep the dog, and whenever the dog approaches the wire, a transmitter sends a signal to a receiver in the dog's collar, and the dog gets a shock. (The shock is only about one-sixth the power of the shock you get from dragging your feet across the rug and touching a doorknob.) Plant small flags above the wire, and the dog soon learns its boundaries and avoids future shocks.

A word of warning: The fence will keep your dog in, but it won't keep other dogs out. If other dogs are likely to bother your dog, this fence probably isn't for you. If you do decide to install a pet fence, buy one of the kits that has all the materials you'll need in it.

Transmitter

Flag

Underground wire

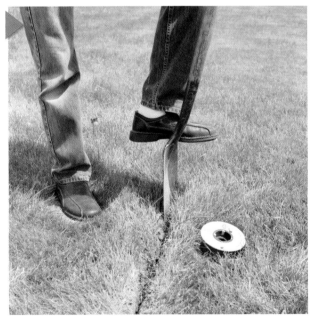

1 Position the transmitter as directed by the manufacturer. Dig a narrow trench 2 to 3 inches deep, beginning at the transmitter and running around the area you want to fence. Connect the wire to the transmitter and run it through the trench.

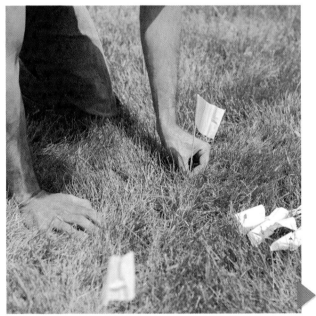

2 Refill the trench and mark it with flags. Plug in the transmitter and put the collar/receiver on the dog. Take the dog on a few daily walks near the flags so it learns its boundaries. Once it does, you can remove the flags.

Repairing fences and gates

| **Skill level:** ★☆☆☆ | **Time to complete:**
Experienced Variable
Handy Variable
Novice Variable | **Materials:** Cleaners, 1×4s, 2×4s, 4×4s, nails, deck screws, lag screws, carriage bolts, mesh, premix concrete, antisag kit | **Tools:** Fiber scrub brush, cloth, wire brush, hammer, screw gun, ratchet and socket wrenches, handsaw, circular saw, drill and bits, spade, shovel, cold chisel, 3-pound sledgehammer, wood chisel, post level, pliers, wire cutters, mason's trowel, clamps, fence puller, pull bar, safety glasses, work gloves, rubber gloves. |

All good fences need help staying good. When faced with damage, the first decision is whether to repair or replace. Armed with the tricks shown here, you can make a fence as good as new (or nearly so) with minimal need to replace sections. Begin by removing any parts that get in the way of the repair. You can either remove the fencing with a pry bar or cut out the damaged section with a handsaw. When repairing a post, remove the fencing and rails connected to it. Once the repair is complete, use new nails to replace fencing and rails.

Cleaning fences

Scrub wood fences with a fiber scrub brush and a mild detergent solution to remove most stains. For tougher stains, add 1 to 2 cups of bleach to a bucket of warm water. **Wear rubber gloves and safety glasses when working with strong cleansers.**

Clean vinyl fences with a sodium-bicarbonate-based cleaner. Bleach may stain the fence. Use a cloth instead of a brush so you don't scratch the surface of the fence. **Wear safety glasses.**

Pressure washing

Rent a pressure washer for hard-to-reach crevices in basket-weave and other fences or for stubborn stains on vinyl fences. Spray about 6 to 10 inches away from the fence. Don't use more than 1,000 psi of water pressure or the force may damage the wood. Many companies make commercial deck cleaners that are also good for cleaning fences. Consult the manufacturer's instructions before starting.

Clean metal fences with a wire brush, scrubbing away old paint, dirt, and rust from metal posts, hardware, and other areas. You can take care of most stains with 1 cup of strong household detergent mixed with a gallon of warm water.

Bracing wood rails

1 Reinforce rail ends with 2×4 cleats fastened to the posts.
Screw the cleats in place with No. 8 deck screws or nail with galvanized 10d (3-inch) nails. Taller fences often have third rails in the center, which can be reinforced using this method as well.

2 Add a sister rail to bolster a damaged rail. It can span the entire rail or just part of it, depending on the damage. Clamp the sister rail under or on top of the original, then drill holes through both rails, bolt them in place with ³⁄₈×4-inch carriage bolts, and remove the clamps.

3 Add a third rail between the top and bottom ones if the fencing seems loose. Screw the rail to the posts with No. 8 deck screws or toenail with galvanized 10d (3-inch) nails. Fasten the fence boards to the new rails with No. 8 deck screws.

Replacing a rail

1 Remove the fence boards.
Remove all of the fence boards from the damaged rail. Unscrew the boards, as shown here, or pry off the boards and pull out the nails. Try not to damage the fence boards so you can reinstall them later.

2 Remove the rail. Pry out the nails or remove the hardware holding the old rail in place. Cut a new rail to fit between the posts. Nail or screw the rail in place, then reinstall the fence boards.

Splicing a rail

Save yourself some work when you need to replace a short section of rail on a fence that has an exposed rail by splicing a new piece of rail in place. Remove the boards from the damaged section of rail, then cut off the damaged section at an angle. Put the new piece in place alongside the cut and trace along the cut in the old piece to transfer the angles to the new piece. Cut along each line, drill holes, and bolt the new piece in place with ³⁄₈×4-inch carriage bolts.

Repairing fences and gates (continued)

Fixing posts that lean

1 Dig out the post. Dig around the post until you reach the bottom. As you dig, pile the soil on a plastic garbage sack or tarp so you can easily refill the hole later.

2 Break up the footing. If the post is set in concrete, break up the concrete with a 3-pound sledgehammer and cold chisel. Wear gloves and protect your hands from the hammer with a shielded chisel, as shown here.

3 Plumb and brace the fence. Screw braces to the post, plumb it with a level, then screw the braces to stakes driven in the ground. Check again for plumb and reset the braces, if necessary.

Adding a sister post

You can reinforce a damaged post with a small post called a sister post. (If the post wobbles in the ground, either brace it or pour a new footing.) A sister post is half the thickness of the original post and the same width, but no higher than the fence's top rail. Cut the base of the sister post at a steep angle so you'll be able to drive it in like a stake. Put it in place against the original post. Place a block on top of the sister post to avoid splitting it and hit the block with a 3-pound sledgehammer to drive it 2 to 3 feet into the ground. Bolt it to the original post with 3/8x4-inch lag screws. Using a handsaw, cut a 45-degree angle on the top of the sister post so it will shed rain.

4 Pour a concrete footing. Mix bagged concrete, following the directions on the bag. You want it to be about as thick as oatmeal. Fill the posthole with the mix, sloping the concrete away from the posts for drainage.

Repairing underground rot

1 Remove the soil around the damage. If a post has rotted in the ground, you can put a second, shorter post next to it and tie the two together. Begin by digging around the footing. Dig deep enough to reach the bottom of the post or concrete.

2 Break up any footings. Wearing safety glasses, break up any concrete with a 3-pound sledgehammer and cold chisel. Break the concrete into small, manageable pieces.

3 Brace the post. Temporarily screw or nail 2×4 supports to the post. Plumb the post and hold it while a helper screws the braces to stakes driven in the ground.

4 Remove the damage. Cut off the old post just above the damaged part and pull the bottom section out of the ground. Cut a new post section 1 foot or so longer than the section you removed, and bevel the top. Place the new section in the hole next to the undamaged part of the original post.

5 Bolt the old and new parts together. Clamp the two post sections together. Counterbore 1-inch-wide holes for the heads of carriage bolts, drill ½-inch through holes, and insert ½-inch carriage bolts with washers. Put washers and nuts at the other end of the bolts and tighten with a socket wrench.

6 Pour a footing. File the posthole with concrete. Slope the top to help drain water away. Let the concrete harden for two to three days before removing the braces and supports.

Repairing a chain-link fence

1 Loosen the mesh. Remove the tie wires from the mesh with pliers. Connect a fence puller to both the post and fence and draw the fence tight enough to take tension off the tension bar. Remove the tension bar by loosening the bolts in the tension band. Loosen and remove the fence puller.

2 Remove the damaged section of fence. Open the loop at the top and bottom of a strand just outside the damaged area. Twist and pull the strand free. Take out a strand on the other side of the damage and remove the damaged section.

3 Weave in a patch. Cut a section of mesh the same size as the one you removed. Weave it into the remaining fence using the strands you removed in Step 2. Loop the wire at the top and bottom of the strand back around the fence with pliers.

4 Attach a fence puller. Slide a pull bar through the mesh about 4 feet from the end post. Reattach the fence puller. Crank the bar until the strands in the mesh press together no more than 1/4 inch when you squeeze them.

5 Reattach the tension bar. Reattach the tension bar to the tension band and release the fence puller.

6 Tie the fence to the posts. Attach new tie wires to hold the mesh firmly against the top rail and line posts. Thread a new tension wire through the bottom openings in the mesh.

Straightening metal fencing

1 **Break up the footing.** Dig around the post footing, then break up the concrete with a 3-pound sledgehammer and cold chisel. If other posts are also leaning, break the footing around them too.

2 **Plumb and brace the fence.** You can't nail into a metal fence, so drive a stake into the ground first, then screw it to the brace with a single screw. Plumb the fence, then clamp it to the brace.

3 **Pour new footings.** Once the fence is plumb and in position, mix bagged concrete and pour new footings. Slope the concrete away from the posts so water will drain away from them. Remove the braces after the concrete has hardened for 48 hours.

Fixing gates

 Gate stop

If a gate droops and you don't have diagonal crossbraces, install an antisag kit, which includes a turnbuckle, some cable, and some eye hooks. Screw an eye hook into the corner on the hinge side and a second eye hook in the lower corner on the opposite side. Attach the turnbuckle and tighten to remove the sag.

If a chain link gate gets out of alignment, you can usually fix it by adjusting the hinge pins. Loosen the pins with a socket wrench and reposition them with a wood block and hammer. Check the gate's swing and reposition, if necessary, before tightening.

A gate that swings too far will gradually loosen its own hinges. The low-tech solution is to screw a 1×2 or 2×4 stop to the gatepost so the gate stops when it's flush with the fence. The high-tech solution is a hydraulic gate closer (available at home centers), which gently pulls the gate shut and stops it at the right point.

159

CHAPTER 5

Landscaping walls

Make no mistake about it: Building a landscape wall is a lot of work, but it is extremely rewarding. Sometimes it's necessary; sometimes it's just attractive. Walls are usually necessary in yards that slope. Anything that's supposed to be flat, such as a garden, patio, or driveway, will cut through the contour of the land. You can plant gentle rises to hold back the soil, but anything higher than about a foot will keep sliding downhill.

As you'll see, these walls need a certain amount of strength. They also need to drain well—water that builds up behind them only adds pressure to the face of the wall. Landscaping block walls are designed to drain on their own; they're also built to automatically slope back into the hillside for strength.

Walls that are built for their aesthetic appeal don't have to be quite as strong as retaining walls. Stone and brick are good choices, built either with or without mortar. Cement block looks a bit utilitarian, but a coat of stucco changes its appearance entirely, and you can trowel or brush on a finish that gives it a handmade texture.

Any stone or brick wall over 48 inches tall requires steel reinforcement for strength and stability. If you are planning a wall over 48 inches tall, you should have the installation done by a professional mason or bricklayer to ensure that the wall will stand and that you comply with local codes.

Contents

All walls are not created equal

Here's the big question: Should you build a mortared wall or dry-set? Dry-set stone walls may have been the first built by humans, and if the stones are stacked carefully, the wall is pretty stable. These walls require very little foundation—a course of stones set underground does the trick. Mortared walls, of course, are stronger and more rigid. Before you start building, you have to realize that the ground is constantly moving under your feet. Though it's not moving enough for you to notice, it is enough to cause a rigid wall to crack over the course of the year. Dry-set walls can flex with changes in the ground, so for them, movement isn't a problem.

Once you put mortar in a wall, however, it can no longer flex, and if you look at an old house, you can often see cracks above spots where the ground has shifted. Consequently, a mortared wall requires a foundation that is thick enough and strong enough to support it if the ground underneath shifts. Concrete and rebar do the trick, but they will need to extend below the frost line. Therefore, if you count the footing, you'll often find as much wall underground as above.

Whichever type of wall you settle on, have the materials delivered. They're far too heavy for even a large pickup, much less the family car, to transport.

Landscaping walls tool kit

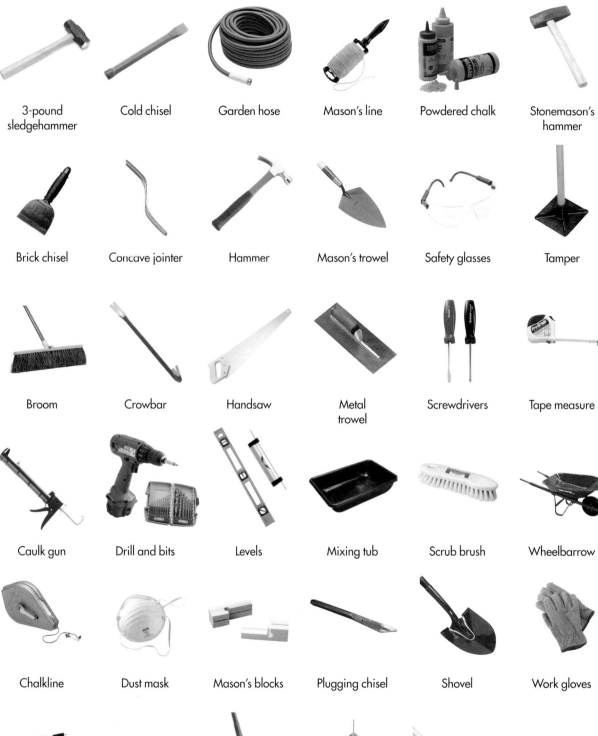

3-pound sledgehammer	Cold chisel	Garden hose	Mason's line	Powdered chalk	Stonemason's hammer
Brick chisel	Concave jointer	Hammer	Mason's trowel	Safety glasses	Tamper
Broom	Crowbar	Handsaw	Metal trowel	Screwdrivers	Tape measure
Caulk gun	Drill and bits	Levels	Mixing tub	Scrub brush	Wheelbarrow
Chalkline	Dust mask	Mason's blocks	Plugging chisel	Shovel	Work gloves

Circular saw	Framing square	Mason's hoe	Plumb bob	Spade

Materials

Once you have your tools in order, you need to choose your materials. Make a list of all the materials you need and buy them all at the same time. Have the materials delivered so you don't end up overloading your own vehicle.

▶ **Pressure-treated lumber** *is chemically treated for rot resistance. Timbers are anchored into the ground with lengths of reinforcing steel better known as* **rebar.** *Join courses of timbers with* **spikes.** *Make retaining walls with* **lipped landscape blocks. Bricks** *are popular for building freestanding walls.* **Concrete blocks** *are less expensive, making them a good choice for heavy-duty walls where appearance doesn't count. Dry walls (those without mortar) are best built with* **rubble stone,** *which is uncut like stones you might find in a field. Once concrete has been poured, cover it with* **burlap** *to help keep in moisture while it cures.* **Perforated plastic drainpipe** *drains water away from the bottom of a wall.* **Landscape fabric** *stops soil from getting into a gravel drainage field and blocking the flow of water.*

◀ *You can buy bags of* **premix concrete.** *Or make your own mix out of* **building sand, gravel,** *and* **portland cement.** *You can buy* **premix mortar.** *Or make your own mortar by mixing sand, portland cement, and* **hydrated lime. Muriatic acid** *is actually a solution of hydrochloric acid and is used to clean masonry. Some walls require an application of* **construction adhesive** *to help hold the top course in place.*

Mixing and working with mortar

Mixing mortar

A good mortar is what masons call workable. It sticks to the brick or block you're working with, and it's strong enough to support the masonry above it but not so thick that it won't squeeze out when you push a brick down on it.

The trick to making mortar workable is water. Too much water and the mortar becomes runny; too little, and the mortar is crumbly and hard to manage.

But how much is the right amount?

The amount of water you'll need depends on so many variables—temperature, humidity, the moisture of the mix in the bag, the quality of the ingredients— that it's pointless to think in terms of cups, pints, or gallons.

Instead think in terms of consistency. Work with a bagged mortar and mix it according to the directions on the bag, putting in about half or three-quarters of the water recommended. Mix it

thoroughly with a mixer if you have one or a mortar hoe if you don't. Once the mortar and water are thoroughly mixed, make ridges in it with the hoe. If the ridges fall, the mixture is too wet; add more dry ingredients. If the ridges remain sharp and distinct, the mixture is right. If they crumble, add water.

Once you think you have it right, double-check with your trowel: Scoop up some mortar and turn the trowel on edge. If the water-to-mortar ratio is right, the mortar will stick to the trowel.

To test mortar, put ridges in it with a trowel or hoe. If the ridges collapse, the mortar is strong but too wet to support the weight of the masonry above it.

If the ridges crumble, the mortar will support weight, but it won't stick to and isn't strong enough to handle the masonry.

If the ridges remain and the mortar sticks to the side of your trowel, the mix is strong enough to stick to and to support the weight of the masonry above it.

 ## Making your own mortar

Most books, including this one, include recipes for mixing cement, sand, and lime to make your own mortar. And you'll find piles of sand and bags of lime and cement that masons use to mix their own mortar at most construction sites. So why would you buy mortar in a bag?

Mortar made from scratch isn't any better than mortar from a bag: It's less expensive, but it's not better. In fact, unless you've had some experience mixing mortar, you won't know how to adjust for the moisture in the materials or how the quality of the materials affects the mixture. Unless you have a mixer, you won't be able to get a homogeneous mix before you add the water.

In short, the recipes on the next page appear so you can understand what mortar is. When it comes to mixing the dry ingredients, however, bagged mortar is worth the price and may even be better than the stuff they mix on-site. Factories can balance the mix of ingredients more accurately because they can control the moisture of the contents. They also sell it in manageable sizes that are easier for you to transport and small enough so you don't end up mixing more than you can use.

▶ **Mixing mortar from scratch is less expensive** than buying it pre-mixed in bags, but it's not better.

Retempering

About 30 minutes after you mix mortar, it will start to thicken. That's because some of the water will have evaporated. You can "retemper" and continue to use the mortar at this point by adding more water.

Around 2 hours after mixing, mortar will start thickening for a different reason: It's beginning to harden. The mortar is spent at this point. Don't use it, and don't retemper it. Mix a new batch.

In between these two points, the mortar is likely to thicken at least once or twice more. Unfortunately, you can't tell if it's drying out or hardening. The closer you get to the 2-hour mark, the more likely the mortar is hardening and the less likely retempering is to succeed. Retempering is generally successful during the first 1½ hours, though hot weather can shorten the time. Always replace mortar that's over 2 hours old.

Because the lime in most mortars stains stones, the mortars for laying stone are lime-free but rich in cement. Whether you're working in brick, concrete block, or stone, make sure you have the right mortar. If you're building a mortared stone wall, mix the mortar a bit on the dry side so it can support the weight of the stones while you work.

Estimating for brick patios

Unlike a wall, a patio is laid with the wide faces exposed, so you'll only need 4⅓ bricks to cover a square foot. A 60-pound bag is enough to mortar between about 68 square feet of bricks.

An 80-pound bag is enough for about 90 square feet.

You'll need one-third more mortar if you're using ½-inch joints.

You'll need an additional 60-pound bag for every 10 square feet of ½-inch mortar bed underneath the brick. If you're buying 80-pound bags, each one will cover 13 square feet.

☑ WORK SMART
USE THE RIGHT MORTAR FOR THE JOB

Different types of premixed mortar cater to different applications and it's important that you use the proper mix for the job you're doing. There are three basic applications—masonry in contact with the ground, masonry that is above ground, and masonry that is exposed to strong winds. Tell an associate at your local home improvement center what you're doing with the concrete and they will lead you to the right material.

Consistency

Consistency is the key when mixing multiple batches of concrete. Unevenly mixed batches won't bond and cure as effectively, so take the time to be consistent.

Estimating the mortar you'll need for walls

Brick walls with 8×2×4-inch bricks and ⅜-inch joints: In simplest terms, you'll need a 60-pound bag of mortar for every 28 bricks you lay, or 4.1 square feet. An 80-pound bag is enough for 36 bricks, or 5.25 square feet. If you are using ½-inch joints, you'll need approximately one-third more mortar. Since most walls are actually two bricks thick, figure out how much mortar you'll need for one face, and then double it.

Concrete block walls with 8×16× 8-inch blocks and ⅜-inch joints: A 60-pound bag is enough for 11 concrete blocks. When combined with the mortar around it, a concrete block covers an area of about 1 square foot. An 80-pound bag is enough for 15 blocks, or 15 square feet.

Laying out a wall

Skill level:	Time to complete:	Materials: 2×4s, 10d (3-inch) common nails, 2×2s, masking tape	Tools: Tape measure, circular saw, hammer, mason's line, line level, 3-pound sledgehammer, plumb bob, powdered chalk, safety glasses
★☆☆☆	Experienced 40 min.		
	Handy 55 min.		
	Novice 90 min.		

Even the most complicated wall starts out as a few lengths of mason's line stretched between sets of stakes and crosspieces—what builders call batterboards. (You could use a single stake with no crosspiece, but batterboards let you reposition the line without having to move one of the stakes.) The ability to make adjustments is especially important when you're squaring up the layout using the 3-4-5 triangle, shown at right.

The wall you lay out can be as long as you like, but you're limited when it comes to height. If the wall stands more than 4 feet high, building codes require a professional engineer's design. If you're taking on a 6-foot hillside, however, you can avoid the cost of engineering work by terracing the hill with a pair of 3-foot-high retaining walls.

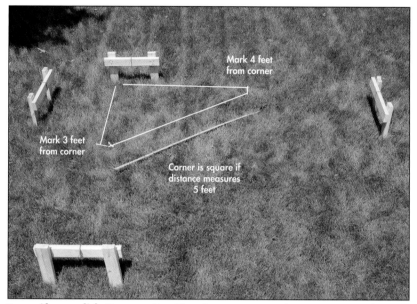

Mark 4 feet from corner

Mark 3 feet from corner

Corner is square if distance measures 5 feet

Even if you didn't pay attention in geometry, the easiest way to lay out a right angle is the 3-4-5 triangle. Lay out the corner by eye using batterboards and mason's line. Mark one line with a piece of tape 3 feet from the corner. Mark the other line 4 feet from the corner. Slide the lines until the distance between the two pieces of tape is 5 feet, at which point the corner is square.

Laying out a straight wall

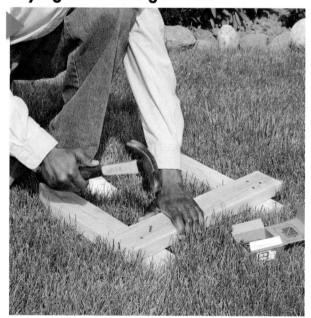

1 Build batterboards. Start by cutting points on the bottoms of two 2×4s, creating stakes. Nail a crosspiece to the stakes about 2 inches from the top.

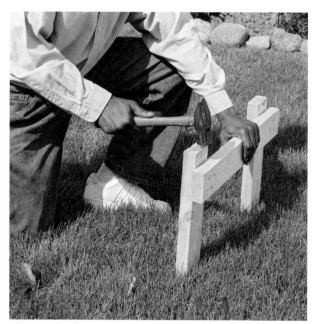

2 Set the batterboards. Drive a batterboard into the ground 12 to 18 inches beyond each end of the planned wall. Drive the stakes so they sit firmly in the ground, then level the crosspiece by hammering the top of the higher stake.

3 Run line between the batterboards. Tie a mason's line to the crosspieces. Attach a line level to the line and, if necessary, tap the batterboard that is at the high end to level the line.

4 Position the line. Slide the line along the crosspieces until it marks an edge of the wall. Tape the line to mark the point you've decided on for each end of the wall. Drop a plumb bob from the taped points and use powdered chalk to mark where it meets the ground.

5 Drive stakes to mark the ends of the walls. Drive in 2×2 stakes at the chalked marks. Sprinkle chalk, sand, limestone, or flour along the mason's line to mark the edge of the wall. Before digging, mark where the line meets the batterboards and untie it. You'll put the line back in place later.

Laying out a square corner

1 Lay out one wall; drive batterboards for the second.
Lay out the wall on one side of the corner with batterboards and mason's line, following the steps above. To lay out the second wall, drive in a second set of batterboards 12 to 18 inches beyond the corner and beyond the end of the second wall. Stretch a mason's line between the batterboards and position it by eye. Attach a line level and level the line.

2 Square up the corner. Square up the corner using the 3-4-5 triangle. Mark one line 3 feet from the corner with a piece of tape. Mark the other line 4 feet from the corner. Measure between the two pieces of tape. Have the helper slide the line until the distance between the two pieces of tape is 5 feet. When it is, the corner is square.

3 Mark the Ground. Drop a plumb bob where the lines cross and mark the ground with powdered chalk. Measure to find the end of the wall, drop a plumb bob, and mark that point on the ground with chalk as well. Drive 2×2 stakes into the ground to mark the corner and ends of the wall.

Providing drainage for retaining walls

Skill level:	Time to complete:	Materials: Landscape fabric, gravel, perforated plastic drainpipe	Tools: Shovel, tape measure, level, garden rake, tamper, utility knife or scissors
★★★☆☆	Experienced 4 hrs. Handy 5 hrs. Novice 6 hrs.		

The life span of a retaining wall depends largely on its drainage. Dry soil places very little stress on a wall, but wet, heavy soil causes the wall to buckle or lean, which means extensive repairs can't be far behind.

No drainage system can handle a flood, but a good drainage system will prevent most water damage. The biggest trick—short of the excavation—is finding a place for the water to go. Bring the drainage pipe around the wall and continue running it until it comes to the surface.

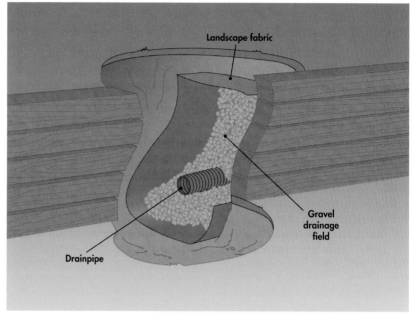

The parts of a drainage system work together. Gravel, which won't absorb water, replaces soil, which does. A layer of landscape fabric keeps the soil from clogging the gravel. A perforated drainpipe collects the water as it gathers at the base of the wall then guides the water along the wall into another part of the yard.

1 Dig a trench. Lay out the wall with batterboards and level lines, and dig into the hill to create a level trench as deep as is required by the wall you're building. Place some of the excavated soil on the slope's low side to help flatten the area.

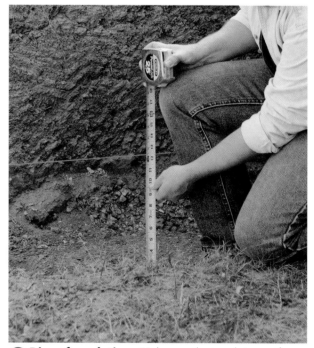

2 Dig a foundation. Make sure the trench is a uniform depth (and level) by taking measurements at various points along a level mason's line. If the measurements vary, add dirt (and tamp it) or remove dirt where necessary.

3 Cover with landscape fabric. Landscape fabric prevents the soil from clogging your drainage system. Unroll enough fabric to run along the length of the trench twice, plus an amount a little more than the depth of the excavation. Pull the fabric across the back and bottom of the trench.

4 Lay the first courses of the wall and then add a gravel bed. Leave space at one end for the drainpipe to exit through the wall. Behind the wall, lay a gravel bed that slopes 1 inch every 4 feet as it travels across the hill. Check the slope with a 4-foot level sitting on a straight 2×4 with a 1-inch spacer under one end. Add or remove gravel to get a level reading.

5 Lay drainpipe. Lay drainpipe along the back of the wall. It, too, should slope 1 inch every 4 feet. Continue the pipe around a sidewall, if any, without kinking the pipe. Continue to run the pipe downhill until it reaches the surface.

Backfilling the excavation

1 Lay gravel in the trench. Cover the drainpipe with gravel as you build the wall. Lay the first few courses and fill in behind them with gravel. Tamp the gravel firmly. Continue to build the wall, filling in with 4-inch layers of gravel and tamping as you go.

2 Continue building the wall. Lay gravel behind the wall until it is about 6 inches from the top. Pack down the gravel with a tamper, then fold the landscape fabric over the gravel.

3 Lay topsoil. Fill the remaining space with soil and tamp it in place. Fill any low spots that result, then rake the area level. Sod, seed, or plant with the groundcover of your choice.

Building a wooden retaining wall

Skill level:	Time to complete:	Materials: Landscape fabric, gravel, drainpipe, pressure-treated 6×6s or 2×12s, No. 4 (1/2-inch) rebar, 10-inch landscape spikes, 1/2×4 inch lag screws, concrete	Tools: Tape measure, shovel, 1/2-inch drill and 1/2-inch spade bit with extension, chainsaw, level, framing square, paintbrush, 3- and 6-pound sledgehammers, shovel, tamper, posthole digger, socket wrenches, safety glasses, work gloves
★★★☆☆	Experienced 10 hrs. Handy 14 hrs. Novice 18 hrs.		

If you want to move the earth, build a retaining wall—by the time you're done, you'll feel as though you've moved half the planet.

Because a retaining wall is going to be in contact with the ground, make sure you use lumber that's rated for ground contact. Your best choice is a pressure-treated wood that has a rating of .40 or higher. (Regular pressure-treated wood, which is commonly used on decks, has a .25 rating; it holds less preservative and won't hold up well.) Avoid railroad ties—they're heavy and soaked with creosote, which is messy and can harm plants.

This retaining wall's hefty 6×6 timbers hold back the soil.
A drainpipe at the base of the wall carries water away. Set the first course of timbers below grade as a foundation and anchor them with rebar. To counteract the pressure caused by the soil pushing against the wall, offset the courses so the back of each timber overhangs the back of the timber below by 1/2 inch. Anchor the wall with deadmen and tiebacks spaced at least 4 feet long installed every 4 feet along the wall.

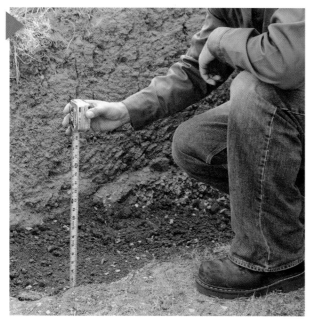

1 Remove soil and dig a trench. Lay out the wall, excavate the soil behind it, and dig a trench 8 inches deep for the first course of timbers. Line the trench and excavation with landscape fabric, then add 2 or 3 inches of gravel and tamp it in place. (See "Providing drainage for retaining walls," pages 168–169.) Make sure the trench is level and flat.

2 Prepare the timbers. Drill a 1/2-inch hole 6 to 12 inches from the end of each timber to hold the rebar stakes (see Step 4). If necessary, cut the last timber to fit with a chainsaw. Treat cut ends with a preservative to keep them from rotting, and set the timbers in the trench.

3 Level the first course. Any irregularity in the first course will show up in all the other courses. Use a level to make sure the timbers are level from end to end and from side to side. At corners, check for square with either a 3-4-5 triangle or with a framing square. Add or remove gravel and move the timbers as necessary.

4 Drive rebar stakes. Drive 42-inch lengths of No. 4 (½-inch) rebar through the holes in the ends of the timbers with a 6-pound sledgehammer. Mark the location of the rebar on the face of the timber so you'll know where they are when you fasten the next course.

5 Lay the second course of timbers. Offset the ends of the second course by at least 4 inches from the ends of the course below. Place the timbers so the front of the upper timber steps back ½ inch from the face of the lower timber.

6 Drill holes for spikes. Each row of timbers is fastened to the one below with 10-inch landscape spikes. Lay out holes for the spikes 6 to 12 inches from each end of the timbers and every 4 feet in between. Make sure the holes won't hit the rebar that holds the first row in place. Drill the holes with a ⅜-inch bit in an electric drill.

7 Drive the spikes. Drive the spikes into the holes with a 3-pound sledgehammer. Mark the location of the spikes on the face of the timbers with chalk so you won't hit them when you drive the spikes for the next course.

8 Lay the drainpipe. Once you have nailed the second course in place, lay a thin bed of gravel on the ground behind it, sloping it 1 inch every 4 feet. (See "Providing drainage for retaining walls," pages 168–169.) Lay drainpipe on the gravel and against the wall. (If a sidewall turns uphill, lay the drainpipe before you put in the sidewall's second course.)

Building a wooden retaining wall (continued)

9 Dig trenches for the deadmen and tiebacks. Deadmen and tiebacks are installed every other course as anchors, offset from the ones on lower courses. Fold the landscape fabric out of the way, cover the drainpipe with gravel, and dig trenches for the deadmen and tiebacks at 4-foot intervals. Make each trench large enough for a 4-foot tieback and a 3-foot deadman. Dig the bottom of the trench level with the top of the first course. Cut a hole in the landscape fabric for each deadman.

10 Put the deadmen and tiebacks in place. Cut the deadmen and tiebacks. Set one end of each tieback on the second course of timbers, the other end on the deadman. Make adjustments as needed to level and square the deadmen and tiebacks.

11 Nail the deadmen and tiebacks together. Bore two 3/8-inch pilot holes through each tieback and deadman for a 10-inch landscape spike. Drive spikes into the holes, attaching the tiebacks to the deadmen and the wall.

12 Lay the next course. Lay the next course, offsetting the timber ends by at least 4 inches from the ones below. Position the timbers so the front edge of the upper course steps back from the lower course by 1/2 inch. Drill and spike as before.

13 Fill the trench with gravel as you build. Fill the trench with gravel to the top of each course as you lay it, and firmly pack down the gravel with a tamper.

14 Lay the remaining courses. As you lay the timbers, the front of each course should step back from the front of the one below. Install deadmen and tiebacks every other course. Spike the courses to each other. For the top course, drive a spike through the corner.

15 Fill with topsoil. After installing the top course, fold the landscape fabric over the gravel and fill the remaining space with topsoil. Tamp it, fill any resulting low spots, and rake it smooth.

If you live in a wet area, bore a 1-inch drainage hole every 4 feet at a slightly upward angle through the second course. If you'd rather not drill holes, leave 1-inch gaps between the timbers and cover the back of the openings with galvanized screening.

Building a post-and-board retaining wall

If digging trenches for deadmen takes you into a neighbor's yard or presents other problems, a post-and-board wall gives you the look of wood with a fraction of the digging.

Begin by digging for a drainage pipe as explained in "Providing drainage for retaining walls," pages 168–169. Then dig holes for 6×6 posts—the holes need to be half as deep as the wall is high. Align, plumb, and brace the posts, then pour the concrete footings.

The wall itself is made of 2×12 or 2×6 boards, which you screw onto the posts once the concrete has dried for at least three days. Use a level to make sure the first row is level, then screw the boards to the posts with deck screws before putting in the drainpipe and gravel. Put in the remaining rows, filling in behind them with gravel as you go.

1 Dig postholes. Lay out the wall, then level the ground at the base of the hillside. Dig postholes about 10 inches in diameter at 2-foot intervals along the length of the wall. Dig until the hole is at least half as deep as the wall is high. In cold climates, dig 6 inches below the frost line.

2 Plumb and brace the end posts. Enlarge the bottom of all the holes to a diameter of about 14 inches. Begin by setting the end posts so their tops are 1 inch shorter than the finished wall height. Trim the posts, if necessary, with a chainsaw. Screw boards to the posts, plumb the posts, and nail the boards to stakes to brace them.

Building a wooden retaining wall (continued)

3 **Place the line posts.** Run a level mason's line between the tops of the end posts and align the tops of the other posts with it. Set, plumb, and brace all the posts, then fill the holes with concrete. Slope the concrete away from each post so water drains away from it.

4 **Put the 2×12s in place.** Put the 2×12s for the first course on the uphill side of the posts. Level the boards and cut them, if necessary, so they'll meet at the center of the posts. Butt the ends together and hold them against the post. Bore two $^7/16$-inch-diameter holes slightly smaller than the diameter of a $^1/2$×4-inch lag screw through the boards into each post.

WORK SMART
NO MORE THAN FOUR FEET

Building codes usually require that a licensed engineer design the system for a retaining wall that is more than 4 feet tall. This is to ensure that the wall can support the weight of all the dirt behind it.

If you need a tall wall and don't want to hire a professional, consider terracing the hill with a series of lower walls. But don't attempt to build a single wall; it isn't worth the risk.

DESIGN TIP
CHAMFERED POSTS

When you chamfer the tops of the posts, you give a wall a more finished look that helps drain water from the top of each post. Cut the chamfer after you've braced the posts and cut them to length but before you attach the boards. The chamfer can be any width you like. Experiment by cutting a sample 2-inch bevel on a piece of scrap. If it's not quite what you like, keep cutting samples until you find one you do like. Note that the finished wall is one inch higher than the post.

5 **Bolt the boards in place.** Put washers on the lag screws and drive them into the holes. Line the area behind the wall with landscape fabric, add gravel, and lay drainpipe. Cover with gravel and tamp. Fill in behind the wall and tamp the gravel as you build. About 6 inches from the top of the wall, fold the fabric over the gravel and fill the remaining space with topsoil.

Building a landscape block retaining wall

Skill level: ★★★☆☆

Time to complete:
Experienced 10 hrs.
Handy 14 hrs.
Novice 18 hrs.

Materials: Landscape fabric, gravel, drainpipe, landscape blocks, construction adhesive

Tools: Tape measure, shovel, tamper, level, circular saw, 3-pound sledgehammer, rubber mallet, torpedo level, brick chisel, caulk gun, safety glasses, work gloves

LANDSCAPING WALLS

Landscape blocks are some of the best things to happen to walls in a long time. Made of precast concrete, they have textured faces that make them look a lot more like stone than concrete. They require neither footing nor mortar, and stacking them automatically creates a wall that leans into the hillside for strength.

Two major types exist: lipped and pinned. The ones with lips work best for this project. The ones with fiberglass pins are used for large structural walls that require engineers and earthmoving equipment. Solid landscape blocks are durable and can easily be cut into smaller pieces to offset courses as you build your wall.

1 Dig and level a trench. Lay out the wall with batterboards and mason's line. Dig a trench as wide and deep as the manufacturer recommends. Line the bottom with an inch or so of sand, rake it level, and compact it with a tamper. Place some of the soil you remove on the downhill side of the trench to level the slope.

2 Lay landscape fabric. Line the back and bottom of the trench with landscape fabric. Unroll enough fabric to cross back over the trench later, plus about a foot more than the height of the wall. If you have to piece together lengths of landscape fabric, overlap any adjoining edges by 3 to 4 inches.

 Laying curves

The keystone shape of most blocks makes it easy to create a curved wall—the shape and size of the block determines how tight the radius can be. Lay out free-form curves with a garden hose. To lay out a precise arc, drive in a pipe at the desired center point. Tie one end of a mason's line to the pipe and the other end to a bottle of powdered chalk. Pull the line tight and walk around the pipe in a circle, marking the ground as you go.

Building a landscape block retaining wall (continued)

3 Lay the first block. Some manufacturers instruct you to set the first block lip up; others instruct lip down. Follow the directions. Lay the first block and check for level from side to side and front to back. Tap with a rubber mallet to make small adjustments. Put sand under the block to solve bigger problems.

4 Lay the rest of the first course. Lay the remaining blocks one at a time. Make sure each block is level, checking both side to side and front to back. Put the level across the new block and at least one of its neighbors to make sure the tops of the blocks are level with each other. The spaces at the ends of the course may not require a full block. Buy smaller blocks or trim larger ones to fit.

5 Lay the second course. If the first course ended with a full block, begin the second course with a half block. If you started the first course with a partial block, trim a full block so it overlaps the seam below by at least 3 inches. (Check the manufacturer's instructions.) Lay a second course of blocks with their lips pointing down, over the back of the wall. Position each block so it spans a joint in the course below. As you work, verify that the blocks are level; if not, shim the low end with asphalt shingle or some landscape fabric.

 Building corners

If your wall turns a corner, lay full blocks for the first course. On the second course, cut a block in half. Place the block as shown. On the remaining courses, lay the half block at a right angle to the one below. Chisel the lip off a block if it interferes with construction, then secure the block in place with a bead of construction adhesive.

WORK SMART
CUTTING BLOCKS

If you're working with solid blocks, you can trim them to fit smaller openings. Score along the line you want to cut with a circular saw and masonry blade. Split the block at the scored line by striking it with a brick chisel and 3-pound sledgehammer. If you're working with hollow-core blocks, don't plan on cutting them to size because they'll break. Instead buy half blocks and smaller blocks to fit openings that are less than a full block long.

6 Trim blocks for the end of the wall. As you come to the end of the wall, trim a block to fit in the opening. When you begin building the rest of the wall, alternate so one row begins with a full block and the next with a half block.

7 Lay a third course and some drainpipe. Not all block walls require a drainpipe, though it's never a bad idea. Lay the third course the same way you laid the second course, leaving an exit point for the drainpipe at one end of the wall. Add a bit more gravel behind the wall to create a flat surface that slopes 1 inch in 4 feet, and tamp the gravel. Tuck a drainpipe behind the wall. Fill in completely behind the wall to the top of the course and tamp.

8 Lay the remaining courses. Continue building the wall, adding gravel and tamping after every course. When you're a course or two below the top of the wall, fold the landscape fabric over the gravel and trim off any excess.

9 Lay capstones. The keystone shape of the blocks leaves triangular gaps between the stones, which are covered up with special blocks called capstones. Apply a bead of construction adhesive along the top of the wall and set the capstones in place.

10 Fill in around the wall. Put topsoil in the space between the landscape fabric and the top of the wall and fill what remains of the trench in front of the wall. Rake to make a flat surface and tamp.

One block short of a full load

If you're trying to calculate the exact number of blocks you'll need for your wall, you wouldn't be the first do-it-yourselfer to do so. A slight miscalculation, however, or a couple of blocks that break during trimming will leave you short. An extra trip to the store is bad enough, but when you get home you might discover that the color of the new blocks differs from the blocks you already have. Dying concrete is not an exact science, and the color can vary from batch to batch. When you buy the blocks, make sure they come from the same batch. Verify that the store will let you return any extras, and add 10 percent to the number of blocks you think you'll need.

Building a dry stone wall

Skill level:	Time to complete:	Materials: Gravel, stones, 1×2s, 4d (1½-inch) common nails	Tools: Shovel, mason's line, tamper, circular saw, hammer, stonemason's hammer, level, safety glasses, work gloves
★★★☆☆	Experienced 16 hrs.		
	Handy 20 hrs.		
	Novice 24 hrs.		

Dry stone walls are built without mortar, which has many advantages and saves a lot of work. Unlike mortared stone walls, a dry stone wall will flex as the ground beneath it shifts, eliminating the need for a foundation. Because no mortar is drying as you work, you can work at your own pace, and no mistake is permanent. (A dry stone wall is a bad choice in areas prone to earthquakes, however, and codes in such areas may prohibit building one.) If you choose to build a dry stone wall, remember that you'll be working with large, heavy stones. After a few days, working on a stone wall feels like a sentence to hard labor.

Sort stones into groups according to their functions before you start. Look for bondstones—those with a solid base, flat top, and one or more straight sides. Corners require stones with two sides that meet at 90 degrees. Save the flattest stones for the wall cap.

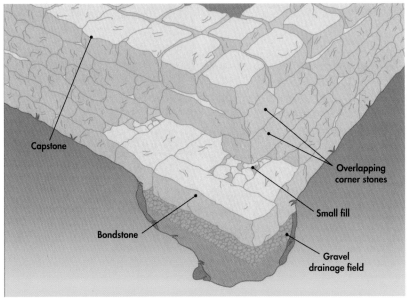

A typical dry stone wall has two parallel faces, called wythes.
A wythe is any continuous vertical section of a wall one masonry unit thick. The face of the wall is made of large stones; smaller stones fill the center. Bondstones— long stones that run the width of the wall—are positioned every 4 to 6 feet to tie the two sides of the wall together. Bondstones are also placed at the corners, with their long faces at 90 degrees to each other from course to course. For stability, the wall has a broad base that supports a narrower top. The resulting inward slope, or batter, should be 1½ to 2 inches for every vertical foot.

1 Lay out and dig a trench for the wall. Stretch a mason's line between stakes to mark each edge of the wall. Sprinkle powdered chalk or sand over the lines to mark the wall's path on the ground. Dig a trench about 8 inches deep within the marked outlines.

2 Line the trench with gravel. Place a 4-inch layer of gravel in the trench. The gravel will drain water away from the finished wall. Tamp the gravel and use a level to make sure the bed is flat and even.

3 **Lay the front face of the first course.** Begin the first course by placing a long stone, a bondstone, across each end of the trench. Then lay the front face of the first course, with bondstones every 4 to 6 feet. Because the top and bottom of a stone are seldom parallel, arrange the stones so any resulting slope inclines toward the middle of the wall.

4 **Lay the rear face of the wall.** Lay the rear face along the back edge of the trench. Fill the spaces between the two faces of the wall with small stones or rubble.

5 **Lay the second course.** Start the next course by laying a long stone at a right angle to the bondstone below it. Work your way down the wall one face at a time. Lay the stones so the space between two stones is always spanned by another stone. Lay bondstones every 4 to 6 feet, varying the positions from course to course.

6 **Check the batter.** Constantly check the batter with your batter gauge and a level. Reposition stones as needed to get a plumb reading. Continue to build the wall, checking the batter after every few courses. Pick the flattest, broadest stones for the top course. Slope the top stones slightly outward by propping them up on small stones. The slope helps drain water away from the top of the wall.

TOOL TIP
BUILD A BETTER GAUGE

For strength, a wall needs to be narrower at the top than at the bottom. Because of this, the face of the wall slopes slightly. Build a batter gauge to check the slope, or batter. Cut two 1×2s equal to the wall's final height. Screw two ends to a spacer that is 1½ to 2 inches long for every foot of wall height. Screw the other two ends together and tape a level to either outer face of the 1×2s. Hold one leg of the gauge against the wall. The batter is correct when the level's bubble is centered in the vial.

Building a footing for a stone or brick wall

Skill level:	Time to complete:	Materials: Gravel, 2×4s, 2×8s, 1×2s, 10d (3-inch) nails, concrete, burlap	Tools: Spade, tamper, mason's line, plumb bob, level, crowbar, 3-pound sledgehammer, circular saw, wheelbarrow, mason's hoe, garden hose, dust mask, safety glasses
★★★☆☆	Experienced 8 hrs. Handy 12 hrs. Novice 16 hrs.		

Whether you're building a brick wall, a stone wall, or any other wall that requires mortar, the job starts underground with a footing. A mortared wall is rigid and won't flex as the ground moves with seasonal changes. Without the footing, the wall would crack, and weather would compound the damage. With a footing, the wall sits on a strong, rigid platform. If the ground shifts enough to move the platform, the platform and wall move as one piece, minimizing cracks.

Foundation wall

Concrete footing

(Wall width)

Concrete footing

Gravel drainage field

Typically a footing is as thick as the wall it supports and twice as wide. If the wall is one foot wide, the footing should be at least one foot thick. Those in frost-free areas can pour their footings in a trench. Those in colder climates must pour their footings below the frost line—anywhere from 6 to 48 inches below the surface. If your footing needs to be deep underground, pour it at the bottom of a deep trench, then build a foundation wall on top, as shown at left.

WORK SMART
HOME DELIVERY

Concrete and gravel are heavy. Have them delivered—it's not worth the wear and tear on your car or truck.

Regional variation

In a climate where the ground freezes, pour a footing so the bottom is at least 6 inches below the frost line. Check local building codes to find out exactly how deep that is in your area. In deep-frost areas, pour the footing and build a foundation wall on top of it once it's dry.

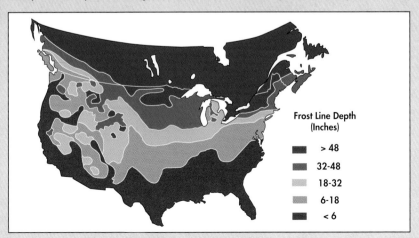

Frost Line Depth (Inches)
- > 48
- 32-48
- 18-32
- 6-18
- < 6

Preparing the site

1 Lay out the edges of the footing with batterboards and mason's line. The footing should be as thick as the wall it supports and twice as wide. Stretch mason's line to lay out the width, then use sand or flour to lay out lines on the ground that are 4 to 6 inches outside the lines. Measure the distance between the ground and the mason's line and write it on the batterboard for reference later. Mark the positions of the lines on the batterboards, then untie the lines.

2 Dig a trench for the footing. Start the trench at the lines you made on the ground, then dig it about 3 inches deeper than the wall is wide. If the ground freezes where you live, dig down at least 6 inches below the frost line. In either case, line the trench with an inch of gravel, and tamp it down.

Assembling the form

1 Lay out the outside of the forms. The lines you originally tied to the batterboards marked the inside edge of the forms. Move them 1½ inches closer to the outside edge of the trench in order to mark the outside edge of the form. Drop a plumb bob from the line and mark the end of the foundation with a nail put through a piece of paper.

2 Drive stakes to support the form. Drive stakes into the ground just outside the nails and run mason's line between them. Drive the stakes no more than 8 feet apart to ensure that the forms won't bow from the weight of the concrete.

3 Attach the forms to the stakes. Place a 2×8 against the stakes on each side of the trench. (Use 2×8s even if the footing will be deeper than 8 inches because excess concrete can flow underneath the form and make the footing stronger.) Measure down from the mason's line to make sure the board is both level and a couple inches below ground level (the distance you wrote on the batterboard in Step 1). Clamp the boards to the stakes and attach them using double-headed nails. If you need to join two boards, drive a stake so it straddles the ends and nail it to both of the boards.

Building a footing for a stone or brick wall (continued)

4 Attach ends to the forms. For the ends of the form, cut 2×8s that are long enough to span the existing forms and the stakes. Attach each end to the forms and stakes. Trim all the stakes flush with the top of the form, using a handsaw. Apply form release agent to the inside surfaces of all the forms.

5 Drive stakes every 2 feet. Lay a level across the form to make sure the sides are level. Hammer on the stakes as needed to adjust the boards. Drive in additional stakes flush with the top of the side boards every 2 feet along them. If two boards meet end to end, drive in a stake that spans the seams. Nail the stakes to the boards and trim them flush at the top.

6 Attach spreaders. Concrete weighs enough to bend the boards outward when it's poured. Reinforce the forms with 1×2 spreaders nailed every 2 to 3 feet.

When the ground is too soft to hold the stakes securely, brace the sides of the form with kickers, pieces of 1×2 that extend out to firmer soil. Drive a stake into firm ground and nail the kicker to it. Nail the end of the kicker to the form.

 Regional variation

In areas prone to earthquakes or hurricanes, footings may need special reinforcement. (Walls more than 4 feet high also need reinforcement, but leave that job to professionals.) Check your local building codes for special requirements in your area. Often a footing must be reinforced with rebar; No. 4 (1/2-inch) rebar is a common standard. You may need to lay two parallel runs of rebar the entire length of the form. Wire the rebar to wire supports (sold separately) that hold the rebar in the middle of the slab. Overlap any lengths of rebar by at least 12 inches and tie them together with wire. If vertical reinforcement is required, drive rebar into the ground, spacing it as local codes require.

Pouring concrete

1 Mix the concrete. Mix pre-mixed concrete following the directions on the bag. Empty out the dry ingredients, then make a crater in the middle and pour in about half the required water. Fold the ingredients together and slowly add the rest of the water.

2 Test the consistency. Properly mixed concrete has the consistency of oatmeal. A more accurate way to test the mix is to smooth out the concrete and make grooves in it with a hoe. If the edges hold, the concrete is ready. If they fall in (like these did), add dry ingredients. If they crumble, add water.

3 Dump concrete in the forms. Set up a wheelbarrow ramp that leads to the edge of the form. Prop up the high end on a 2×4 or bricks. Resting it on the forms could knock them out of alignment. Pour the concrete into the form from the wheelbarrow, dumping one load up against another until the form is filled to the top.

4 Remove trapped air. Work a shovel or spade in and out of the concrete to remove air pockets. Pay particular attention to corners and edges, where air often gets trapped. Gas powered, portable vibrators are available for rent.

$ BUYER'S GUIDE
HOW MUCH IS ENOUGH?

Concrete is sold by the cubic yard, so you'll have to round up the numbers to the next highest cubic yard after you've done the math. To find out how many cubic yards you'll need, first figure out how many cubic feet you'll need: Multiply the footing's width by its length and thickness in feet (W'×L'×T'). Divide the answer by the number of cubic feet in a yard, 27, to get the number of cubic yards you'll need. For example, if a footing is 2 feet wide, 50 feet long, and 8 inches (.67 feet) thick, you would need: 2 × 50 × .67/27 = 2.48 cubic yards. You will need to order three cubic yards for the job.

☑ WORK SMART
DELIVER THE MIX

If you're doing a job that involves less than 2 cubic yards of concrete, bags of premix concrete are probably easiest to handle. Anything bigger is going to take quite a few bags: One 90-pound bag of concrete yields only two-thirds of a cubic foot. You'll need 41 bags to get a cubic yard.

For large jobs, let the professionals do the mixing, whether they're at the factory that bags the mix or driving the concrete truck that pours it for you. Tell the suppliers what you're building so you get the right mix. Have plenty of help when the truck arrives. You may have to pay for more than you use but if you consider that your time has value, it may offset the extra cost.

Building a footing for a stone or brick wall (continued)

5 Screed the form. Lay a 2×4 across the form and pull it along the length of the footing, shimmying from side to side and removing the spreaders as you go. This process, called screeding, levels and smooths the concrete.

6 Cover with burlap. Cover the footing with burlap and keep it damp, but not soaked, with water for two or three days while the concrete cures. The moisture keeps the concrete from drying too quickly and cracking.

7 Remove the form. Once the concrete has cured, pull the nails out of the form. Work stakes loose with a crowbar and remove them, then gently pry the boards off the footing.

8 Replace the dirt. Fill in around the footing with soil and tamp it firmly. Wait until you've finished the wall to replant.

$ BUYER'S GUIDE
USE A FORM RELEASE AGENT

Concrete forms have to come apart as well as go together. Typically they're nailed together with duplex nails. A duplex nail has a head at the end of the shank just like every other nail, but it also has one about 1/4 inch down the shank. This head hits the form as you're driving the nail, stopping it so there will be enough nail to grab and pull out with your hammer.

Once you've removed the stakes, you'll want to remove the forms themselves. At this point, if you didn't use an oil-like form release agent, you'll wish you had. Without the agent, the boards stick to the concrete, and some of the concrete may break away as you pry them. With the agent, the boards come off easily. Form release agent is sold in the same department that sells concrete.

OOPS
SMOOTH OPERATOR

Even the most experienced do-it-yourselfer can get carried away sometimes. If you're the kind of worker who takes great pride in your work, that's good, but don't get carried away. It can actually cause you to waste a lot of your time—something you don't want to do when building a wall. For example, you may want the surface of your footing troweled smooth as glass so it shows off. The surface of the footing will be buried below ground and no one will see it. Screed the footing and leave it alone. A rougher surface holds mortar better.

Building a running bond brick wall

Skill level:	**Time to complete:**		**Materials:** 1×4, spacers, bricks, mortar, metal 2-ties	**Tools:** Tape measure, chalkline, level, mason's trowel,

Skill level:
★★★☆☆

Time to complete:
Experienced 12 hrs.
Handy 16 hrs.
Novice 20 hrs.

Materials: 1×4, spacers, bricks, mortar, metal 2-ties

Tools: Tape measure, chalkline, level, mason's trowel, brick chisel, pencil, 3-pound sledgehammer, mason's line, line level, mason's blocks, concave jointer, safety glasses, work gloves

You can build a wall in countless ways, all of which have the same goal—strength. Every pattern relies on the ends and corners, called leads, to create straight and true starting points. Leads are built first. They can be as high as the finished wall or you can build them in stages. Then you fill in between the leads to the center of the wall. The pattern, right, called running bond, gains its strength from its staggered joints—each mortar joint is bridged by a brick above and below it. On common bond walls, the two sides of the wall are tied together by occasional rows of bricks laid perpendicular to the others. Directions for building a common bond wall are on pages 188-190.

Use grade SW brick in freezing climates and MW or NW elsewhere.

Make a story pole to check that courses of bricks are properly spaced. Mark the thickness of each brick on a 1×4, including the thicknesses of the mortar joints.

A running bond wall is nothing more than bricks stacked on top of each other. The bricks are offset so the joints don't line up. Because mortar is the only material tying the two sides of the wall together, use metal Z-ties to link the two wythes. (A wythe is any continuous horizontal section of a wall one masonry unit in thickness.)

TOOL TIP
USING MASON'S OR LINE BLOCKS

Mason's blocks (or line blocks) ensure that the front and the top of each brick in the course are positioned correctly. Cut a piece of mason's line the length of the wall, and tie a knot in each end. Slip the knots in the slots provided so that the line comes out through the inside corner.

Hook one block on a corner of the lead while a helper hooks the other block on the opposite lead. Adjust the blocks until the line is about 1/16 inch from the surface of the wall and aligned with the top of the course you're laying. Move the blocks up the wall as you add courses.

Building a running bond brick wall (continued)

Dry-laying runs

1 Lay out the wythes of the wall. If necessary, have a friend help you snap chalklines on the footing to lay out the front and rear sections, or wythes, of the wall. Separate the lines by the length of one brick.

2 Make a trial run. Dry-lay the first course of both wythes. Begin one row with a half brick so joints are staggered. Leave gaps between the bricks using plywood spacers. Leave a $\frac{1}{2}$-inch gap for bricks $7\frac{1}{2}$ inches long and a $\frac{3}{8}$-inch gap for bricks $7\frac{5}{8}$ inches long. Mark the location of the bricks on the footing.

3 Dry-lay a corner lead. Mark the location of the bricks on the footing.

Building the wall

1 Lay mortar. Remove the bricks and spread a $\frac{3}{4}$-inch-thick mortar bed for the first three bricks at one end of the wall. To lay the mortar, load a mason's trowel with mortar and slowly turn it on edge as you drag it along the footing.

2 Set the bricks. Push the first brick into the mortar until it sits $\frac{1}{2}$ inch above the footing. Butter the next brick, patting mortar onto one end of it. Push the brick into the mortar and up against the first brick. Repeat for the third brick.

3 Check for level. Scrape off the excess mortar that squeezes out of joints. Check the bricks for level and tap them into place with the end of the trowel handle. Lay a second wythe of three bricks parallel to the first.

4 Build the leads. Follow up with courses of bricks so each brick spans the joint below it. Begin courses with half bricks as needed. Place metal Z-ties between wythes as your local code requires. Press each tie into some mortar and spread a little more mortar on top. Check the spacing of the courses with the story pole.

5 Build up the corner and end leads of both wythes to a height of five courses, checking the bricks often for plumb and level.

6 Fill in between the leads. Attach mason's blocks to the ends of the first course and run a mason's line between them, 1/16 inch away from the bricks and flush with the top edge of the course you're laying. Working from each end, throw mortar lines the width of the brick and lay the first course of the front wythe three bricks at a time. (Throwing is laying down a bed of mortar with a trowel.)

7 Lay the closure brick. The last brick in each wythe's course is called a closure brick. If you've followed the marks you made during the dry run, the brick should fit without trimming. Test the brick's fit, then butter each end of it and the neighboring bricks and push it into place. Now finish the first course of the back wythe.

8 Work your way up the wall. Build between the leads and check your progress, course by course, with mason's blocks and line, a level, and the story pole. As you work, scrape off the excess mortar from the joints. When the rest of the wall reaches the top of the leads, build the leads higher, then fill in between them.

9 As the mortar between bricks begins to get firm, press it with your thumb. If your thumb leaves an impression, run over the joints with a concave jointer. After you've laid the last course, cap the wall as explained on page 190.

Laying a common bond brick wall

Like running bond, the common bond design features bricks that run the length of the wall. However, it also has headers, which are bricks that run across the wall to tie the faces of the wall together.

For the pattern to work, you need nominal 4×8-inch bricks. Nominal bricks are those that are less than the stated dimension by the thickness of a mortar joint. In fact, 4×8-inch bricks actually come in two nominal sizes: If you measure a brick and find that it's off its nominal dimension by $\frac{3}{8}$ inch, use a $\frac{3}{8}$-inch mortar joint; if it's off by $\frac{1}{2}$ inch, lay a $\frac{1}{2}$-inch joint.

In addition to adding strength, a common bond makes for a prettier wall, sometimes accented with headers that are a different color.

One of the most common ways to lay bricks is called, fittingly enough, common bond. Both of the wall's faces begin with a row of bricks placed long edge out—masons call them stretchers. This stretcher course is followed by a course with the narrow edge out, called a header course, which ties the wall together. A header course is followed by four courses of stretchers which, in turn, are followed by another header course, and so on. The top of this wall is capped with rowlocks, bricks set on edge.

Building end leads

1 Lay the first course of the lead. Dry-lay two rows of bricks on the foundation, each starting with a full brick. Then spread mortar for three bricks. Butter the ends, set them, and check them for level. Repeat for the second row of three bricks.

2 Start the second course. Start the second course with two bricks cut to three-quarters of their length. Spread mortar lines and lay the bricks, buttering the inner edge of one just enough to close the faces, or wythes. Press the bricks into place, using a story pole to space them correctly.

3 Lay headers. Butter the long edge of a full brick and push it into the mortar up against the end bricks. Lay three more header bricks the same way. The next four courses of the lead are stretchers followed by a header course. Continue building up the lead as high as you are comfortable.

Building corner leads

1 Lay the first course. Throw mortar lines and lay the first course, beginning with the front wythe. Lay a corner brick and two more along each arm. Lay two bricks along each arm of the rear wythe. Check for level along and across the wythes, adjusting the bricks as you need to.

2 Trim bricks for the corner. For the second course, cut two bricks into one-quarter and three quarter pieces, called closures. Lay the two three- quarter closures on the front wythe. Lay the two one-quarter closures on the rear wythe, as shown. Then begin laying headers in both directions.

3 Lay headers. Continue laying header bricks to complete the second course of the lead. Then lay the next four courses of both wythes with stretchers. Check for level and plumb after each course.

Filling in between the leads

1 Fill in between the leads. Attach mason's blocks to the ends of the first course and run a mason's line between them, 1/16 inch away from the bricks and flush with the top edge of the first course. Working from each end, spread mortar and lay the first course of the front wythe three stretchers at a time until you reach the center. Lay the last brick, called the closure brick, to finish the front wythe and then lay the rear wythe.

2 Lay a header course. The next course is made entirely of headers, or bricks laid across both wythes. Move up the mason's blocks and line, lay a bed of mortar, and butter the long edge of each brick before setting it into place.

The last brick in a wythe is placed after you have filled in from the leads to the center of the wall. It's called the closure brick and offers you a margin for error if the joints between bricks aren't uniform. If the wythes are laid out perfectly, the closure brick will fit easily, but if the space is a little tight you can trim the closure brick to fit the opening.

Laying a common bond brick wall (continued)

3 Fill in between the leads of the front wythe. Once you've laid the row of headers for the second row, build up the front wythe between leads. Row two consists entirely of headers; the next four rows are stretchers, followed by a row of headers, after which the pattern repeats itself. Move up the mason's blocks and line as you go, and check your progress with the level and story pole.

4 Strike the joints. As you lay the bricks, use the trowel to scrape off the excess mortar. Test the mortar between the bricks by pressing with your thumb. When your thumb leaves an imprint, run a concave jointer over the joints.

5 Fill in between the leads of the rear wythe. When the front wythes are done, shift the mason's blocks and line to the rear wythe. Continue to build between the leads, moving up the mason's blocks and line for each course. Check often for plumb and level. When both wythes are at the heights of the leads, build the leads higher and fill between them until the wall is the desired height.

Building a cap

1 Lay out the bricks. Cap the wall, regardless of the pattern you used. Use a course of rowlocks, or bricks set on edge across the wythes. First place the story pole on the last course and mark where the bricks will lie. You may have to trim one of the bricks. If so, place it a few bricks from an end or corner to hide it.

2 Work from one end toward the middle. To start the cap, lay mortar for a short distance along one end and place bricks on edge in the mortar. At corners, lay mortar and place a brick at the end of one arm, then butter the face of the next and butt it against the first. Lay a few more bricks along that arm, then begin along the other arm, as shown. Slope the cap slightly to allow drainage off the top.

3 Work from the other end back toward the middle. As you approach the end of the wall, skip a few bricks and lay the end brick. Then work your way back, filling in the gap. Dry-lay the last brick, or closure brick, to check its fit. Trim it, if necessary, with a masonry saw. Butter the brick and its neighbors, then tap it into place with the trowel handle.

Building a mortared stone wall

Skill level:	Time to complete:	Materials: 1×2s, 2×2s, 4d (1½-inch) common nails, stones, mortar	Tools: Tape measure, chalk line, level, mason's trowel, mason's line, line level, concave jointer, scrub brush, safety glasses, work gloves
★★★☆☆	Experienced 16 hrs.		
	Handy 20 hrs.		
	Novice 24 hrs.		

It was while restacking the stones of a dry stone wall that Robert Frost observed that "good fences make good neighbors." Better fences make better neighbors, and if you'd like a better wall, build one that's mortared together.

Buy the stone from a dealer and have it delivered—scrounging stones from a field is a tremendous amount of work. Ashlar is cut stone, rubble is uncut quarried stone, cobblestones are naturally rounded, and fieldstones are those found on the ground. What type of stone you choose is largely a matter of taste and expense.

Like any other mortared wall, a mortared stone wall needs a foundation. Leave anything taller than 4 feet to the skills of a professional.

Overlapping corner stones

Front wythe

Bondstone

Concrete footing

Small fill

Mortar joint

Rear wythe

A mortared stone wall needs a footing (see "Building a footing for a stone or brick wall," pages 180-184). Building one is extra work, but the stones won't shift and crack once the wall is set on it. A typical mortared wall of this type has two parallel faces, or wythes, made of large stones. Smaller stones fill the gap between wythes. Bondstones, which stretch the width of the wall, are placed every 4 to 6 feet to tie the wythes together. For strength, the wall is wider at the bottom than at the top, and each side has a slope, or batter, of 1 inch per vertical foot. Stagger the mortar joints so each is bridged by a stone above and below.

 Checking the wall's slope

Build a batter gauge to check the wall's slope. Nail two 3-foot 1×2s together at one end and separate them at the other end with a 3-inch spacer. To check the wall, hold one leg of the gauge against it and a level against the other leg. If the level reads plumb, the wall has the correct batter.

 TOOL TIP
STONEMASON'S HAMMER

One of the nice things about working with ashlar is that the stones are cut with square edges, eliminating the need for you to cut them. On occasion, however, you may find that a stone is troublesome to place because of a small irregularity. Keep a stonemason's hammer on hand for such times; the pointed end of this heavy tool is ideal for trimming off small bits of stone.

Building a mortared stone wall (continued)

Dry-laying runs

1 Lay out the wall. Pour a foundation as described in "Building a footing for a stone or brick wall," pages 180-184. Working with a helper, snap a chalkline on the footing outlining the front and rear faces of the wall.

2 Lay bondstones at the end. At each end of the wall, lay a bondstone that is the width of the wall. The bondstones tie the front and rear wythes together. You'll need one of these stones every 4 to 6 feet.

3 Make a trial run. Dry-lay the first course of both wythes, choosing stones that fit neatly between the bondstones at the ends of the wall.

Building end leads

1 Lay the first course. Remove 3 to 4 feet of stones at each end of the wall and set them aside in order. Apply a 1-inch-thick layer of mortar to the exposed section of footing and furrow it lightly. Set the first course in the mortar. Pack the joints between stones with mortar.

2 Begin constructing leads. Allow the mortar to set slightly so it isn't dislodged by subsequent stones. Dry-lay a few stones at each end of the second course to make sure they bridge the joints below. When you're satisfied with the fit, lay the stones in mortar. Fill between the wythes with smaller stones and mortar.

3 Complete the leads. Continue building courses. After each one, check the slope, or batter, of both the wythes and the wall end with the batter gauge and a level. When the mortar is firm enough to hold a thumbprint, run a concave jointer over the joints to remove excess mortar.

Building a corner leads

1 Lay the first course. Start in the corner, setting two stones at right angles to each other in each wythe. Dry-lay the rest of the stones in the first course. Remove the first 3 or 4 feet of stones, then set them in an inch of mortar. Fill the space between the wythes with rubble and mortar.

2 Lay the second course. Test-fit the stones, overlapping them as shown. When you're satisfied with the fit, set the stones in mortar. Continue building up the lead one course at a time, test-fitting, setting them in mortar, and filling the gap between with stones and mortar.

3 Check the slope, or batter, of each wythe with the batter gauge and a level as you build up the corner lead. When the mortar is firm enough to hold a thumbprint, run a concave jointer over the joints to remove excess mortar.

Building between leads

1 Set the first course of stones. Put the stones in a 1-inch mortar bed. Drive stakes into the ground at the ends of both wythes and run mason's lines between them at the height of the leads' second course. Dry-lay the second course of both wythes between the leads, choosing stones that sit roughly 1/2 inch below the lines.

2 Set the second course. Put the stones from each wythe aside, keeping track of how they fit together. Apply a 1-inch-thick layer of mortar on the first course of stones, then lay the second course of stones. Once the course has been completed, move up the mason's lines and dry-lay the third course.

3 Continue laying stones. Build the wall a course at a time, test-fitting the stones before you set them in mortar. Fill the space between wythes with rubble and mortar. Move the mason's lines up at the start of each course to help you keep the wall level.

Building a mortared stone wall (continued)

4 **Check the batter of the wall.** Check your progress often with the batter gauge and a level.

5 **Reposition stones as necessary.** If you make a mistake, remove the stone and scrub it with a wet brush before repositioning it. Dirt, grit, and dried bits of mortar weaken the joint.

6 **Fill the joints with mortar.** As you work, pack mortar into the joints between the stones. Scrape off the excess mortar that squeezes out as the stones are set.

 OOPS
STAY FOCUSED

Be careful you don't get so caught up with building your wall that you forget to strike the mortar joints as you work. By the time you get to the top of the wall, the mortar on the lowest stones will already be hard, and the raking tool will be ineffective. The result? You can chip away at the joints, but, in the end, you'll leave a sloppy-looking job. Stay focused on the process and finish each step before you move on. That's how you really save time.

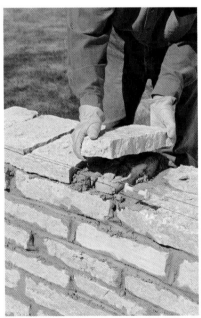

7 **Tool the joints.** When the mortar between the stones is firm enough to take a thumbprint, run over the joints with a concave jointer 1/2 inch deep or so.

8 **Set the cap.** For the cap, choose the flattest stones you can find. Line up the stones with mason's lines set at the finished height of the wall. Lay a 1-inch-thick bed of mortar and set the stones in place, tapping them with a trowel handle.

Building a concrete block wall

Skill level:	Time to complete:		Materials: 1×4, concrete blocks, mortar, screening	Tools: Tape measure, circular saw, brick chisel, 3-pound sledgehammer, chalkline, pencil, mason's trowel, level, line level, mason's blocks, wheelbarrow, concave jointer, safety glasses, work gloves
★★★☆☆	Experienced	8 hrs.		
	Handy	10 hrs.		
	Novice	12 hrs.		

A concrete block wall is a fast, inexpensive alternative to brick. Unfortunately the wall also looks like a fast, quick alternative, so you might want to consider applying a stucco finish to the blocks.

Concrete blocks measure $7\frac{5}{8} \times 7\frac{5}{8} \times 15\frac{5}{8}$ inches. Mortar joints $\frac{3}{8}$ inch thick bring this to a full 8×8×16 inches—use this size to figure out how many blocks you'll need. If you look at a block, you'll see that the thickness of its walls varies. Lay the blocks with the thick-walled side up—it holds more mortar.

Make sure you get the right type of mortar: Use Type N for general outdoor use and Type S in an area prone to strong winds. If you plan to stucco the wall, don't bother to strike the joints with a jointer. Simply cut them flush with a trowel.

Like other mortared walls, a concrete block wall requires a concrete footing that extends at least 6 inches below the frost line. (See "Building a footing for a stone or brick wall," pages 180-184.) The wall is built with several types of blocks. Stretcher blocks have flanges, or "ears," at each end to hold mortar. Corner blocks are used at corners and ends. They have one flat end and come in half and full sizes. In straight walls, half corner blocks are laid every other course to stagger joints. Cap blocks seal the top of the wall, protecting it from water.

Make a story pole to help space courses correctly. Cut a 1×4 to the finished height of the wall. Lay out and mark the courses on the board, separating them by $\frac{3}{8}$ inch for mortar joints.

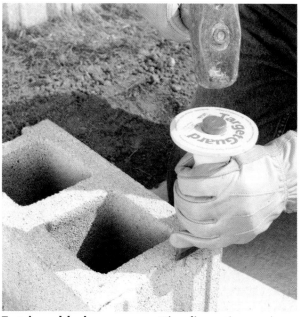

To trim a block, score a cutting line with a circular saw and a masonry blade. Split the block at the scored line by striking it with a brick chisel and sledgehammer.

Building a concrete block wall (continued)

Making a trial run

Half corner block

Full corner block

1 Lay out the first course. Snap chalk lines on the footing to lay out the front and back faces of the wall, separating the lines by the width of a block.

2 Lay the first course without mortar. For a wall with no turns, start with a corner block, which is half the length of a regular block. Space the blocks with a ⅜-inch plywood spacer. Adjust the wall's length, if necessary, so it ends with either a full or half block. Mark the position of each block on the footing.

3 To start a corner on a wall that turns, lay one full corner block, which has one flat end, then lay two stretcher blocks along each arm. Once again, follow the chalk lines, space blocks ⅜ inch apart, and mark joints on the footing. Remove the blocks.

Constructing end leads

1 Lay the first two blocks. Build the ends, or leads, first. Lay a mortar bed 1½ inches thick. Push the first block—in this case, a full corner block—into the mortar until it's ⅜ inch above the footing. Mortar the ears at one end of the second (stretcher block), and push it up against the corner block as shown.

2 Lay the third block. Mortar the ears on the next block, and set it into place. Check the level of the first three blocks from side to side and front to back. If necessary, tap the blocks into position with the end of the trowel handle. Trim away any excess mortar with the trowel.

3 Build up the lead. Lay the next few courses, with leads alternating half and full corner blocks at the end of each course. Check your work often to make sure the lead is both plumb and level.

Building corner leads

1 Start with a full corner block. Lay a 1½-inch-thick mortar bed along the first three blocks of each arm. Put a full corner block on the bed. Mortar the ears and place two stretcher blocks along each arm.

2 Lay the second and third courses. Build up the lead by laying a full corner block so it's at 90 degrees to the one below it. Lay stretchers until you reach the end of the lead. Repeat for subsequent courses. As you go, check that the lead is plumb and level from front to back and side to side.

3 Check the spacing with a straightedge laid diagonally across the blocks at each end of the lead, as shown. If gaps occur between any of the blocks and the level, tap the errant block into place with the end of the trowel handle.

Building between leads

1 Stretch a guide line. Attach mason's blocks to the leads and run a mason's line level with the first course of blocks between them. Lay a mortar bed 1½ inches thick on the footing and start the first course, working from each lead to the center.

2 Lay the center block. Lay the first course until you reach the center of the wall. Test-fit the last block, called a closure. If you've followed the marks you made on the footing, the closure block should fit without trimming. Mortar the block and its neighbors, then set it in place.

3 Reposition the line. Move the mason's blocks and line up to the top of the next course. Apply mortar to the top of the blocks in the first course. Mortar the ears and lay the second course, working from the leads inward.

Building a concrete block wall (continued)

4 Tool the joints. Scrape off excess mortar from the joints as you go. Test the mortar every so often by pressing it with your thumb. When the mortar is firm enough to hold a thumbprint, shape the joints by running a concave jointer across them.

5 Check your progress. Use a level and your story pole to make sure each course is aligned, level, and plumb. Tap blocks into position with the end of the trowel handle.

If you're laying cap blocks, apply a 1½-inch-thick mortar bed on the top edges of the last course of blocks. Mortar the ends of the cap blocks and set them in place. Tap them into position, leaving a ⅜-inch-thick mortar line. Make sure the caps are level and centered on the wall.

For a mortar cap, lay wire mesh into the mortar before laying the last course of blocks. Lay the blocks, then fill the gaps between the webs with mortar to the top of the blocks. Level the mortar.

 WORK SMART
FIBERGLASS TO THE RESCUE

Mortar has been used for decades to join concrete blocks despite the fact that it's time-consuming to butter the blocks and lay down a bed of mortar for each course. A faster alternative is to apply a commercially made surface-reinforced bonding cement. Lay the blocks with no mortar between them, then cover the wall with a ⅛-inch-thick layer of the cement and your wall is done.

DESIGN TIP
FINISHING TOUCHES

You can top off your wall with any style block you like. Ask to see the entire line at the store and get your favorite even if it requires a special order.

Stuccoing a block wall

Skill level:	Time to complete:	Materials: Stucco, 2×2s, 10d (3-inch) nails	Tools: Mason's trowel, mixing tub, metal trowel, texturing trowel, broom or brush, safety glasses, work gloves
★★★☆☆	Experienced 8 hrs. Handy 10 hrs. Novice 12 hrs.		

Stucco—a mixture of portland cement, hydrated lime, sand, and water—is a durable covering for exterior walls. Simply put, it's outdoor plaster. One of the advantages of stucco is that you can create different textures (page 201) while masking minor imperfections in the wall. You also can add color to it or buy a pretinted mix.

Stucco goes on block walls in two coats: a scratch coat and a finish coat. The scratch coat is mixed to stick to the wall and gets its name because you scratch the surface when it's wet so the finish coat sticks better. For brick walls, (which require metal lathe) you'll apply three coats: scratch, brown, and finish to guarantee that the stucco will adhere solidly to the wall.

If you're building a block wall that you plan to stucco, cut the mortar joints flush with a trowel as you build the wall. If the wall already exists, clean it with soap or detergent and water before applying stucco.

Finish coat

Scratch coat

Concrete footing

Two layers of stucco are applied to walls made of concrete blocks: a scratch coat and a finish coat. (Three coats—scratch, brown, and finish are applied to brick walls.) If you want a colored wall, buy bags of pretinted mix so the color varies as little as possible from batch to batch.

 ## Making stucco

It's easiest to make stucco from premix bags, so do it whenever you can. But you also can prepare your own mixture. The basic ingredients are portland cement, lime, and sand. The only difference between the coats is the proportions.

Scratch Coat: 1 part portland cement, 1 part hydrated lime, 2½ to 4 parts sand

Brown Coat (for brick walls only): 1 part portland cement, 1 part hydrated lime, 3½ to 5 parts sand (1 part more than scratch coat)

Finish Coat: 1 part portland cement, 1 part hydrated lime, 1½ to 3 parts sand (1 part less than scratch coat)

 ## Mixing stucco

Mix the dry ingredients, then add water until the mixture is a uniform color and the consistency of a thick paste. Make only as much stucco at one time as you can apply in an hour or so. If the stucco starts to stiffen, you can retemper it once—but no more—by adding water and mixing.

Stuccoing a block wall (continued)

Applying a scratch coat

1 **Apply a scratch coat of stucco** ³⁄₈ inch thick onto the wall with a mason's trowel. Spread the stucco with smooth strokes of the trowel, angling the blade slightly to keep it from catching.

2 **Scratch grooves into the stucco.** Use a homemade tool called a scarifier (a 2×2 with 10d [3-inch] nails hammered through it at 1-inch intervals). The grooves provide grip for the next coat. Let the stucco cure for two days, misting it occasionally with a fine spray of water to prevent it from cracking.

Applying a finish coat

1 **Apply the finish coat.** Mix a batch of stucco for a finish coat and spread a ¹⁄₄-inch layer uniformly over the scratch coat. Apply the stucco in smooth back-and-forth strokes, holding the blade of the trowel at a slight angle.

2 **Smooth out the surface.** Smooth the stucco with a metal trowel. Make broad, sweeping passes and apply even pressure, lifting the lead of the blade slightly to avoid catching an edge.

3 **Smooth out the corners.** To make crisp corners, hold a scrap board gently against one surface and sweep the trowel along the other. Texture the finish coat (opposite), if desired. Mist the wall lightly with water every few hours to prevent it from cracking while it cures.

Texturing a finish coat

Texturing stucco takes a little practice—not to mention patience—in order to achieve the right effect consistently. Begin to texture the finish coat as soon as it begins to set.

Don't be afraid to experiment. It might take a combination of techniques to get the texture you like best.

Your texturing technique need not be complicated. You can create a coarse, uniform texture simply by making passes with a wood float. For a rougher finish, dab the stucco with a piece of carpeting that has a thick pile. Or don't texture the stucco at all—the surface created by a metal trowel is a finish coat in itself.

Textured or not, the stucco needs a few days to cure. To keep it from drying out too quickly and cracking, mist it lightly with water every few hours.

Stipple the finish by pressing the tips of a stiff brush into the stucco without sweeping or overlapping passes. Use a wet rag to wipe off stucco that builds up on the bristles.

Make an English-cottage texture by dabbing small amounts of stucco onto the finish coat with a round-nose trowel. Hold the trowel at an angle and twist it slightly to create ridges in the stucco.

For a marbled finish, jab the smooth finish coat with a stiff brush. When the mortar begins to set, smooth out the high spots with a metal trowel, moving the tool back and forth in even strokes.

Spatter the finish by loading a paintbrush with stucco and striking it against a wood block. For a more uniform texture, repeat the process in an hour.

 DESIGN TIP
ADD SOME COLOR

Want something a little more exciting than white, white, and white? Use a tinted stucco. You can buy tints and make the color yourself, but it can be hard to get a uniform color. For best results, buy a premixed tinted stucco. You'll find many colors available, and the results will be more consistent than what you'd get by tinting the stucco yourself.

Applying stucco to brick

A brick wall needs metal lath to hold three coats of stucco. Fasten standard lath to the wall with self-furring nails. Such nails hold the lath a little bit out from the wall, allowing the stucco to squeeze through and lock itself in place. (You can also get self-furring lath and install it with standard masonry nails.) Whichever lath you use, apply three coats of stucco: scratch, brown, and finish.

Maintaining walls

Skill level:	Time to complete:	Materials: Muriatic acid, mortar, brick, stone, concrete block, stucco	Tools: Garden hose, scrub brush, 3-pound sledgehammer, plugging chisel, cold chisel, screwdriver, brick chisel, mortar hook, mixing tub, mason's trowel, pointing trowel, metal trowel, concave jointer, burlap, texturing trowel or brush, safety glasses, work gloves
★★★☆☆	Experienced 2 hrs. Handy 4 hrs. Novice 6 hrs.		

LANDSCAPING WALLS

Nothing lasts forever, not even a well-made wall. Eventually the time will come to repair what you've built. The next few pages show you how to deal with some of the most common problems—from washing off the white, powdery substance called efflorescence to repairing joints and replacing cracked bricks, stones, or blocks. Most repairs are minor, some are labor-intensive, and some involve using muriatic acid. **Whatever you're doing, wear work gloves and safety glasses to protect yourself.**

Repairing efflorescence

1 Wash the wall. To wash off white, powdery mineral deposits (efflorescence), first soak the wall with a garden hose. Then scrub the surface with a stiff fiber brush and rinse.

2 Scrub with muriatic acid. For efflorescence that recurs on brick or stone, scrub the surface with a solution of 1 part muriatic acid and 12 parts water. Work carefully: Muriatic acid is extremely strong. Rinse with water. On concrete blocks, use only water; acid can damage them. **To avoid dangerous splashes, pour acid into water. Never pour water into acid.**

Repairing mortar joints

1 Break up damaged mortar. Chip away the damaged mortar with a plugging chisel and a 3-pound sledgehammer.

2 Remove the residue. Rake loose mortar out of the joints with an old screwdriver. Wash out the joints with water from a garden hose.

3 **Mix the mortar.** Add water a little at a time to the dry ingredients until the mortar reaches an oatmeal-like consistency that holds its shape when it's furrowed.

4 **Apply mortar.** Hose the joints with water again so the bricks don't suck all the water from the mortar. Pack the joints with mortar. Scrape off excess mortar with the blade of the trowel.

5 **Tool the mortar.** Run a concave jointer over the mortar when it becomes firm enough to hold a thumbprint. Use the type and size of jointer originally used for the rest of the wall so the repair blends in well. Remove excess mortar by rubbing it with dry burlap before it dries.

Replacing a brick

1 **Remove the mortar.** Knock out the mortar around the damaged brick with a plugging chisel. Then break the brick into pieces with a cold chisel.

2 **Remove the brick.** Pry out the brick pieces. Chip off remaining mortar and brush away all fragments. Flush the cavity with a spray of water.

3 **Mix mortar.** Mix mortar in a mixing tub with a trowel. Add water slowly, mixing well until the mortar is the proper consistency—it should cling to an inverted trowel.

Maintaining walls (continued)

4 **Apply mortar.** Soak the cavity with water, then spread mortar onto the cavity's bottom and sides. Apply mortar to the top of a replacement brick.

5 **Put the brick in place.** Slide the brick into the cavity. Tap the brick gently with the end of the trowel handle until it's flush with the rest of the wall. Scrape off excess mortar.

6 **Shape the joint.** Once the mortar is firm enough to hold a thumbprint, shape the joints with the type and size of jointer used on the original bricks so the repair blends in well. When the excess mortar is crumbly, rub it with dry burlap to remove it.

Replacing a stone

1 **Remove the mortar.** Replace a mortared stone if it is badly cracked or crumbling. Chip away the mortar around the stone with a cold chisel and a 3-pound sledgehammer. Clear out particles of mortar with a mortar hook.

2 **Remove the stone.** Pry the damaged stone out of the wall, brush away remaining fragments, and flush the cavity with water. Butter the edges of the cavity and the new stone with mortar, then set the stone in place.

3 **Rake the joints.** Once the mortar is firm enough to hold a thumbprint, scrape or rake out the joints to a depth of about 1/2 inch. Work with a concave jointer, as shown, or a piece of wood.

Repairing stucco

1 Chip away the damage.
A repair will be visible no matter how well it's done, so leave minor blemishes alone. With a cold chisel and a 3-pound sledgehammer, chip away the damaged stucco down to the wall behind it.

2 Clean the area. Hose down the exposed wall and surrounding area with water and scrub it clean to remove loose masonry particles.

3 Mix stucco patch. Mix a batch of premixed stucco patching compound following the instructions on the bag. Add water slowly and blend the ingredients until the mix is thick enough to cling to the trowel.

4 Apply the patch. Fill the cavity with the premixed stucco patch. Fill the damaged area within 1/4 inch of the adjacent surfaces. Smooth the patch with a metal trowel.

5 Scratch the surface. Make a tool called a scarifier: Drive 10d (3-inch) nails at 1-inch intervals through a length of 2×2. Use it to scratch grooves into the patched surface, making a rough area for the finish coat of stucco to grip.

6 Apply the finish coat. Keep the first, or scratch, coat moist for a couple of days while it cures. Then apply a finish coat of stucco patch and texture it to match the rest of the surface.

CHAPTER 6

Sheds

Lawn mowers, bicycles, snowblowers, basketballs, shovels, rakes, hoes, and hoses…. Solving the problem may be as easy as building a storage shed.

But how easy is it? Building one from scratch can be an undertaking. The materials list is extensive, and the framing is as complicated as framing a garage or even a house. Unless, of course, you buy a kit.

Kit manufacturers have made shed building much easier. To begin with, you have all the pieces and hardware you need. All of the pieces are cut to the right length, and the ends are cut at the right angles. Complicated assemblies are color-coded so that Tab A fits in Slot B as it's supposed to. Best of all, you can call a customer support number if things go wrong.

Until recently sheds were made of either metal or wood. The differences between the two were practical as well as aesthetic; Wood rotted and metal rusted; metal came prepainted, wood didn't; wood required nails, metal required screws. Recently, however, vinyl entered the scene. It doesn't rot or rust, needs no painting, and requires no nails and only a few screws.

The choice between materials is a matter of taste, budget, and application. You may want a wood shed in the backyard to match the house, a vinyl shed beside the cottage to avoid rust, and a metal shed any number of places because a metal shed is economical and easy to build.

Contents

A shed needs somewhere to sit

Whether you choose a vinyl, metal, or wood shed, it will need a place to sit. This seat can be as simple as a couple of beams on some gravel or as finished as a concrete slab, often called a pad.

Of all the sheds, vinyl gives you the least as far as flooring options go. It is designed to sit only on a concrete slab. You screw a metal channel into the slab and mount the panels in the channel.

Metal sheds sit on a wood platform or a concrete slab. You can also buy a "foundation" kit, a metal grid that houses sheets of plywood. It requires that you dig up the sod, create a flat surface, and set the plywood and metal grid on it. (Though the frame holds the plywood slightly off the ground, use a pressure-treated ply.) Because you walk on the foundation and because it requires further anchoring, a kit is really more floor than foundation. In fact, if you buy a foundation kit, you should also buy an anchor kit, with cables and augers that you twist to seat in the ground.

Manufacturers of wood sheds make floor kits that are designed to fit perfectly inside the shed. Because they truly are floors, they'll need a foundation. The simplest foundation is a series of beams set and leveled on the ground. The beams act as both foundation and floor joists, reinforcing a floor that is otherwise pretty flexible.

The foundation is a good deal more permanent if you put the beams on footings that begin below the frost line and extend at least 6 inches above grade. Cylindrical forms for concrete give you a nice, neat footing that is easy to smooth and level.

A good concrete slab may outlast your shed. Slabs are durable and convenient. Getting the lawn mower off a floor at or slightly above ground level is a lot easier than pulling the lawn mower from a shed that's 8 to 12 inches off the ground. All good things come with a price, however; of all the foundations, concrete slabs are the most labor-intensive.

Sheds tool kit

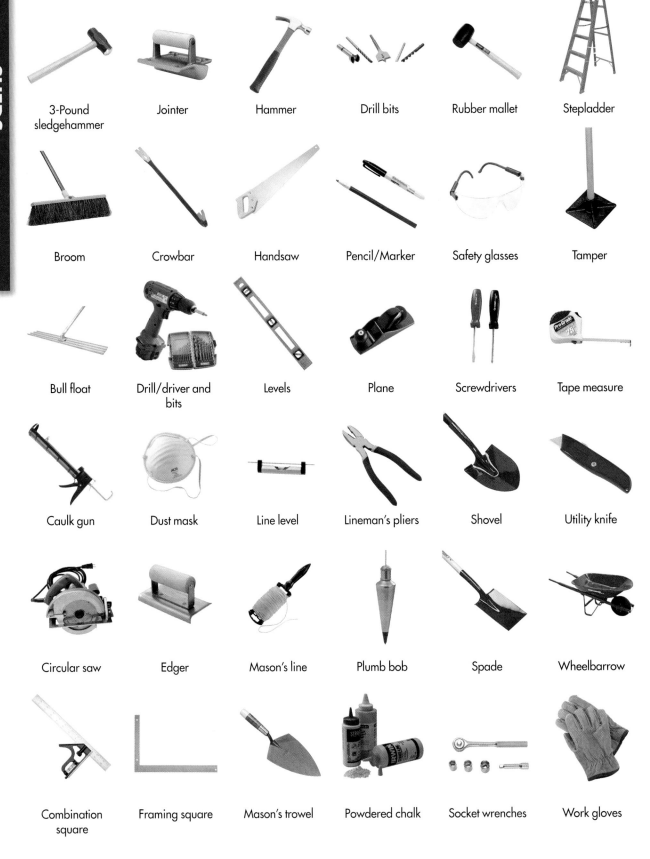

3-Pound sledgehammer	Jointer	Hammer	Drill bits	Rubber mallet	Stepladder
Broom	Crowbar	Handsaw	Pencil/Marker	Safety glasses	Tamper
Bull float	Drill/driver and bits	Levels	Plane	Screwdrivers	Tape measure
Caulk gun	Dust mask	Line level	Lineman's pliers	Shovel	Utility knife
Circular saw	Edger	Mason's line	Plumb bob	Spade	Wheelbarrow
Combination square	Framing square	Mason's trowel	Powdered chalk	Socket wrenches	Work gloves

Materials

Foundations

Beams

Fiber foam tube

▲ **A shed foundation is made of beams, concrete footings** cast in a cylindrical form, or a poured concrete slab. If you pour a concrete slab, reinforce it with **6×6-10/10 wire mesh** (a 6"×6" mesh made of 10-gauge wire).

Foundation and floor kits

Wooden floor kit

Metal shed foundation kit

Metal shed anchor kit

▲ **Kit manufacturers make kits that serve as either a foundation or floor in their sheds.** The kits are sold separately from the sheds. **Metal shed foundation kits** are pieces of metal that you assemble into a grid. You'll have to buy the plywood separately that fits in the grid. A separate **metal shed foundation kit** is called an **anchor** and has guy wires and augers that you twist into the ground. **Wooden floor kits** contain studs and plywood that are precut to give you the right size floor.

Shed kits

▼ **You can buy kits for three different kinds of sheds: metal, vinyl, and wood.** Metal sheds get their strength from ribs in the siding and a frame that runs around the top, bottom, and sides of the shed. Thick walls with interior ribs give vinyl sheds their strength. Wood sheds rely on stud walls and siding.

Metal

Vinyl

Wood

Laying out a shed

Skill level: ★☆☆☆	Time to complete: Experienced `Variable` Handy `Variable` Novice `Variable`	Materials: 2×4s, 2×2s, 10d (3-inch) nails, landscape fabric, ¾-inch gravel, perforated plastic drainpipe	Tools: Tape measure, circular saw, hammer, 3-pound sledgehammer, mason's line, line level, plumb bob, powdered chalk, shovel, tamper, 4-foot level, safety glasses, work gloves

Laying out a shed is the first part of building a shed, but before that, you need to plan. Does your municipality require you to set the shed back from the property line? Does it require a building permit? Is your site easy to access? Does it use space wisely? Think it through. Once your shed is up, you won't want to move it by even a few inches.

1 Build batterboards. Build four pairs of batterboards with 2×4 stakes and crosspieces that are about 2 feet long. Nail the crosspieces a few inches below the top of the stakes with 10d (3-inch) common nails.

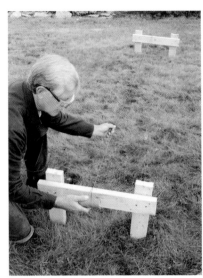

2 Lay out the first wall. Put batterboards about 2 feet past the ends of one of the walls. Tie mason's line between the batterboards along the path of the wall. Level the line with a line level.

3 Lay out the second wall. Lay out the next wall at a 90-degree angle to the first with batterboards and a level mason's line. Square the corner using the 3-4-5 triangle method, adjusting the lines until points 3 feet and 4 feet from the intersection are exactly 5 feet apart.

4 Lay out the remaining walls. Drive in the remaining batterboards and stretch lines to mark the locations of the third and fourth walls. Make sure you square the third wall with the second wall and the fourth wall with either the first or third.

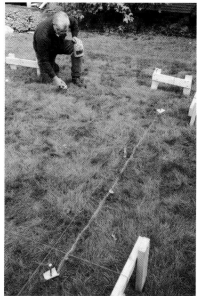

5 Double-check for square. Measure diagonally between the corners. If the measurements are equal, the layout is square. If not, recheck all the corners using the 3-4-5 triangle method and make the necessary adjustments.

6 Mark the shed's corners on the ground. Use a plumb bob and powdered chalk to mark the ground where the lines cross. To make a more permanent mark, drive a landscape spike through a small piece of paper.

7 Using the mason's lines as guides, mark the shed's edges on the ground with powdered chalk, sand, or fluorescent layout paint. Mark where the lines meet the batterboards and remove the lines until you need them again during construction.

Laying drainpipe

If you're building a shed on a site that drains poorly, install perforated plastic drainpipe to prevent water from pooling around the foundation. Slope the drainpipe 1 inch every 4 feet. For a 6×8-foot shed on skids or piers,

lay the drainpipe across the center of the site. For a shed that develops a drainage problem after it has been built, install drainpipe around the perimeter if the shed sits on a concrete slab.

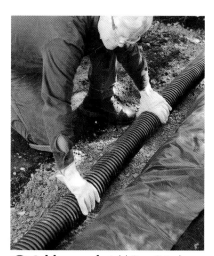

1 Dig a trench. Start it at a depth of 6 to 8 inches at the top of the run and drop 1 inch every 4 feet. Continue the trench to a point where the pipe can exit the ground. Line the trench with landscape fabric, leaving enough overlap to fold it over the top.

2 Add gravel. Add 2 to 3 inches of gravel to the trench and tamp firmly. Lay the drainpipe and add or remove gravel until it slopes 1 inch every 4 feet. Cover the pipe with 2 to 3 inches of gravel, then fold the landscape fabric over it. Fill the trench with soil and tamp firmly.

SAFETY ALERT CALL, THEN DIG

Locate underground utilities before starting to excavate.

SAFETY ALERT SLOPE CHECKER

To check for a slope of 1 inch over a distance of 4 feet, slip a 1-inch spacer under one end of a 4-foot level and set both on a straight 2×4. The slope is correct when the level's bubble is centered.

SHEDS

Installing a skid foundation

Skill level:	Time to complete:	Materials: 4×6s, ¾-inch gravel, landscape fabric	Tools: Tape measure, circular saw, handsaw, level,
★★★☆☆	Experienced 6 hrs.		mason's line, line level, tamper, dust mask, safety glasses,
	Handy 8 hrs.		work gloves
	Novice 10 hrs.		

The fastest way to lay a skid foundation for your shed is to set 4×6 or larger timbers on patio pavers that are set in a gravel bed. To keep the timbers from rotting, use pressure-treated wood that's rated for ground contact. If you like, bevel the ends of the timber to dress up the skids.

Once all materials are in place, shim between the pavers and the skids to level the foundation.

For frost-free ground that drains well, dig trenches 4 to 6 inches deep, fill them with gravel, and rest the timbers on the gravel.

Pressure treatment doesn't get to the center of timbers, so treat cut ends with a preservative. **Wear safety glasses and a dust mask when cutting pressure-treated timbers.**

Your shed can sit on 4×6 or larger pressure-treated timbers placed parallel to each other and no more than 8 feet apart on center. To provide drainage, excavate the entire site to a depth of 3 to 4 inches, lay landscape fabric, and fill to ground level with gravel. Tamp the gravel to create a firm surface and space a line of brick to support the skids. Level the skids with each other and from end to end and side to side.

Installing skids

1 Lay a gravel bed and patio stones. Remove the grass and dig out an area 3 to 4 inches deep underneath your shed. Fill the excavation with gravel and tamp firmly to create a hard surface. For larger sheds, use a power tamper. Lay patio brick to support the timbers, spacing them 4 feet on center.

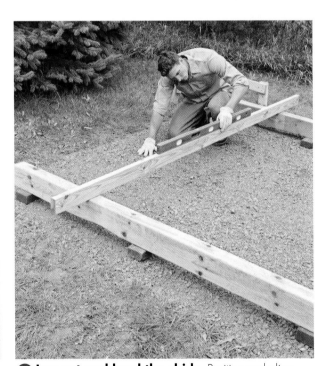

2 Lay out and level the skids. Position and align the skids using mason's line and batterboards. Shim between the pavers and skids to level one of the skids. Put a straight 2×4 across the skids and level them with each other at one end of the shed. Shim the second skid to level it along its length.

Installing concrete footings with fiber forms

Skill level:
★★★☆☆

Time to complete:
Experienced Variable
Handy Variable
Novice Variable

Materials: 2×2s, 2×4s, 4×6s, 10d (3-inch duplex nails, fiber-concrete forms, J-bolts and anchoring brackets, ¾-inch gravel, landscape fabric

Tools: Shovel, line level, mason's line, tape measure, posthole digger, plumb bob, powdered chalk, hammer, level, safety glasses, work gloves

Concrete footings provide a more stable foundation than skids. The footings support 4×6 pressure-treated timbers which are fastened to them with a metal bracket. The beams, in turn, support the shed. Lay out the shed, dig the site to a depth of 3 to 4 inches, and dig holes 6 inches below the frost line for footings. Line the holes with leveled, round fiber forms, and add about 4 inches of gravel before you pour in the concrete. Put bolts for the hardware in the concrete while it is still wet. Once the concrete cures, add achoring brackets, lay down landscape fabric and a gravel drainage bed, then install the beams.

Footings extend 6 inches below the frost line and their tops protrude at least 6 inches above grade. Space the beams 8 feet apart and support them with footings spaced 4 feet apart on center. Attach the 4×6 beams to the footings with concrete anchors.

Pouring fiber footings

1 Lay out and dig for the shed. Lay out the shed and centers of the beams with batterboards and mason's line. Mark the ground with chalk about 1 foot outside the outline of the shed. Remove the lines and dig along the chalk line and remove sod and 3 to 4 inches of soil in the entire area.

2 Dig for the footings. Reattach the lines for the beams to the batterboards and mark them every 4 feet with pieces of tape. Transfer the marks to the ground with a plumb bob and dig a hole large enough to hold a concrete tube form. Dig 10 inches below the frost line and shovel 4 inches of gravel into the holes for drainage. Tamp with the end of a 2×4.

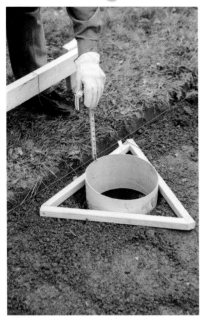

3 **Put forms in the holes.** Build a triangular frame like the one shown and nail it to a tube form from inside the tube. Seat the forms in the holes. Measure to make sure each one is exactly the same distance below the layout lines (6 inches is the minimum).

4 **Level the forms.** Check each form for level. Shim underneath the frame to correct any problems. Double-check that each form is still at the right height.

5 **Pour concrete.** Mix concrete and shovel it into the forms and holes. Work the shovel up and down in the concrete to help eliminate air pockets. Level the concrete to the top of the forms by pulling a 2×4 across the surface.

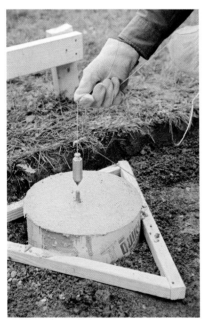

6 **Set J-bolts in the footings.** Drop a plumb bob at each piece of tape and push a J-bolt into the wet concrete. When the concrete dries, you'll use the bolt to attach the anchoring bracket. When the concrete is cured cut away the forms above ground level.

7 **Install the anchoring bracket.** Put anchoring brackets (made to hold a 4×6) over the J-bolts and align them so you can put the beams in them. Tighten the nuts over the bolts.

8 **Level the beams.** Cover the excavation with landscape fabric and fill with gravel for drainage. Place beams into the anchors on the footings. Level the beams from end to end and side to side and with each other by slipping shims under them as needed. Nail the beams to the anchors.

Constructing a concrete slab foundation

Skill level:
★★★☆☆

Time to complete:
Experienced 18 hrs.
Handy 24 hrs.
Novice 30 hrs.

Materials: 2×2s, 2×4s, 2×8s, 10d (3-inch) duplex nails, ³/₄-inch gravel, No. 4 (¹/₂-inch) rebar, tie wire, 6×6 10/10 wire mesh, wire supports (chairs), concrete, 6-mil poly, concrete release agent or vegetable oil, J-bolts

Tools: Hammer, tape measure, mason's line, powdered chalk, shovel, tamper, 6-pound sledgehammer, power tamper, paintbrush, wheelbarrow, bull float or darby, mason's trowel, broom, concrete edger, control jointer, knee pads, safety glasses, work gloves

SHEDS

Though it isn't strictly necessary, a concrete slab makes the best foundation for your shed. Exactly how you build it varies. If your soil is firm (such as clay), remove the grass and pour the slab on grade. If your soil is unstable, excavate and pour a gravel bed, compact it, and build the slab on top. A heavy-duty shed may require a footing below the slab, as shown here.

You will need a building permit for your shed. Talk to your local building inspector or zoning official to learn the local requirements for a foundation, including the need for a footing.

Wire mesh

Rebar

Gravel drainage bed

Soil

Concrete

Build a concrete-slab foundation (called a pad) the appropriate size for your shed at grade level on a 4- to 6-inch-thick gravel drainage bed. Make the slab a minimum of 4 inches thick and the same amount above grade. Codes and manufacturer's instructions often require footings as part of the slab to stabilize it. Footings are edges typically 12 inches deep, 8 inches wide at the bottom, and 18 inches wide at the top. Reinforce the footings at the top and bottom with continuous runs of rebar. Install wire mesh with wire supports (chairs) to reinforce the slab.

Excavating and building forms

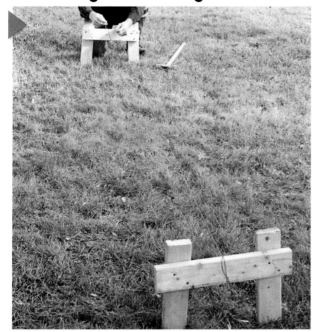

1 Lay out the shed. Put batterboards 3 feet outside each corner, stretch mason's line, and square up the lines. (For more on layout see "Laying Out a Shed," pages 210–211.) Sprinkle flour or powdered chalk along the lines to mark the layout on the ground. Remove the mason's line but not the batterboards.

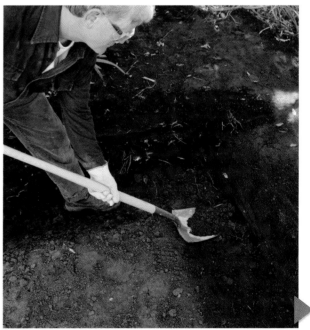

2 Excavate for the slab and footings. Dig out an area that extends 6 inches beyond the foundation on all sides. Remove the sod, then dig 4 inches deeper for the gravel bed. (If a footing is required, dig out a footing the size and depth required by code.)

Footing trench

3 Lay a gravel bed. Pour 2 inches of gravel in the footings, dampen with water to help compact it, then compact with a hand tamper. Repeat. Lay about 2 inches of gravel in the rest of the excavation. Dampen and compact with a power tamper. (Rent, don't buy.) Add, dampen, and compact gravel until the surface is at ground level.

4 Build the forms. Nail together a 2×4 box that has an inside dimension the size of the pad. Restring the layout lines. Align the box with the lines and square it by adjusting until the diagonal distances are equal. Use a level to make sure the form doesn't slope.

5 Brace the forms. Drive 2×6 stakes at the corners and nail them in place with duplex nails. Drive and nail additional stakes every 2 to 3 feet. For extra support, add kickers made with 2×2s and 2×4s.

$ BUYER'S GUIDE
ESTIMATING CONCRETE

A slab requires more concrete than you want to mix by hand, so have it delivered premixed by truck. To estimate how much to order, multiply the slab's length, width, and thickness in feet. (Four inches equals ⅓ or .33 feet.) Multiply this amount by 2.1 to take the footings into account and to allow for waste. Divide the answer by 27 to convert the total to cubic yards.

You'll have to round up to the nearest full yard. The calculations for a 6' × 8' × 4" pad are shown below:

$$([6 \times 8 \times .33] \times 2.1) / 27 =$$
$$(15.84 \times 2.1) / 27 =$$
$$33.26 / 27 =$$
$$1.23 \text{ cubic yards.}$$

Round up to 2 cubic yards of concrete.

$ BUYER'S GUIDE
REINFORCE

Rebar is sold by the number. No. 2 rebar is ¼ inch thick; No. 3 is ⅜ inch thick, and No. 4, the most common, is ½ inch thick.

Mesh is sold by size and wire gauge: 6×6 10/10 has 6-inch squares, all sides of which are made of 10-gauge wire.

Installing a plastic vapor barrier

In poor drainage areas, lay a vapor barrier of 6-mil plastic on the gravel drainage bed to keep moisture from working its way into the concrete. Overlap strips of plastic by at least 12 inches, being careful to avoid tears and punctures. If the vapor barrier isn't continuous, the slab may curl upward or develop high spots.

6 Reinforce the footing. Put two runs of No. 4 rebar about 4 inches apart around the trench and support them with commercially sold wire frames called chairs. Tie the rebar to the chairs with tie wire. Overlap the ends of rebar at joints and corners and wire them together.

7 **Reinforce the pad.** Lay down 6x6-10/10 wire mesh to reinforce the slab, keeping it 1½ inches or so from the edges. Prop the mesh on chairs so it runs through the middle of the form. Overlap sections by 4 to 6 inches and wire them together.

8 **Brush on a release agent.** Apply a commercial release agent or vegetable oil to the forms so concrete won't bond to them. Though once a popular substitute for a release agent, motor oil leaches into the soil and causes damage. Use a release agent instead.

9 **Hang two runs of rebar at the top of the trench** about 2 inches below the wire mesh. Suspend the rebar from the mesh with wire and tie the ends at joints and corners so the runs are continuous.

Pouring and finishing concrete

1 **Pour the concrete.** Build a sturdy ramp over the form so the wheelbarrow won't move the forms. Start in a corner and dump each load of concrete against the one before it. If you spread the concrete too much with a shovel or rake, the ingredients separate.

2 **Remove the air pockets.** Work a shovel or rake slowly up and down the concrete to rid it of air pockets. Tap the outside of the forms with a hammer so the edges of the concrete don't become honeycombed by trapped air.

3 **Level the top.** Enlist a helper to level the concrete with the top of the forms using a 2x4 as a screed. Rest the screed on the forms and pull it forward with a side-to-side sawing motion. Make a second pass at 90 degrees to the first. **Wear long sleeves, safety glasses, and gloves to protect yourself from contact with concrete.**

3 **Float the surface.** Smooth the surface with a bull float if the slab is large, moving it in broad, sweeping arcs with a slightly side-to-side sawing motion. Float with a darby if the slab is small and easy to work from the edges. Stop floating when water appears on the surface.

4 **Broom the surface.** Push a broom made for concrete work across the surface. The resulting surface will be nonslip, but brooming will not cover any flaws, so be sure to use a float or darby first, as described in Step 3.

5 **Separate the pad and forms.** With a trowel, cut carefully along the inside edges of the forms to separate the concrete from them. This makes the forms easier to remove after the concrete cures.

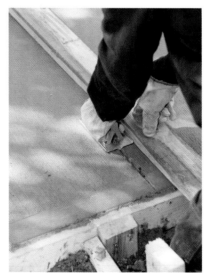

6 **Round over the edges.** If you leave the edges square, they will chip. Round them over with a tool called an edger, guiding it along between the form and the pad.

7 **Cut control joints every 4 feet.** If your pad is more than 8 feet long in any direction, cut control joints with a control jointer to help prevent cracking. Get a jointer that will cut one-quarter of the way through the pad. Put a 2x across the pad, resting it on the forms. Guide the control jointer against the 2x to cut the joint. Cover the slab with 6-mil poly that does not touch the concrete until the slab has cured.

Anchoring the shed

Put ½-inch J-bolts into the concrete before it sets so you can attach the shed to the pad later. Sink the bolts 1¾ inches from the edges, leaving 2½ to 3 inches of the threads exposed. The bolts will pass through the midpoint of the shed's 2×4 soleplates that are set flush with the slab edges. Starting 6 to 8 inches from a corner, space the bolts about 4 feet apart.

Building a subfloor

Skill level:	Time to complete:	Materials: 2×6s, 8d (2½-inch) nails or No. 8	Tools: Tape measure, circular saw, clamps, hammer,
★★★☆☆	Experienced 8 hrs.	2½-inch deck screws, 10d (3-inch) nails, corner brackets,	combination square, cordless drill and bits, safety glasses,
	Handy 12 hrs.	hurricane/seismic ties, joist hangers,	work gloves
	Novice 16 hrs.	¾-inch exterior-grade plywood	

Most shed kits don't come with a floor, so you have to decide what you want and build it yourself. The subfloor that is shown here sits on wood skids, but the assembly on beams and piers is identical.

If you're building on a concrete slab, a subfloor is optional: The concrete is its own subfloor. If you choose to build a subfloor over a concrete pad, anchor it to the slab with angle irons, lag screws, and anchor shields.

Corner bracket
Joist hanger
Hurricane / Seismic tie
Inner joist
Header joist
Plywood
Skid
End joist

Build a subfloor made of ¾-inch exterior-grade plywood on a frame of pressure-treated 2×6s. Strengthen the corners with corner brackets and anchor them to the foundation—in this example, wood skids—with hurricane/seismic ties. Hang the inner joists with joist hangers at 16-inch intervals. Place the plywood so joints are staggered and fall at the center of joists.

Framing a subfloor

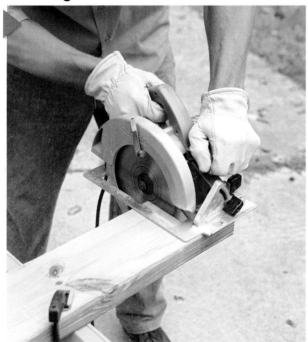

1 Cut the joists. Cut 2×6s to make the four sides of the platform. They're called end and header joists. The headers are the ones that all the other joists nail into. Cut end joists 3 inches shorter than the frame dimension to account for the thickness of header joists.

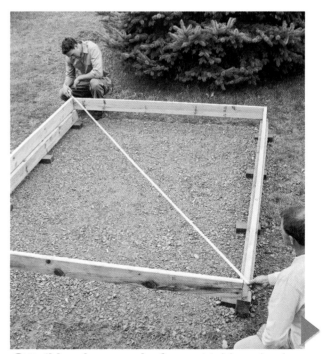

2 Build and square the frame. Nail the end and header joists together with 10d (3-inch) common nails. Set the frame in place on the foundation. Check for square by measuring across opposite corners. Adjust the frame as needed until the two diagonal distances are equal.

3 Attach metal hangers. Nail a corner bracket at each corner of the frame to reinforce the joint. Attach the frame to the skids with hurricane/seismic ties. Recheck the corner for square. **Wear safety glasses when cutting lumber or driving nails.**

4 Lay out the joists. Mark joist positions every 16 inches on the opposing header joists. Extend the lines down the inside face of the header joists with a combination square.

5 Attach the joist hangers. Center a joist hanger at each mark. Drive nails through the flange on only one side of each hanger so you can insert the joists easily.

6 Cut the joists. Cut 2x6 joists to length and set them in the hangers. Press each hanger closed, nail the other flange to the header joist, then nail the hanger to the sides of the joist.

7 Lay the subfloor. Lay ¾-inch exterior-grade plywood on the joists. Trim panels so joints are at the center of joists, but stagger the joints so no joint runs into another joint. Leave a gap of ⅛ inch between edges to keep the panels from buckling.

8 Screw the subfloor in place. Fasten the panels to the joists with 8d (2½-inch) nails or No. 8 2½-inch deck screws. Space the fasteners every 6 inches along the edges of panels and 12 inches elsewhere.

Building a wood shed

Skill level:	Time to complete:		Materials: Shed kit, foundation, floor, No. 8 phillips head concrete screws or $^3/8 \times 3$-inch lag screws and anchors, roofing felt, shingles, nails, paint	Tools: Tape measure, cordless drill and bits, stepladder, hammer, circular saw, clamps, caulk gun, jigsaw, safety glasses, work gloves
★★★☆☆	Experienced	Variable		
	Handy	Variable		
	Novice	Variable		

A shed is basically a small house with stud walls, windows, doors, and a roof. Shed kits are for do-it-yourselfers who want a shed without the hassle of building a house, no matter how small. The parts come precut and ready to nail. If six pieces are supposed to be exactly the same length, they are. If a piece is supposed to be notched, it is. If a roof truss is supposed to be cut at a special angle, it is.

With the details taken care of, you're left with just the fun of building. Nothing is ever foolproof, but kits are foolproof enough that you can tackle some things you otherwise might not try, such as the gambrel roof on the shed shown on the following pages.

Wood sheds include neither floor, roofing, nor paint—allowing you to choose a wood or concrete base and shingles that match the paint scheme you choose.

Kits vary from manufacturer to manufacturer and model to model. This one starts with the construction of the rear wall. Follow the directions that come with your kit.

Building the floor

You can build the floor for your shed in one of three ways: You can buy a floor kit made to go with the shed you're using; you can build your own wood floor; or you can pour a concrete floor. If you buy a floor kit, make sure it's made to go with the make and model of the shed you're building. If you build a wooden floor, follow manufacturer's recommendations so it will fit inside the shed you're building. If you're pouring a concrete slab, attach 2×4 sill plates to the floor with masonry screws, which drive directly into the concrete, or lag screws. If you're using lag screws, drill into the concrete to set anchors for the lag screws, then attach the 2×4 sill plates to the slab. The kit directions should provide dimensions for the sill.

Once the slab has cured, lay out and attach the sills. Concrete screws are designed especially to anchor the sills securely into the slab. Drill a pilot hole slightly smaller than the size of the screw.

SHEDS

Building a wood shed (continued)

Building the rear wall

SHEDS

1 **Nail the rear crossbrace together.** The heart of the back wall framing in this shed is a T-shape assembly in the center of the wall. Fit the two pieces together, then nail them together with 2-inch nails.

2 **Nail the outer studs in place.** Measure to find where the outside studs are attached to the crossbrace. Nail each in place with 10d (3-inch) nails.

3 **Apply a wide panel.** The back wall is made of four panels: two wide panels and two narrow extension panels. Nail in one of the wide side panels as directed. On this shed, the panels stick out beyond the bottom of the framing, creating a flange that you'll nail to the floor framing later.

4 **Apply a narrow extension panel.** Put a narrow extension panel in place next to the wider panel. Prop an edge of the extension on a spare piece of framing to help support it while you nail.

5 **Install the remaining panels.** Repeat the process to cover the unpaneled section of the back wall.

Building the front wall

The front wall also is made of two wide pieces and two narrow extensions. The wide pieces attach to each other via a gusset nailed across the center seam. The extensions are attached to the wider pieces with a piece of framing that spans the joint between the two.

Read over and familiarize yourself with the manual that comes with your shed before you begin assembly. The order of work as outlined is usually the easiest way to guarantee a successful installation.

1 Nail in the gusset. Lay one of the wide pieces on the ground. Support it with a wall extension brace on one side and a spare piece of framing on the other. Slide the gusset under the panel, positioning it as directed. Nail it in place.

2 Nail in the extension brace. Position the extension brace so half of it is under the panel and half of it is exposed. Make sure the panel overhangs the bottom of the brace as directed, then nail the brace in place.

3 Nail in the extension panel. Put the extension panel over the brace and snug it up against the wide panel. Nail the extension panel to the gusset.

4 Install the remaining panels. Put the remaining wide panel in place so it overlaps the gusset and is tight against the first panel. Nail it to the gusset, then toenail through the trim to tie the two wide panels together. Nail in the remaining extension brace and attach the remaining extension panel as before.

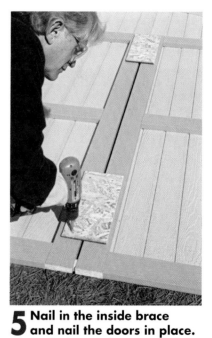

5 Nail in the inside brace and nail the doors in place. On this shed, a crossbrace travels the width of the shed above the door to help support the front wall. Position the brace as directed and slip framing not yet in use under an edge to keep the panel from rocking. Nail the crossbrace in place. Position the doors as directed, then screw temporary braces across the opening between them to prevent them from opening while you work.

SHEDS

Building the sidewalls

Unlike the framing on the front and back walls, the framing on the sidewalls is a fairly traditional stud wall. The bottom of the panel once again extends beyond the studs so you can nail it to the floor framing. The paneling extends beyond the corner of the framing, too, for easy nailing into the front and back walls.

If your arm gets tired of driving nails into studs, rent a pneumatic nailer and air compressor from your local home center to make the job easier. Lower tech, slower solutions include drilling pilot holes or lubricating the nails with soap.

1 Lay out the wall. Put the top plate on a flat surface and put a stud against it. (The exact location will depend on the make and model of your shed.) Put your foot on the stud and nail through the top plate into the stud. Attach the remaining studs, positioning them as directed.

2 Position a side panel. Put a side panel on the framing, positioning it as the manufacturer directs. On this shed, one edge of the panel is cut to lie on the corner of the shed; the other is cut to lie in the middle of the shed. The panel extends beyond the end of the top plate and below the bottom of the studs. These areas get nailed to other parts of the shed later. Double-check that everything is properly aligned.

3 Nail the panel to the center stud and top plate. Nail the edge of the panel to the center stud, leaving half the stud exposed. Nail the entire edge in place, spacing the nails as the manufacturer directs. When you're done, nail the top edge to the top plate.

4 Nail the panel to the remaining studs. Measure between the end of the center stud and the next stud to make sure they're still properly spaced. Once you're sure, nail the panel to the stud. Repeat for any remaining studs.

5 Repeat for the remaining panels. Put the remaining panels in place as directed, positioning them to get the proper overhang and making sure the corner edges are where they belong. Nail the paneling to the center stud and top plate, check the position of the next stud, then nail the paneling to it. Repeat for remaining panels until you've covered the framing.

Raising the front and sidewalls

With the walls assembled, you're ready for the modern-day equivalent of a barn raising. Get a couple of friends to help you put the walls in place. The sidewalls get nailed in place first, followed by the front wall. What you nail them to depends on what you've chosen for a floor. If you have a concrete floor, you'll nail to the 2×4s you've attached to it. If you have a wooden platform, you'll nail the walls to its sides.

Wearing gloves while you're hammering nails may seem a bit cumbersome at first, but they'll protect your fingers, especially when you're working in tight spaces.

1 Raise the first sidewall. Have a couple of helpers put the wall in place on the floor so the paneling overhangs the framing. Nail through the paneling into the framing. Support the wall while the helpers toenail through the studs and into the floor framing.

2 Raise the second sidewall. Install the second sidewall the way you installed the first one: Put the wall in place, nail through the siding, then toenail through the studs.

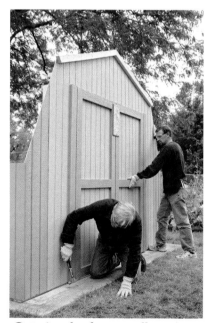

3 Raise the front wall. Put the front wall in place with the paneling overhanging the floor framing. Nail through the wall into the top plate of the side walls. Nail or screw through the bottom of the wall into the floor framing as directed. Once the wall is firmly attached, toenail through the braces into the floor framing.

4 Remove the door braces. Now that the front wall is in place, remove the braces that hold the doors shut by unscrewing the screws that hold the braces in place.

WORK SMART
WORKING WITH FRIENDS

When you ask friends to help you with a project, you're asking a big favor. Make the job as easy as you can by having a solid understanding of the project and how you want your friends to assist. Nothing is more frustrating for people than standing around on a Saturday afternoon while you solve problems or figure out how something is supposed to fit together. The more problems you've solved before everyone gathers in the backyard, the more pleasant their volunteer experience will be.

Prioritize! You're more likely to need your friends for tasks you can't handle by yourself, so don't waste valuable labor by asking someone to hand you a few nails.

Assembling the trusses

With three walls up, you'd think it was time to install the fourth. Some manufacturers, however, recommend that you assemble the trusses first. The floor makes a good work surface, and the absence of the back wall gives you easy access to it. Placing the ends of the trusses against the sidewalls helps align the trusses and ensures that they will be the right width. In this kit, the trusses come partially assembled, and the ends are color-coded to help you put them together in the right order.

Even if trusses come partially assembled, it's up to you to finish the job properly. Otherwise you'll have problems when it's time to put on your roof.

1 Lay out the pieces. Put the pieces for one of the trusses on the floor of the shed. In this kit, half of each truss is pre-assembled. Put the black ends against the wall and the red ends against each other in the center of the shed.

2 Apply construction adhesive. Slip a section of newspaper under the center seam to protect the floor. Put the gusset temporarily in place and trace around it. Apply construction adhesive to the mating ends of the trusses and to the surface to be covered by the gusset.

3 Attach the gusset. Put the gusset in place, pushing it into the adhesive. Nail according to the pattern the manufacturer recommends.

4 Turn the assembly over. Hold on to the peak of the truss while a helper holds on to the lower section. Turn the gusset over. Put a section of newspaper under the peak to catch any construction adhesive that squeezes out.

5 Nail on a second gusset. Attach a gusset to this side of the truss the same way you attached one to the other side. Clean up any construction adhesive on the floor with paint thinner—it will be nearly impossible to remove once it dries. Assemble the remaining trusses.

Raise the rear wall

Once the rear wall is in place, the walls are relatively stable, and you can begin nailing on trim and ultimately the roof trusses. Putting the rear wall in place is essentially no different from putting the front wall in place, and you will need some helpers to get the wall into position and make sure it's square. Once again, the siding should overlap the sidewalls and the floor framing. When the wall is in position, nail the siding to the top plate in neighboring walls, then nail the paneling to the floor framing. Next comes the trim. Nailing on the trim before you install the roof makes the job easier because you won't have to reach around obstacles to get into corners.

1 Put the rear wall in place. Have helpers put the rear wall in place. Make sure the siding overlaps the floor framing as well as the sidewalls.

2 Nail the siding to the top plates. Drive nails through the siding of the back wall into the top plates in the sidewall.

3 Nail paneling to the floor framing. Working from the outside, drive nails through the siding into the floor framing. Working from the inside, toenail the vertical braces to the floor.

4 Attach the roof trim. Clamp the roof trim in place, aligning it per the manufacturer's directions. Drive screws from the inside to hold it in place or attach as directed.

5 Attach the corner trim. Put the corner trim on the corner, butting it against the bottom of the roof trim. Nail through the trim into the paneling. Repeat for the remaining corners.

Building a wood shed (continued)

Raising the roof

Yes, you're ready to raise the roof. You'll begin by resting the trusses on the top plates and toenailing them in place. Toenailing supplies minimal support, so don't climb on the roof yet. Wait until all the panels have been nailed in place. Cover the roof with tar paper and then apply shingles—neither of which comes from the manufacturer.

1 Nail a truss in place. Have helpers hold a truss in place. Toenail through each end of the truss into the top plate. Repeat to attach the remaining trusses.

2 Nail a roof panel in place. Put a lower roof panel in place and nail the corners of one end to the side wall. Align the other end of the panel with the other end of the shed, pushing against the wall, if necessary, to pull it into alignment. When the panel and wall are properly in place, nail the corners.

3 Nail the panel to the trusses. Measure to make sure the first truss is the correct distance from the wall and parallel to it. Drive a nail through the top of the panel into the truss. Repeat on the remaining trusses. When you're finished, install the lower panel on the other side of the shed.

SAFETY ALERT
KEEP OFF THE ROOF

The structure may look secure once the walls are up and the trusses are in place, but it's still relatively fragile. Do not climb on the roof until all panels have been nailed in place. Otherwise the structure could collapse, and you could get hurt.

4 Nail the upper panel in place. Put the upper panel in place and nail down two corners. Rack the panel as needed to align the other end properly, then nail those corners in place. Nail the top edge to the trusses, making sure they are spaced properly. Repeat on the other side of the shed.

5 Drive nails every 8 inches. Once all the panels are properly in place and nailed along the edges, drive nails every 8 inches into the trusses or trim beneath the panels.

Roofing a shed

When it comes to keeping out water, roofing is an art. Most of this is done in layers: Roofing felt overlaps the sheathing, and shingles overlap the paper. Each row of shingles overlaps the one below, and a full shingle overlaps the joint between shingles below it. In one way or another, each seam is sealed by another shingle. Any water that wants to get in will have to do what it is least inclined to do—flow uphill.

Unfortunately, roofing supplies don't come in a shed kit. Here's what you'll need:

■ Enough 15-pound roofing felt to cover the roof.

■ Drip edge to cover the eave and rake edges of the roof (also known as the bottom and ends of the roof).

■ Enough shingles to cover the roof. Multiply the width in feet by the length in feet of each slope of the roof. (There are four on this shed: the two lower panels and the two upper panels.) Write down the amounts, and ask a salesperson to help you purchase the right amount.

■ Hot-dipped galvanized roofing nails. (Electroplated nails have a thinner coating and don't last as long.) Roofing pros suggest you buy nails long enough to go $3/4$ inch into the deck. If the deck is thinner than $3/4$ inch, get nails that go through and stick out at least $1/8$ inch.

■ Staples. They hold down the roofing felt until you cover it with shingles.

1 **Install drip caps along the bottom edges of the roof,** called the eaves. Nail at 10-inch intervals into the roof sheathing, using 2d (1-inch) roofing nails. **Wear safety glasses when hammering nails and driving staples.**

2 **Staple 15-pound roofing felt to the sheathing.** Start with a double layer along the eaves and work up toward the ridge—the peak of the roof. Overlap strips by about 2 inches at the edges and by 4 inches at the ends.

3 **Install drip caps along the rakes** on top of the roofing paper. Drive 2d (1-inch) roofing nails every 10 inches.

4 **Install a starter course of shingles.** Cut the tabs off a shingle. Nail the shingle in place with four nails so the shingle overlaps the drip cap on the end and bottom of the roof by $1/2$ to $3/4$ inch. Continue nailing cut shingles along the bottom row to create a solid strip of shingles at the bottom of the roof.

Roofing a shed (continued)

5 Snap a chalkline. Measure up the width of a full shingle from the drip edge and make a mark at each end of the roof. Snap a chalk line between the marks.

6 Nail a row of full shingles on top of the starter course. Align the upper edge of the shingle carefully with the chalkline. Nail in place with galvanized roofing nails long enough to come out the bottom of the roof panel. Follow manufacturer's instructions for nails.

7 Start the second row. The tabs of the second row overlap the solid portion of the first row. Snap a chalkline to mark the upper edge of the row. Begin the row by trimming 6 inches off the end of the first shingle. This positions the shingles so a tab covers the joints in the row below. Lay the rest of the row with full shingles.

WORK SMART
A LITTLE DAB
WON'T DO YOU

For some reason, the myth that you need to dab roofing cement over each nailhead when roofing persists.
But you don't. Asphalt shingles have a self-sealing adhesive that bonds each shingle with the row below. It probably doesn't hurt to dab roofing cement over each nail, but it doesn't help either. In fact, roofing cement is a thick, sticky, tarlike substance, and anyone who works with it is bound to get a substantial coating on their hands. Forget the roofing cement. Roofing is dirty enough work as it is.

8 Work your way up the roof. Trim the first shingle of every row so it is 6 inches shorter than the first shingle of the previous row. Start the seventh row with a full shingle, then begin shortening the first shingles in 6-inch increments again. Work your way all the way up the roof, then shingle the other side of the roof, using the same technique.

9 Shingle the ridge. Roof the ridge with 12-inch squares cut from standard shingles. Bend each edge over the ridge and drive nails 1 inch from each edge and $5\frac{1}{2}$ inches from the butt.

Applying trim, hardware, and paint

1 **Apply trim over the door.** Clamp in place the trim piece that goes over the door. Measure to make sure the overhang is equal on each side of the door. Screw the trim in place from inside the shed.

2 **Install door stiffeners.** The doors will flex unless you reinforce them with battens. Clamp the battens in place directly in line with the crosspieces on the front of the doors. Screw through the battens into the crosspieces.

3 **Install a door lip.** Sheds with double doors have a strip of wood that covers the gap between the doors screwed to one of the doors. Screw it in place as directed.

4 **Put in a barrel bolt.** When locking double doors, one of the doors needs to lock to both the shed and the other door. Install a barrel bolt on the inside of the door to lock the door to the shed (refer to manufacturer's instructions).

5 **Attach a hasp.** Attach a hasp to the outside of one of the doors so you can close them. Put in a padlock so you can lock the shed when not in use.

SHEDS

Applying trim, hardware, and paint (continued)

6 Cut the side vent. The shed must be ventilated, especially if you will store gas-powered equipment in it. Lay out a vent on the lower front corner of a sidewall or as directed by the manufacturer. Drill holes inside the layout lines at each corner and cut along the lines with a jigsaw.

7 Cut the rear vent. Lay out the rear vent toward the top of the rear gable or as directed by the manufacturer. Drill holes and cut out as before.

8 Caulk the seams. Use a long-lasting, paintable acrylic caulk to caulk all the seams in the shed. Be sure to caulk between the trim and the wall, as well as around all the door trim.

9 Paint the shed. Paint helps keep moisture from causing rot that could eventually destroy the shed. Paint all the outside surfaces, including the top and bottom of each door, the top edge of the trim, and the bottom edge of each wall.

10 Screw the vents in place. Put a vent in each of the cutouts and screw it in place.

11 Check for protruding nails. Look for nails that protrude (other than roofing nails; the protruding end of roofing nails help keep the shingles in place) on the inside and outside of the building. Bend them over with a hammer or cut them flush with a pair of diagonal cutters.

Installing a shed window

Skill level:	Time to complete:	Materials: Window, shims, 2×4s, ½-inch plywood, 8d finishing nails, caulk	Tools: Tape measure, circular saw, hammer, level, drill and bits, jigsaw, caulk gun, safety glasses, work gloves
★★★☆☆	Experienced 1.5 hrs. Handy 2.5 hrs. Novice 3.5 hrs.		

If you often find yourself fumbling around the shed for the snowblower on cold winter mornings or putting away tools on a late summer evening, sooner or later you're going to want more light. Electricity is one solution; a window and the light it sheds is a lower-tech solution.

In addition to cutting a hole in the siding and putting in a window, you'll need framing to support the window; and if the window is more than about 14 inches wide, you'll need headers and framing to replace the studs you'll have to cut out of the way. Make sure you have the window to get accurate measurements.

The key to installing a window is making sure it sits level and square in the opening. A noticeably out-of-level window will be disconcerting from inside the shed and embarrassing when viewed from the outside. An out-of-square window, on the other hand, won't open. Because it's so important to get it right, standard practice is to build an oversize opening, called the rough opening, and shim the window to get it where you want it.

Top plate

Stud to be removed for rough opening

Rough window placement

Soleplate

■ **Window framing explained.**
Because windows are in exterior walls, which are always load-bearing, they have built-up headers consisting of 2×4s or 2×6s sandwiched around a piece of ½-inch plywood and 2×4 rough sills to hold the bottom of the window. They are supported by cripple studs, which hold the frame of the window in place and help support the weight of the roof.

Header will go here

Rough sill will go here

1 Measure for new studs. The opening for a window is always slightly larger than the window and is called the rough opening, which will be noted in the directions that come with the window. You will need to remove at least one existing stud and cut at least one or two new studs depending on the location of the window. Measure between the soleplate and the top plate and cut the new studs (called king studs) to fit between them.

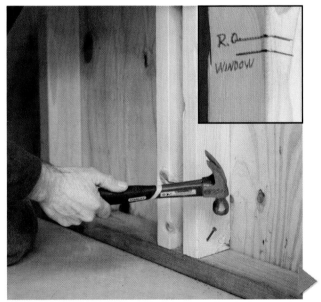

R.O.

WINDOW

2 Toenail the king studs in place. Put the king studs between the soleplate and top plate, spacing them so that the inside surfaces are separated by the width of the rough opening. Plumb them and double-check the distance between them. Toenail them in place. Mark the studs to show where the top and bottom of the window will be and make a second set of marks showing the top and bottom of the rough opening.

3 Nail cripple studs to the king studs. Cut three cripple studs 3½ inches shorter than the distance between the rough opening and the top plate and nail two of them to the king studs. Cut two more supports, each 1½ inches shorter than the distance between the rough opening and the soleplate. Cut any studs that fall between either set of cripple studs to the same length. Toenail the cripple studs in place.

4 Install the rough sill and header. Cut three 2×4s to fit between the king studs. Nail one in place as the rough sill. Put ½-inch plywood between the other two. Nail the sandwich together and nail it in place as a header across the top of the opening. Cut a 2×4 to fit on each side of the opening and nail them in place.

5 Cut an opening for the window. Working from inside the shed, drill ½-inch-diameter holes at the four corners of the rough opening. Working from the outside, cut between the holes with a jigsaw to remove siding and create a hole for the window.

6 Put the window in the opening. Slide the window into the rough opening. Put shims underneath to level the window in the opening and above the window to fill in the space. Shim to the sides of the window to hold it in place. Check to make sure the window operates and is square. Re-shim as needed.

7 Nail the window in place. Drive 6d nails into the window frame, through the shims, and into the framing, leaving a bit of the nail exposed so you can remove it if necessary. Verify that the window works and remove the nails and re-shim if needed. Nail the flange to the framing per the window manufacturer's instructions.

8 Apply window trim. Cut a 1×4 to fit around the window and to cover the nailing flange. Nail the 1×4 pieces in place. Caulk taking special care to fill any voids created by the siding.

Building a vinyl shed

Skill level:	**Time to complete:**		**Materials:** Shed kit, concrete, caulk	**Tools:** Rubber mallet, tape measure, pencil, stepladder, drill with screwdriver and drill bits, masonry bit, framing square, level, slot-head screwdriver, phillips screwdriver, safety glasses, work gloves
★ ☆ ☆ ☆	Experienced	Variable		
	Handy	Variable		
	Novice	Variable		

Ridge cap · Ridge beam · Roof panel · Wall panel · Hinged double doors · Bottom rail

▲ **Because vinyl sheds are rather basic** in terms of design, they're relatively easy to assemble. They also provide almost indestructible storage. Properly situated and cared for, a vinyl shed will shelter your garden tools for decades.

Vinyl sheds are the low-maintenance solution to your outdoor storage problems. The thick vinyl panels that make up the shed are durable and will neither rust nor rot. The color you buy is the color you get—no painting required.

Building a vinyl shed is completely different from building a wood shed. It requires no framing, no siding, no nails.

Vinyl panels—about 2 inches thick— do the job of both framing and siding. The edges of the panels are grooved, and splines slip into the grooves to tie neighboring panels together.

While this simplifies construction, be prepared for a couple of hidden problems. First, the edges of the panels can be surprisingly sharp. Wear work gloves while assembling the shed. Second, beware of the wind. The panels are both wider and lighter than wood. In fact, they're light enough to get caught in the wind but heavy enough to knock you over as they sail across the yard. Work on days when the wind is calm.

Flooring and foundations for a vinyl shed

Vinyl shed kits do not include a floor. Most are designed to sit on a concrete pad. A metal channel screws to the concrete, and the vinyl panels are held in place by the channel. You won't need to drill and install anchors. Masonry screws, which screw into holes in the concrete, are strong enough. Manufacturers recommend that you make the pad somewhat larger than the shed, but they give no specific guidelines.

Pour the pad before you start installation and position it so each side has at least 4 feet of clearance—you'll need the room to put on the roof. (See "Constructing a Concrete Slab Foundation," pages 215-218.)

OOPS
LOCATION IS EVERYTHING!

Everyone has had a laugh about painting themselves in a corner, but it isn't just inside where people get into trouble. Some DIYers do the same thing in their back yards. The decision about placement of an outdoor structure is really important because once the slab is in place, you're stuck. It's not just about where the door goes, it's also about clearance on both sides and maybe even about how close the structure is to that big tree. Take some time deciding where you want the shed to go before you pour the slab.

Mounting the channels

1 **Put in the rear channel.** Put the rear channel in place. Measure to make sure it's centered from side to side. Attach a corner block to each end.

2 **Attach the side channels.** Put side channels into the corner blocks. Use a framing square to make sure they're square. If the side channel is made of more than one piece, use one of the vinyl panels as a guide to make sure they're in a straight line.

3 **Double-check for square.** To make sure the sides are square with the back, measure the diagonals. If the diagonals are equal, the sides are square. If not, adjust them until they are and double-check with the framing square.

4 **Attach the front channels.** Put corner blocks on the side channels and put the front channels in the blocks, leaving room for the door. Measure to make sure the opening is the right size and for layout of any screws that will hold the threshold. Some kits have a special tape that shows where the screws go.

5 **Screw the channels to the floor.** Check again for square— you'll find it virtually impossible to assemble the shed if it's out of square. Trace the screw holes in the channels to mark the concrete and drill pilot holes one size smaller than the screws you'll be using. Screw the channels in place with phillips masonry screws that don't need anchors.

Mounting the panels

1 **Put pieces for the rear corner in the track.** Put a sidewall panel in the track at the corner. Put a rear panel in the rear track (all of the side panels are usually the same, but the tops of the rear panels follow the slope of the roof and are different lengths). Make sure you have the right panels.

2 **Install the corner post.** Slide a corner post over the two panels. Slide it all the way down and seat it in the corner block.

3 **Work your way across the back wall.** Once the corner is in, put in the next panel of the back wall. Align the grooves and join the two panels by sliding a connector into them.

4 **Work your way along the wall.** Make sure the panel follows the roofline. When you reach the middle, a panel with two square ends supports the vent. Install the panel and work your way across the rest of the wall.

5 **Install the vent.** Put the vent in its opening in the wall and put the vent panel over it. Slide connectors to hold it in place.

> ☑ **WORK SMART**
> ## EASIER SLIDING
>
> **Vinyl is a relatively high-friction material,** which can make assembling a vinyl shed tricky because the connectors may not slide in easily. This is especially true as you complete more of the assembly and the structure becomes more rigid. Some manufacturers recommend lubricating the connectors with dishwashing detergent before you slide them between the panels. And, of course, the more square the assembly, the easier it is to connect.

Building a vinyl shed (continued)

Building the front wall

1 Install the corner panel. Put the shortest front panel in place in the corner and slide a corner post over it. Repeat on the other side of the shed.

2 Install the remaining panels. Put the next longest panel in place and attach it with a connector. Work your way to the doorway and repeat on the other side of the shed.

3 Put in the hinge posts. The doorposts are reinforced with metal, and the hinges are already mounted on them. Put one on each side of the door and attach it to the adjacent panel with a connector.

4 Hang the upper door frame. The upper door frame also is reinforced with metal. Put the frame at the top of the doorway and gently slide each end into the sockets in the hinge posts.

5 Install the upper door panels. Put the panels that form the peak of the roof in place on the beam and attach them with connectors.

Installing the main roof beam and the doors

1 Slide the caps onto the main beam. Slide the mounting caps onto each end of the main roof beam. Screw the caps in place.

2 Hang the beam. With a helper, put the beam in place. Align it with the marks on the panel and screw each end in place.

3 Hang the doors. Lift the half hinge on the door above the half hinge on the shed and slide the hinge pin into the hinge barrel. Repeat on the other side.

4 Align the doors. Eye the top edge of the doors to see if the top edge of one and the top edge of the other form a straight line. If not, push gently on the appropriate side of the shed to bring the doors into alignment.

5 Check the gap between the doors. If the gap between the doors isn't parallel, neither are the sides of the shed. Correct the problem at the bottom of the shed. Put a piece of wood against the appropriate side along the bottom and tap with a hammer until the space between the doors is uniform.

Installing the roof

The roof is made of several panels that slip into grooves on the beam and the walls. At the front and back of the shed, the panels fit into the trim too. Work from one end toward the center of the roof, then work from the other end toward the center. This gives you wiggle room when working with the end panels.

Have a helper stand inside the shed to feed the panel into the groove on the beam. Then have the helper use a drill with a phillips bit to drive a single screw into the panel and the beam. This will prevent the panel from falling down while you work on the next panel. Once all the panels are in place, drive several screws into each panel to secure them.

1 Install roof guides. Put a roof guide over one of the exposed ends of the rear wall so the channel faces the inside of the shed. Repeat for the other exposed end of the rear wall and the front wall.

2 Install the side moldings. These moldings go over the tops of the sidewalls. Put one on each wall with the angled flange on the inside of the wall.

3 Put in the first roof panel. Have a helper work inside the shed while you work from the outside. Put a roof panel into the main beam and against one of the roof guides. Attach with a connector by screwing the connector to the inside of the main beam.

4 Work your way toward the center of the shed. Put in as many panels as it takes to get to the center of the shed, connecting them and screwing the connectors to the main beam as you go.

5 Start on the other end of the shed. Once you reach the center, go to the opposite end of the roof, install a panel against the side molding, and screw it in place. Work your way back across the roof, screwing the connectors in place as you go. Attach the two center panels with a connector, and screw the connector in place. Repeat on the other slope of the roof and tap with a hammer until the space between the doors is uniform.

6 Attach the roof trim. Snap the roof trim to the lower edge of the roof. You'll screw it in place later.

7 Attach the corner cover. Snap the corner trim over the gutter. You'll screw it, too, in place later.

8 Double-check the alignment of the doors. If the doors are out of alignment, one or more of the sides is out of plumb. To check, close the doors against a thin strip of wood such as a stir stick; then remove the stick without moving the doors. Next see if the gap is the same at the bottom. If not, correct as before: Push against the side of the shed to align the tops and tap against the bottom to make the door edges parallel.

9 Screw the shed together. Once the shed is properly aligned, drive screws into the connectors as directed by the manufacturer. Screw the gutter in place.

10 Hang the door hardware. Screw the doorstop, the door handles, and the latch in place.

11 Apply caulk. Apply caulk between the ends of the panels and the metal channels, working from the inside. Use a clear, long-lasting silicone caulk.

Building a metal shed

Skill level:	Time to complete:	Materials: Metal shed kit, plywood for floor	Tools: phillips screwdriver, stepladder, utility knife, pliers,
★★★☆☆	Experienced `Variable` Handy `Variable` Novice `Variable`		level, tape measure, drill with phillips bit and nut driver, safety glasses, work gloves

▲ **Installing a metal shed kit requires little more than the ability to drive a screw** or tighten a nut. Make sure you square the assembly as directed by the manufacturer and don't work on windy days. Metal panels fly like kites and cut like knives.

Metal sheds are an economical, relatively simple way of storing things in your yard. If you can use a screwdriver, you can build a metal shed. One of the handier things about metal sheds is that you don't necessarily need to pour a pad or build a platform for it. Cut up a few sheets of plywood and screw them to a metal grid (sold as a foundation kit), and you've laid all the foundation a metal shed needs. (If you prefer a concrete or wooden platform, you can buy hardware that simplifies attaching the shed to these materials.)

The siding and roof of a metal shed are prepainted, unlike wood sheds, so once the shed is up, you're done. The only maintenance concern is rust. Get some touch-up paint from the manufacturer and paint over any nicks and scratches as soon as they occur. Brush leaves off the roof with a soft-bristled broom. If you really want your shed to shine, wash—and wax—it.

Flooring and foundations

Like all other sheds, you can build a metal shed on a wood platform or concrete pad, and most manufacturers sell accessory kits that simplify attaching the shed to the foundation.

Many kits, however, come with their own foundation kit. When assembled, the foundation is a grid of beams to which you screw several pieces of plywood to make a floor. Foundation kits are the simplest way to put down a base for your shed. If your shed comes without such a kit, you can usually purchase one separately.

The time at which you attach the shed to the foundation depends on which type of foundation you are using. Follow the manufacturer's directions.

Assembling the frame parts

The first step in building your shed is to put together the frame around which the structure is built. For the first hour or so, you won't assemble anything you can easily recognize, and most of what you build you'll set aside until later.

Fortunately, the framing for a metal shed is less extensive than for a wood shed. You'll find a floor frame, a rim that goes around the top of the shed, and a parallel frame that encircles the middle. The roof requires a couple beams too.

The framing gives the shed shape and horizontal rigidity. The rest of the shed's strength comes from the siding. Ribs stamped into the siding during manufacture keep it from buckling and give it strength to support the roof.

Assembly, fortunately, is easy Everything is either screwed or bolted together.

1 Assemble the parts for the bottom frame. The bottom frame is the sill upon which you build the entire shed. For now, assemble front, back, left, and right frames separately, then set them aside. **Wear gloves to protect your hands from sharp metal edges.**

2 Assemble the parts for the top and the middle frames. The main frame on this shed is a right angle, called a wall angle, that goes around the top of the walls and reinforces them. The middle frame is called a wall channel and is attached to the walls midway between the floor and roof. You will have a wall angle and a wall channel for each wall. Put them together and set them aside for now.

3 Assemble the roof beams. The roof beams run between the front and back walls and support the roof. Assemble each of the beams and set them aside.

4 Assemble the door beam. Put together the parts that will form the track that the door slides on. Put the slides in the track.

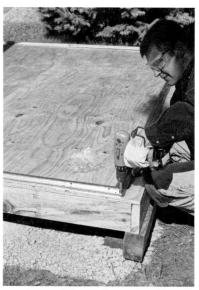

5 Assemble and square the bottom frame. Put the four sides of the bottom frame together with screws. Make sure the assembly is square by measuring the diagonals. If one is longer than the other, push gently on the frame until the diagonals are equal, at which point the frame is square.

Building a metal shed (continued)

Assembling the walls

1 Put in a corner panel.
Put a corner panel in the left rear corner of the bottom frame. On this shed the wider face of the panel goes on the side of the shed. Put a washer over a screw, and screw the panel into the floor frame. Support the panel with a ladder. **Don't work with metal plates on windy days**.

2 Screw a wall panel to the corner panel. Rest a panel on the bottom frame so it overlaps the narrow part of the corner panel. Brace it as shown to hold it in place while you work. Put a washer over a screw and screw the two panels together, then put in the rest of the screws and washers that connect them.

3 Repeat in the remaining corners. Put in another corner panel and screw a flat panel to it. Repeat on the remaining corners, bracing each one as you work.

4 Fasten the rear wall angle. Screw the rear wall angle, which you assembled earlier, to the top of the rear wall.

5 Fasten the rear wall channel assembly. Screw the rear wall channel, which you assembled earlier, across the middle of the wall.

6 Repeat on sidewalls. Fasten the sidewall angle and sidewall channels the same way you attached the assemblies to the rear wall.

7 Assemble the door track over the door opening. Fasten the door track assembly across the top of the front wall. You'll fasten the doorjambs later.

8 Lay out the wall panels. The wall panels are usually not identical. Check the part numbers against the directions and lay out the panels in order along the shed's perimeter. Double-check that you have the panels in the right places. If so, the holes on each panel will align with those on its neighbor.

9 Attach the panels. Put each panel in place so the rib on the edge of the panel fits over the rib of an installed panel. (On this shed, one of the ribs is crimped and should always be covered by an uncrimped rib.) Screw the panel in place at the top and bottom, then screw the middle of the panel to the wall channel.

10 Install the remaining panels. Work your way around the shed, installing neighboring panels one at a time.

11 Fasten the doorjamb. Screw the front wall channel in place. Put the doorjamb in place and bolt it to one adjacent wall panel. Screw through the jamb to attach it to the floor frame, wall channel, and door track. Repeat on the other side.

Building a metal shed (continued)

Attaching the gable and roof

1 Attach roof beam supports. Use brackets to attach the roof beams to the gables. Screw them in place before you put the gables in place.

2 Fasten gable panels to shed. Each gable is made of two panels. Fasten the panels to the front and to the back of the shed.

3 Bolt the gable panels together. At the back of the shed, shown here, attach a brace to the panels while fastening them together. At the front, attach supports for the door track while fastening the gable panels together.

4 Attach the roof beams. Fasten the main beam following the directions supplied by the manufacturer. Once it's in place, fasten the smaller beams as directed.

5 Install left and right rear roof panels. Roof systems vary from shed to shed. On this shed, you screw the left and right rear panels in place first. Follow the directions supplied by the manufacturer.

6 Install left and right front roof panels. Once you've installed the back panels, install the front panels. Then return to the back of the shed to install the wide panels.

7 Attach the ridge cap. Attach weather stripping to the roof panels as you work. The weather stripping should be continuous, so don't cut it between panels. Screw a section of ridge cap over the weather stripping. **Don't put your full weight on the roof.**

8 Install the remaining panels. Put the next two panels in place using the manufacturer's instructions as a guide. Cover with weather stripping and put the ridge cap in place. Continue until the roof is installed.

Installing the door

1 Screw in braces. Several screwed-in braces stiffen the door. Attach them and the door hardware per the manufacturer's instructions.

2 Tilt into place. Put the bottom of the door in place and tilt it so the holes in the door align with the holes in the door slides. Screw the door to the slides.

Anchoring the shed

Shed manufacturers suggest you anchor a metal shed to protect it from the huffing and puffing of the wind. If your foundation is a wooden platform, screw through the floor frame into the platform. If the platform is concrete, drill into the concrete and install anchors for lag screws. You can also anchor the shed to wood posts set into the ground or use special tie-downs. Ask the manufacturer of your shed what accessories are available for anchoring.

Building a shed ramp

Skill level:	Time to complete:		Materials: 2× lumber, ⅜ × 3-inch lag screws, ½-inch J-bolts, concrete, duplex nails, galvanized 8d (2½-inch) and 10d (3-inch) nails or No. 8 2- and 2½-inch deck screws.	Tools: Hammer, socket wrenches, circular saw, tape measure, combination square, pencil, square-point shovel, crowbar, plane, drill, level, 3-pound sledgehammer, safety glasses, work gloves
★★★☆☆	Experienced	4 hrs.		
	Handy	6 hrs.		
	Novice	8 hrs.		

SHEDS

After you've lugged your lawn mower into your shed a few times, you'll definitely be ready to build a ramp to get over the lip. Make it wide enough for the equipment you need to move: 3 feet should be sufficient. To build a ramp, you'll nail 2×6s onto a frame. To attach it, rest the ramp on a ledger and nail it in place. For a sturdier ramp, anchor it on a concrete footing.

Decking

Ledger

Stringer

Crossplate

J-bolt

Concrete footing

The surface of a ramp is supported by three stringers—one on each side and another in the center—and a ledger that ties the ramp to the shed. Pour a concrete footing for the base and nail the upper end of the ramp to the ledger. Anchor the foot of the ramp to the concrete with J-bolts.

Installing a ramp

1 Cut a 2×6 ledger equal to the ramp width and cut the top edge so it is beveled at the ramp angle. Drill three ⅜-inch holes in the ledger, level the ledger so it's 5 inches below the floor, and hold it in place with a couple of nails. Drill ⁵⁄₁₆-inch holes in the shed through the existing holes in the ledger. Attach with ⅜ × 3-inch lag screws. If attaching the ledger to concrete, use anchor shields.

2 Cut stringers. Measure the height of the floor at the door. For a comfortable slope, make the length of the ramp about eight times this height. Cut three 2×4 stringers to this length.

3 Cut the ends of the stringers. Rest the 2×4 stringers on the ledger and make a plumb mark with a combination square. Cut along the line with a circular saw so the ends of the stringers will lie flat against the shed. Cut the other ends of the stringers so they will lie flat on the ground.

4 Pour the pad. Build a 2×6 form 18 inches wide and 12 inches longer than the width of the ramp. Dig a 6-inch-deep hole for the form, level the form in the hole, and drive in stakes. Mix and pour concrete; screed it level. Set two J-bolts in the wet concrete at the center of where you will install cross plates.

5 Screw the stringers in place. Allow the footing to cure for two or three days, then remove the forms. Fasten the top of each stringer to the ledger by driving No. 8 2½-inch deck screws through the stringer at an angle.

6 Attach the surface. Cut 2×6s the same length as the ledger. Leaving a ¼-inch gap between each 2×6, drive 8d (2½-inch) nails or No. 8 2-inch deck screws through each board into the stringers. Wait to attach the last two boards.

7 Bolt to the concrete. Cut two 2×4 cross plates to fit between each side of the center stringer and the outer ones. Then mark the J-bolt locations on the cross plates and drill holes ⅛ inch larger than the bolts to allow for error. Drive screws at an angle through the cross plates and into the stringers, then fasten the cross plates with nuts and washers.

8 Attach the remaining 2×6s. Rip a bevel on the last board to make the transition from ground to ramp smoother, then nail or screw the last two boards to the stringers.

CHAPTER 7

Trellises & arbors

A rose-draped arbor is easy on the eyes, but from a builder's point of view, its strength lies underground. The general rule proclaims that the holes for arbor posts should be half as deep as the arbor is high. An 8-foot-tall arbor belongs in holes that are 4 feet deep. The poles need to be 12 feet long overall—enough to anchor the arbor against wind, top-heavy vines, and 10-year-olds playing baseball. While the lattice, braces, and rafters enhance the structure's attractiveness, they add little strength. Like roses, the arbor has its roots in the ground; what one sees is mostly there for appearance.

An arbor stuck in the middle of a featureless lawn seems out of place no matter how well-built or how healthy the plants. The landscaping at the foot of an arbor planter makes it seem part of its surroundings. Siting this arbor at an angle

to the house visually connects the porch with other plantings. The pink roses that arch over this arbor lead the eye to a red Japanese maple. The green leaves lead the eye back to the green trim of the house. Select the plants you want to grow on your arbor with care. For extra color, combine varieties of flowers; to attract hummingbirds, pair honeysuckle or trumpet vine with colorful flowers at the base of the arbor.

Sometimes an arbor is more than you need or want to build. Climbing plants such as morning glory and clematis will fill out a trellis and thrive. Roses will grow on a trellis, too, though the trellis won't support plants as large as those shown here. Build and install your trellis or arbor in the late fall or early spring to give yourself a full growing season for whatever you choose to plant.

Contents

A rose by any other name

Like fence posts, arbors and trellises face a special challenge: For reasons of stability, one-third of such a structure must be underground. While the upper section has to withstand wind, rain, and perhaps freezing temperatures, the bottom portion has to withstand the rigors of an underground life.

Plan for the bottom section of your arbor or trellis. Whether you opt for cedar, redwood, pressure-treated wood, or vinyl above ground is merely a matter of taste; what you use underground is a matter of survival. The almost constant exposure to water makes buried wood a prime candidate for rot and carpenter ant and termite attacks.

The best candidate for an arbor or trellis material is pressure-treated wood—usually a southern pine (longleaf, shortleaf, loblolly, or slash pine) soaked under pressure in a combination of preservatives. (The specific solutions are alkaline copper quat [ACQ] and copper azole [CA]. Copper chromium arsenate [CCA] is no longer available for residential use).

But not all pressure-treated woods are equally hardy. They fall into three categories depending on how much of the preservative they have absorbed: aboveground use, soil and freshwater use, and permanent-foundation. Aboveground is fine for fence panels, and soil and freshwater works well for raised-bed gardens. But if you want wood to last underground, use permanent-foundation pressure-treated wood.

As its name implies, it is manufactured for use in foundations, and of the three classes, it's the only one that holds up underground. The three types look identical, and the only way to tell them apart is to locate an inked stamp on the wood. The rating is stamped in capital letters that are centered in the upper portion of the stamp.

Above ground, you have a wider range of choices. Pressure-treated wood and redwood both boast excellent above ground durability; cedar is rated as good; and vinyl outlasts them all and needs no paint.

Trellises & arbors tool kit

⅜-inch drill and bits

Clamps

Mason's line

Power miter saw

Shovel

Wheelbarrow

3-pound sledgehammer

Dust mask

Pencil/marker

Router

Socket wrenches

Work gloves

Brick chisel

Hammer

Plumb bob

Saber saw

Speed square

Caulk gun

Level

Post level

Safety glasses

Stepladder

Chalk line

Line level

Posthole digger

Sanding block

Tape measure

Circular saw

Mason's hoe

Powdered chalk

Screwdrivers

Utility knife

Materials

Trellises and arbors are exposed to the elements year-round and need to be made from materials that will last.

Aluminum products are NOT recommended for use in contact with pressure-treated wood. Fastener and connector manufacturer's recommend hot-dipped galvanized, polymer-coated, or stainless-steel fasteners and connectors.

▶ *Common species of naturally rot-resistant wood are **redwood** and **cedar**. A less-expensive alternative is **pressure-treated wood**, which is chemically treated to prevent it from rotting. Frame custom-made panels with prefabricated **U-channels**—get vinyl channels for vinyl, and wood channels for wood. You can buy prefabricated lattice panels made of **wood** or **vinyl** to make your trellis or cover your arbor. Lattice isn't the only material you can use to cover your arbor; **shade fabric** and **reed or bamboo** make attractive as well as practical alternatives. (Both products are not available in all parts of the country and may have to be special ordered.) Anchor the posts of your arbor in the ground with **premix concrete. Fiber tube forms** help create a level surface to work from.*

Fiber tube form · Pressure-treated wood · Premix concrete · Shade fabric · Redwood · U-channels · Vinyl · Cedar · Wood

Flanged-style post anchors · Rebar-style post anchors · Platform-style post anchors · Hurricane/seismic ties · Post/beam connector · J-bolt · Grommets · Lag screws · Galvanized carriage bolts · Lag shields · Angle brackets

◀ *Building trellises and arbors that last is easy with the right fasteners and hardware. Make strong wood joints with **galvanized carriage bolts** instead of nails or screws. Hang a trellis on wood with **lag screws**. For a masonry wall, you'll also need **lag shields**. Reinforce corners with **angle brackets**. **Hurricane/seismic ties,** also known as rafter ties, secure the top of your arbor to the beams—and may be required by your local building codes. **Post/beam connectors** allow you to secure beams on the top of posts. Three basic types of post anchors are available to secure posts to concrete piers. **Flanged-style post anchors** and **rebar-style post anchors** can do the job, but they aren't adjustable once the concrete sets. You'll want the leeway to make minor positioning corrections that are possible with **platform-style post anchors,** which are secured to **J-bolts** placed in the wet concrete. Reinforce holes used for hanging shade fabric with **grommets** to keep the fabric from tearing.*

Building a trellis panel

Skill level:	Time to complete:	Materials: U-channels, 2×4 for frame, galvanized	Tools: Circular saw, power miter saw, clamps,
★★★☆☆	Experienced 1 hrs.	deck screws, wood or synthetic lattice panels	drill and bits, utility knife, screwdriver, dust mask,
	Handy 1.5 hrs.		safety glasses
	Novice 2 hrs.		

Unsupported, a trellis panel is flexible, and thinner ones are downright flimsy. Consequently, the first step in any trellis project is to strengthen it with a frame. The frame begins as a 2×4; a prefab channel that you nail to it holds the trellis in place. Vinyl channels are for vinyl trellis. They're U-shaped and about ½ inch thick and 1 inch wide. Wood channels are beefier, and the groove is stepped in order to handle panels of different thicknesses.

Wood trellis comes in two thicknesses—$^7/_{16}$ inch and $^5/_8$ inch. Get the $^5/_8$ inch—it's more durable. Vinyl panels are a standard thickness.

▲ **Reinforce a trellis panel before you build with it.** Make a frame with mitered corners and hold the trellis in place with prefabricated U-channels. Trellis is available in both wood and vinyl, and thicknesses vary. Buy U-channel made of the same material as the trellis; it will have the right size groove in it.

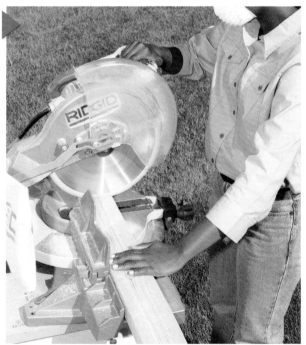

1 Cut the frame pieces so they're a bit long.
To determine the size, add at least twice the width of the frame to the desired length of the piece. For example, if you have a 2×4 frame and want a finished frame that is 6 feet square, cut pieces that are 6 feet plus 2×2, or 6 feet 4 inches. (A 2×4 is really 1½ inches thick. Using the full 2 inches in the formula gives you an extra margin of error.)

2 Screw U-channel to the frame. Cut pieces of U-channel to the same length as the frame pieces. Drill holes in the channel that are slightly wider than the shank of a #8 galvanized deck screw. Screw through the holes to attach the channel to the frame. If the channel is wood, tighten the screws so they're snug. If the channel is vinyl, leave them slightly loose so the channel can expand and contract with changes in temperature.

3 Cut one end of each frame piece. Set your power miter saw to cut a 45-degree angle. Put an assembled frame-and-channel piece in the box so the groove is against the fence. Cut one end of all the pieces you'll need.

4 Miter the second corner of each piece. Measure out the length you want on one of the pieces and mark the edge of the wood with a sharp pencil. Lay out the miter with the help of a combination square. Repeat the process on an adjoining side. Cut the pieces to length with the power miter saw.

5 Lay out the remaining frame pieces. Use the first two pieces as a pattern for laying out the remaining two. Put the finished pieces on top of the unfinished ones. Have a helper carefully align the mitered ends and hold them together. Trace along the other end of the finished piece with a sharp knife to lay out the remaining miters.

OOPS
THEY DON'T MAKE BOARD STRETCHERS ANYMORE

Actually, they never did.
(It's an old carpenter's joke because boards can always become shorter, but they'll never become longer. Once you make the cut, you're committed.) Because it's easy to mess up miter cuts (even the pros occasionally do), leave yourself extra length on the board so you can make little adjustments to ensure a good, tight fit. To avoid mistakes, measure from a miter you've already cut on one end, then lay out the cut at the other end with a pencil. Put the piece in the saw and work toward the mark to hit it accurately. Check the fit when the piece is a little long—maybe you'll get lucky.

6 Miter the remaining pieces to size. To ensure that you hit your mark right on the money, ease into the cut by starting about $1/2$ inch longer than the mark but lower the blade only enough to begin the cut. Slide the piece slowly toward the knife mark until the saw is positioned accurately, then finish the cut.

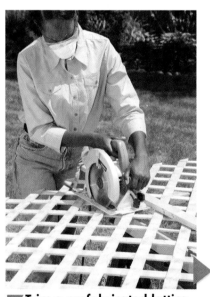

7 Trim a prefabricated lattice panel to fit inside the frame. Measure the opening, add the depth of both grooves, and subtract $1/4$ inch to allow for expansion in humid weather. Clamp a piece of 1×2 to the lattice to serve as an edge guide while you make the cut. Work slowly to keep the slats from splintering. **When cutting lattice with a circular saw, make sure the blade doesn't hit any staples.**

Building a trellis panel (continued)

8 Predrill for screws. Start by putting the pieces next to each other to form the frame. Lay out three holes in each corner: two through one frame piece, one through the other. To prevent splitting, keep the holes at least 1 inch from the tip of the miters. Drill oversize holes through the marked pieces but not into wood behind them.

9 Screw the first corner together. Have a helper hold two sides of a corner in position, or clamp them to a work surface. Drive galvanized deck screws through the holes and screw the pieces together.

10 Assemble the frame. Screw a third piece to the other two, creating a U-shape assembly. Slide the sheet of lattice into the assembly. Have a helper hold the fourth side in place while you screw it to the others.

11 Anchor the lattice. Lattice is flexible and could pop out of the frame if someone were to lean against it or bump into it. To anchor wood lattice, drive 1½-inch deck screws at an angle through the lattice and into the body of the U-channel.

If the lattice is vinyl, drill holes along the top so the screws will go through the lattice. Screw the lattice in place. On the sides and bottom, drill holes that go through the channel but not the lattice, which needs room to expand and contract with seasonal changes in weather.

How oversize is oversize?

Driving screws near the end or edge of a board can cause the board to split. The oversize holes in this project help prevent splitting. The holes you make through the first piece should be big enough that the threads won't grip and small enough that the head won't slip through. To drill the right size, hold the shank of a drill behind the threads of the screw. The right size bit will just peek out beyond the threads. Better yet, use a combination bit that drills the oversize hole for the shank in the first piece and a slightly smaller hole for the threads in the second piece.

Hanging trellises

Skill level:
★ ☆ ☆ ☆

Time to complete:
Experienced 1 hr.
Handy 2 hrs.
Novice 3 hrs.

Materials: Wooden trellis kit, pressure-treated 2×s, 4×4s, 1/4×3-inch lagscrews, washers, anchor shields, No. 8 2 1/2-inch deck screws, premix concrete, hinges, hook-and-eye fasteners

Tools: Tape measure, 3/8-inch drill and bits, masonry bits, circular saw, socket wrenches, level, hammer, screwdriver, mason's line, stepladder, 3-pound sledgehammer, line level, plumb bob, powdered chalk, posthole digger, wheelbarrow, mason's hoe, pencil, safety glasses, work gloves

TRELLISES & ARBORS

You can purchase wooden trellises in kits that are easy to assemble and mount on the side of your house. Mounting depends on the wall itself and the size of the trellis. If you have wood siding, you can fasten furring strips, called ledgers, to studs in the wall with lag screws and attach your trellis to them. Putting a ledger on a masonry wall requires anchor shields. Both vinyl and aluminum siding will dent easily. Mount the trellis on hinged posts as shown on page 258.

Attaching a trellis to siding

Because the trellis frame may not fall over any studs, it's usually necessary to screw a ledger to the studs, then nail the trellis to the ledger. Drill the holes in the ledger slightly larger than the bolt diameter to make it easier to align the holes with those you drill in the studs.

1 Assemble and paint the trellis then hang the ledger. Find stud locations with an electronic stud finder and mark them. position a 2× on the wall, level it, and transfer the marks to it. Bore 5/16-inch holes through the 2×, and 3/16-inch holes into the studs at the marks.

2 Hang the ledger. Slip washers over 1/4×3-inch lag screws and drive them through the holes in the ledger and the studs. Tighten the lag screws with a ratchet and socket wrench. Repeat, installing a ledger to support the trellis at the opposite edge.

3 Hang the trellis. Put the trellis against the ledger strips. Plumb the trellis against an edge or center upright. If necessary, have a helper hold the trellis in place.

Hanging trellises (continued)

Attaching a trellis to masonry

Attaching a trellis to a masonry wall is similar to hanging it on a wall with siding. The only difference is that you'll need to install anchor shields in the masonry for the lag screws. Make the ledger easier to align by drilling the holes in the ledger so they are slightly larger than the 1/4-inch lag bolts.

1 Drill holes. Drill 3/8-inch holes into a 2x ledger for the lag screws. Place and level each furring strip, marking for anchor shields in the mortar. Drill holes (typically 1/2 inch) in the wall with a masonry bit and insert the shields. If a hole is too big, put anchoring cement in it, then insert the shield. The cement will expand as it sets.

2 Hang the ledger. Position each furring strip on the wall, aligning the holes with the anchor shields. Put a washer over a 1/4-inch lag screw and drive the screw into the shield with a ratchet and socket wrench. Fasten the trellis to the furring strips with nails or screws.

Installing a trellis on hinges

Hanging a trellis on 2×4 posts lets you fold the trellis out of the way for cleaning or painting the wall. Space the posts equal to the width of the framed panel and set them in concrete. Buy hook-and-eye fasteners beforehand so you set the posts at the right distance from the wall.

1 Put the posts in holes. Dig the holes. Cut two 2×4 posts about 6 inches above ground. (Half the exposed height of the post will be below ground.) Join the two sections of each post with a hinge and a temporary cleat. Screw the frame to the posts and remove the cleats.

2 Attach the trellis. Screw supports a few inches from the top of the posts to hold them out from the wall. Offset the screws to prevent splitting. Position hook-and-eye-fasteners, screwing the hooks into the posts and the eyes into the wall. Plumb and brace the posts, then fill the holes with concrete. (See page 118.)

Attaching a trellis to posts

Hanging a trellis on posts is a step short of building an arbor. While the structure is less complicated, it can still serve much the same purpose: You can grow vines on it or use it to break your yard into smaller areas.

The biggest task in putting a trellis on posts is actually putting in the posts, but this is a relatively simple undertaking. Set posts in holes that are half as deep as the post is high. For example, a post that extends 8 feet above ground needs to extend another 4 feet underground for stability. Fill the holes with concrete to further anchor the posts.

Lattice panel

Concrete

4×4 post

You can mount trellis panels between posts to provide a private corner in your backyard. Set the posts in holes that are half as deep as the exposed height of the posts. Screw the panels to the posts, then plumb the posts and fill the holes with concrete. Install post caps or angle the tops of the posts so water will drain off them.

1 Lay out the corner. Lay out a corner with mason's lines and batterboards set a foot or so past where the end posts will go. Level the lines, then square them with a 3-4-5 triangle: Mark one line 3 feet and the other 4 feet from where they meet. Slide them on the batterboards until the distance between the marks is exactly 5 feet.

2 Lay out the posts. Measure from the corner to find out the location of the other posts. Put tape on the mason's line to show where each post will be. Transfer the taped points to the ground with a plumb bob and powdered chalk. Mark where the lines are tied to the batterboards, then untie them. You'll put the lines back later.

3 Dig the holes. With a posthole digger, dig holes that are half as deep as the post will be high. Placing the dirt you remove from the posthole on a tarp or garbage bag will make disposal easier. Dealing with the inevitable calluses and blisters that come from digging postholes isn't fun. Wearing gloves will help you avoid sore hands.

Hanging trellises (continued)

Restring the layout lines.
Reattach the mason's lines to the batterboards and slide them along the crosspieces until they mark the outer edges of the posts. Set the posts into the holes, plumb them, and brace them.

5 Install the trellis panels between the posts at the height you want. Make sure each panel is level and sits at least a few inches above the ground. Fasten the panels with No. 8 2½-inch deck screws. Plumb each post again after screwing into it.

6 Mix Concrete. Mix bagged concrete in a wheelbarrow. Add water a little at a time, blending the ingredients with a mason's hoe until the concrete clings to the hoe when you lift it from the wheelbarrow.

Post haste

Make the posts long enough but not too long. Many DIY landscape designers seem to be in a hurry to select unnecessarily long posts for trellis and arbor projects, thinking that way, they'll get an extra sturdy structure. That's overkill. Any post set in concrete in a hole that's half as deep as the exposed height of the post, will break before it ever falls over. So there's no need to install longer posts. You're just wasting time and money. What you should do, of course, is dig the holes at least 6 inches wider at the bottom than the top. Doing so gives the post extra support with the enlarged concrete "foot."

Metal anchor spikes are a quick way to set posts.
Drive the spike into the ground, then install the post in the anchor. Posts set in anchor spikes provide less support than posts anchored in the ground with concrete, but they're much easier to install.

7 Fill the holes. Fill each posthole with concrete, working a 2x4 up and down in it to eliminate air pockets. Allow the concrete to cure for two or three days before removing the braces.

Building an arbor

Skill level:	Time to complete:	Materials: 4×4s, ¾-inch gravel, fiber tube forms,	Tools: Tape measure, mason's line, line level, chalk line,
★ ★ ★ ★ ★	Experienced Variable	1×4s, 2×4s, 2×8s, 1×2s, 1×1s, lattice, duplex nails,	3-pound sledgehammer, plumb bob, post level, powdered
	Handy Variable	No. 8 2½- and 3-inch deck screws, premix concrete, post	chalk, clamps, posthole digger, shovel, level, wheelbarrow,
	Novice Variable	anchors, reed, bamboo, or shade fabric as necessary	mason's hoe, hammer, socket wrenches, circular saw, drill
			and bits, stepladder, speed square, saber saw, pencil, dust
			mask, safety glasses, work gloves

Building an arbor is a big job. It's a big job made of several smaller ones, however, including setting posts, trimming them, attaching beams, and attaching rafters. Double-check your work as you go. A small error at ground level can make a big difference at the top of a post.

Building starts with the posts. You can install them in the ground and fill the hole with concrete, or you can pour a concrete pier and rest the posts on top of it.

An arbor adds an elegant and formal touch to a landscape.
Place your arbor to take advantage of focal points in your garden or in a spot which provides a striking view of the general landscape. Arbors can have built-in or removable seating.

You can either bury posts in the ground or set them on concrete piers. If you're setting the posts in the ground, dig each hole either 6 inches below the frost line or half as deep as the exposed height of the post plus 10 inches (whichever is deeper). Widen the holes at the bottom, set each post on a bed of gravel, then fill the holes with concrete.

To set the posts on a concrete pier, dig holes 6 inches below the frost line, add 4 inches of gravel, and pour a concrete footing and pier. Put a post anchor in the concrete while it's still wet. Once it's dry, you can attach the post to the anchor.

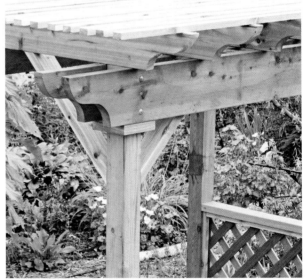

Arbor construction is typical of what you might find in building a deck. The 4×4 posts rest on concrete footings that provide stability. Beams made of 2×8s are bolted to the posts, and 2×6 rafters sit on top of the beams. The rafters support 1×2 slats that provide shade. Braces reinforce the beams, and end rafters provide stability. Lattice panels along the sides enclose the arbor and provide structure for climbing plants.

Building an arbor (continued)

Laying out the posts

1 Install batterboards. Drive batterboards into the ground 2 to 3 feet beyond each post's position. Stretch mason's line between the batterboards, outlining the edges of the arbor. Level the lines with a line level.

2 Square the corner. To square a corner, mark one of the mason's lines 3 feet and the other 4 feet from where the lines cross. Slide the lines on the batterboards until the distance between the marks is exactly 5 feet. The corner is now square.

3 Mark the ground. At each corner, drop a plumb bob and mark the ground below it with powdered chalk or sand. Mark the position of the mason's lines on the crosspieces. Untie the lines, but leave the batterboards in place.

Setting posts below grade

1 Dig postholes. Use a posthole digger or power auger to dig holes at the marked spots. Dig at least 6 inches deeper than half the exposed height of the posts. For example, a post that's 8 feet tall needs to sit in a hole that's 4 feet 6 inches deep. Shovel in 4 inches of gravel, tamp it, pour in a 6-inch layer of concrete, and let it dry.

2 Align the posts. Retie the mason's lines and slide them on the crosspieces to mark the outside edges of the posts. Set each post into its hole, plumb it with a fence post level or regular level, and brace it with 1×4s and 2×4 stakes.

3 Fill the holes with concrete. Pour the concrete and work a 2×4 up and down in it to remove air pockets. Slope the top of the concrete so water drains away from the posts. Let the concrete cure for two to three days.

Setting posts on a pier

1 Place the forms. Dig postholes 6 inches below the frost line, pour in 4 inches of gravel, and tamp. Retie the mason's lines and center fiber tube forms in the corners. Nail pieces of wood to opposite sides of each form so the form sits at least 6 inches above the gravel. Put the form in the hole and level it.

2 Mix concrete. Mix bagged concrete in a wheelbarrow. Start by making a crater in the dry ingredients. Pour in about half the water recommended by the manufacturer. Mix with a mason's hoe, then slowly add the remaining water until the concrete has the consistency of oatmeal.

3 Fill the forms. Shovel concrete into the forms. The concrete will form a footing by spreading out into the 6-inch gap between the form and the bottom of the hole. Keep adding concrete, filling the forms to the top.

 The road not taken

Although it may seem easier, don't cut the posts to height before mounting them in the post anchors. Any slight variation in the terrain can throw the whole arbor out of whack. Instead nail each uncut post to the post anchor, then lay out and make the cut.

4 Release any trapped air. Work a 2×4 or shovel up and down in the concrete to release any trapped air. Pull a short section of 2×4 across the top of the form as a screed to level the concrete with the top of the forms.

5 Mark the center. Reset the mason's lines and drop a plumb bob to mark the centers of the posts. Sink 6-inch J-bolts into the concrete. Coat the J-bolt threads with petroleum jelly or soap so concrete will not stick to them.

Building an arbor (continued)

6 Remove the forms. Allow the concrete to cure for two to three days, then strip off the forms and fill in around the concrete with soil. Tamp the soil with your feet.

7 Install post anchors. Put a post anchor over the J-bolt. Put a washer over the bolt. Fasten with a nut.

8 Attach the posts. Attach rot-resistant 4×4 posts to the post anchors with hanger nails. Cut a recess in the side of the post, if necessary, to fit it into the anchor

Trimming the posts

1 Lay out the cuts. Mark the final height on one post and tack mason's line to it at that point. Run the line to the next post, level it with a line level, and mark the height on the post. Repeat the process for the remaining posts.

2 Make a cutting guide. Clamp a speed square to the post at a measurement that compensates for the distance between the edge of the circular saw's base and the blade so the cut will be on your mark.

3 Cut the posts. Set the saw's base plate against the cutting guide and cut into the post. The blade won't cut all the way through, so finish the cut with a handsaw. (The cutoff may fly off wildly if you finish the cut with the circular saw.) Cut the other posts the same way. **Keep the saw's power and extension cords well away from the blade's cutting action.**

Installing beams

1 Cut the beams to length.
Before installing beams, check your local building department for code requirements. Usually 2×8s are installed, one on each side of the posts. If you want a decorative effect, extend the beams beyond the post and cut a shape in them. Make a cardboard pattern of the shape, trace it onto a board, and cut with a saber saw. Use the board as a template to cut the other beams and the rafters.

2 Screw the beams in place.
With a helper, screw a beam in place on one side of the posts so it's flush with the top of the posts. Place a second beam on the other side. Fit two 4×4 spacers between the double beams as reinforcement and screw them in place on both sides with 3-inch screws. (See Step 1, page 266 for reference.)

3 Drill for bolts. Drill two ¼-inch holes per post that run through a beam into the post and out through the second beam. Offset holes to avoid weakening the wood. Insert a carriage bolt through the hole, slip on a washer and a nut, and tighten.

4 Add a temporary support.
Tack a board to the post under each end of the double beam. Level the board and tack it to the adjacent post. The two boards will serve as a temporary support for the other double beam and ensure that the two beams are square and level.

5 Install the second set of beams. Rest the second set of beams one at a time on the supports. Drill and counterbore holes as before, then install carriage bolts. Remove the temporary support once the second beam has been installed.

WORK SMART
CAN'T TAKE THE PRESSURE

The chemicals that pressure-treating exposes wood to travel from the outside surfaces of the board toward the middle. Unfortunately they never make it all the way to the center.

Usually this isn't a problem. The bug that can gnaw through enough pressure-treated wood to get to the untreated core of a board has yet to be born. Once you cut a board to length, however, you've exposed the core. Every bug known to man (plus several fungi) will be ready to feast on the freshly cut end.

Treat cut ends with a preservative recommended by the manufacturer of the board. The warranty requires it, as does common sense.

Building an arbor (continued)

Adding rafters

1 Lay out the rafters. Start with the end rafters, positioning them so the outside edges align with the outside edge of a post. Measure, then space the rest of the rafters between the end rafters at 16 inches on center.

2 Cut the rafters to length. Cut the rafters 24 inches longer overall than the distance between beams. Cut any desired design at the ends of the rafters. Place an end rafter on the beams and adjust it so the overhang is equal at both ends.

3 Screw the rafter in place. Drill starter holes for the screws at an angle through the rafter, making the holes a bit smaller than the diameter of the screw. Repeat on the other end.

4 Stretch a line between the ends of the rafters. Tack a nail to each end of the end rafters and pull a mason's line taut between the nails. The lines will help align the ends of the rest of the rafters.

5 Attach the remaining rafters. Place the rafters one at a time, spacing them according to the marks you made on the beams. Align the ends of each rafter with the mason's lines, then drill starter holes and toenail the rafter in place with 3-inch deck screws. Repeat, screwing all the rafters in place.

6 Install braces. Cut miters on both ends of short 2×4s to make braces for the rafters. Drill ⅜-inch-diameter holes through each brace, then drill through the brace with a ¼-inch-diameter bit to create a pilot hole. Drive ⅜×3-inch lag screws through the holes. Seal any gaps at the joints with exterior caulk.

Installing roof slats

1 Cut the slats to length. Cut 1×2 slats to length by clamping several together at a time and cutting them with a circular saw.

2 Mark the center of the arbor. Locate the centerpoint of the rafters and snap a chalkline across them.

3 Install the slats. Align the center of the first slat with the chalkline on the rafters. Drill holes into the slat with a combination countersink bit and screw the slat into place with No. 8 2-inch deck screws. Use a slat as a spacer to lay out the next slat and screw it in place. Repeat across the entire roof.

 Working with galvanized hanging hardware

Using galvanized hangers makes installing beams a little easier.
They're stronger than nails, and using them is easier and more effective than toenailing. This means you'll get a better connection and the structure will come together faster. However, there is a potential downside from a design perspective: Nails are effectively invisible; hangers are not. In general, construction hangers are usually hidden from view; consequently, designers give little thought to how they look. The truth is they're not very pretty. So decide whether seeing the hangers will bother you once the structure is complete. If so, use nails. But check your local building codes: In regions subject to high winds and earth tremors, rafter ties—also known as hurricane/seismic ties—may actually be required by those codes.

Nail a post/beam connector on top of the post and you'll find that the problem of holding heavy beams in place while you work has largely been solved.

Put rafter ties on top of the beams to hold the rafters, and the problem of toenailing disappears. Rafter ties also are sold as hurricane/seismic ties. They make great all-purpose hangers even if you don't live in an area that is prone to earthquakes or high winds.

Building an arbor (continued)

Attaching lattice panels and post trim

1 Attach rails. Screw 2×4 top and bottom rails to the posts with galvanized No. 8 2½-inch deck screws. Place 1×1 stops along the outside edges of the posts and rails to support the lattice panel. Secure the stops with galvanized No. 8 2½-inch deck screws.

2 Install the lattice. Place the lattice panel against the stops and install 1×1 stops along the other side, sandwiching the panel.

3 Attach trim. As a decorative touch, add four mitered 2×2s around each post directly below the beams. Cut the pieces to size, then drill pilot holes and nail each piece to the post with galvanized No. 8 2½-inch finishing nails.

Covering with woven reed or bamboo

A woven reed or bamboo covering provides shade but is less durable and less sturdy than slats. To install reed or bamboo, nail a frame of 2×2s to the rafters, then tack the covering to it. Add 1×2s on top of the covering to help hold it in place.

1 Build a frame. Construct a frame of 2×2s and screw it to the rafters with No. 8 2½-inch deck screws. Nail 2×2 supports every 2 feet inside the frame so they're at right angles to the rafters. Unroll the material onto the frame and tack two adjacent corners to the frame.

2 Install the covering. Cut 1×2s to fit over the 2×2s. Lay the 1×2s in place. Have a helper pull the material tight while you screw the first 1×2 to the rafters with No. 8 2-inch deck screws. Pull the material tight and screw in the next 1×2, continuing this way to the other end.

Applying shade fabric

Shade fabric is a meshlike material that lets in air but keeps out sun. Fabric that provides 60 percent shade is best for plants. For people, buy fabric that provides 80 percent. Shade fabric comes in rolls with unfinished edges. Make your own border or roll up the edges before installing grommets. Secure the fabric with cord and eye screws on a 2×2 frame.

1 Build a frame. Build a four-sided frame from 2×2s to sit on top of the rafters. (Unlike the frame for bamboo, this frame needs no crosspieces.) Screw the frame to the top of the rafters with No. 8 2½-inch deck screws. Cut a piece of shade cloth so it's the same size as the outside dimensions of the frame.

2 Lay out the grommets. Roll the edges of the fabric under about 2 inches and pin them in place. Put a grommet in place at a corner and trace around the inside to mark where the hole will be. Repeat in each corner and every 16 inches along the edges.

3 Set the grommets. Cut a hole in the fabric with the hole cutter that comes in a grommet kit. Set up the grommet punch as shown, with the top-hat-shape half of the grommet on the bottom and the flat grommet piece on the top. Strike with a hammer to drive the grommet halves together.

4 Attach screw eyes. Put the fabric loosely in place. Lay out holes on the frame for screw eyes, positioning them to align with the grommets. Drill holes one bit size smaller than the screw shank and screw the screw eyes in place.

5 Tie the fabric in place. Lace a strong, weather-resistant cord long enough to secure the fabric on all sides through the grommets and screw eyes. Pull the cord tight to stretch the fabric taut across the frame. Tie the cord securely and cut off the excess.

Building an arch-top arbor

Skill level:	Time to complete:	Materials:	Tools:

Skill level:
★★★☆☆

Time to complete:
Experienced 8 hrs.
Handy 12 hrs.
Novice 16 hrs.

Materials: Pressure-treated 1×8s, 4×4s, 1×2s, 1×3s 2×4s, tempered hardboard, ½-inch plywood, construction adhesive, galvanized 6d (2-inch) and 10d (3-inch) nails, No. 8 2-inch deck screws, sandpaper, ¾-inch gravel, premix concrete

Tools: Tape measure, mason's line, utility knife, circular saw, saber saw, router and bits, caulk gun, hammer, sanding block, mason's hoe, wheelbarrow, shovel, level, ⅜-inch drill and bits, screwdriver, pencil, dust mask, safety glasses

Arch-top arbors are classic and beautiful, especially when roses are climbing up the sides and over the top. The challenge is building the arches.

Each arch is constructed from three pieces of 1× lumber that are laminated together to provide thickness and strength. Making them is easier than it sounds, and you'll get a chance to use a router to cut them out. The router will eliminate lopsided arcs and uneven lines. You'll use a jig that turns the router into a big compass to cut a template. The template will be your guide for cutting the arches themselves. Once you have cut the pieces to shape with a saber saw and glued them together, you'll use the router again to trim the arches to their finished shape.

The holes for the posts should be half as deep as the structure is high (excluding the arched top). The base of this arbor is 6 feet tall, so the holes should be 3 feet deep (plus 4 inches for gravel fill) and the posts 9 feet long overall. Make sure you use posts rated for ground burial and weather-resistant lumber for the entire structure.

◄ **This arbor has 4×4 posts that are 6 feet high and spaced 47½ inches apart from side to side and 3 feet apart from front to back.** To simplify alignment, the posts are anchored in concrete after the arches are attached. Horizontal 1×3 slats brace the structure and provide a climbing surface for plants.

Making an arch router jig

1 Make a template with a router jig. Make a template of the arch with the help of a jig that turns your router into a giant compass. Cut a 40-inch piece of 1/2-inch plywood to a width of 10 inches. Drill two 1/16-inch-diameter holes in it: one centered 6 inches from the end and the other centered 4 inches from the first hole. Drill a centered 1/2-inch-diameter hole 24 inches from the first hole.

2 Drill for the router. Unscrew the router base, put a 1/2-inch bit in the router, and put the bit in the 1/2-inch hole. Put a pencil through the screw holes in the router base and mark the plywood. Drill stepped holes at each mark: Drill 3/8-inch-diameter holes 1/4 inch deep, then drill 1/8-inch holes that go all the way through the plywood in the center of the first holes.

3 Attach the router to the jig. Screw the router to the jig through the holes you just drilled, propping up the unsupported end of the jig to make the job easier. (You may need to replace the original screws with longer ones.) If the screw heads stick out above the surface of the plywood, make the holes slightly deeper.

Cutting a template

1 Attach hardboard to a work surface. Screw the corners of a sheet of tempered hardboard to a sheet of inexpensive 1/2-inch plywood. Draw a line across the center of the hardboard, dividing the sheet into two 48-inch squares. Accurately drill a 1/16-inch hole in the center of the line. Drive a No. 8 drywall screw through either of the holes in the jig into the 1/16-inch hole in the hardboard until just snug so that the jig will turn smoothly but not wiggle.

2 Rout one edge of the arch. Lower the router bit to barely cut through the hardboard. Swing the jig so the bit is just to the left of the edge of the hardboard. Turn on the router and swing the jig across the hardboard in a slow arc.

3 Rout the other edge of the arch. Put the screw in the other hole and screw the jig back in place. Drive in a couple of drywall screws to hold the arch in place once you cut it free. Make sure the router won't hit any of the screws, then rout out the arch. Cut the ends of the arch along the pencil lines you drew in Step 1.

Building an arch-top arbor (continued)

Building the arbor

Outer layer
(cut two for each arch)

17"
25°
24"
32"
41"
21"
24"
25°

Inner layer
(cut one for each arch)

1 Cut stock for the arches. For stability, each arch is made of three layers, each made of 1×8s and trimmed to shape. Lay out an inner layer and two outer layers for each arch using the dimensions given above. The angles are 25 degrees if cut on a tablesaw or power miter saw and 65 degrees if you use a protractor.

2 Assemble the stock for the arches. Stack up the parts for each arch and lay out the arch on each stack. Glue the layers together with construction adhesive, then nail the layers together with 4d finishing nails placed well away from the layout lines.

3 Cut out the arches. Cut along the layout lines with a saber saw. Cut slowly and carefully, skimming the outside edge of the line as you go. You'll clean up the cut later with your router and a flush trim bit. Get a bit with a flush bearing on top that is long enough to cut through all three layers of wood.

4 Attach the template. For the smoothest possible curve, rout the arch to shape using the template you made earlier as a guide. Wipe the dust off the arch, cover it with two-sided carpet tape, and press the template firmly in place over the tape. Drive finishing nails at the top and sides to secure.

5 Rout the arches. Put a flush trim bit in the router—a bit with the bearing on top will be easiest to use. Clamp the arch so it overhangs a work surface and guide the bearing along the template to trim edges of the arch. Leave the ends of the arch as the saw cut them—if you try to rout them, the wood will split.

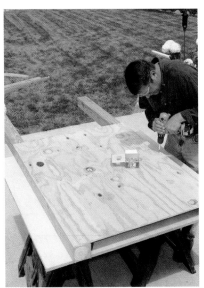

6 Support the posts. The arch will be somewhat flexible until it's anchored in concrete. To support it, cut some leftover plywood into 3×4-foot panels and screw the panels to the posts.

7 **Attach the top plates and slats.** Measure the width of the side, subtract the combined thickness of the arches, and cut a 2×4 top plate to this length. Screw it to the tops of the posts as a support for the arches, as shown. Cut 1×3 slats to length and screw each end to the posts with two screws, spacing the slats 8 inches apart on center. Repeat on the second side.

8 **Attach the arches and slats.** Remove the plywood. Put an arch in place and screw it into the 2×4 top plates. Measure to make sure the legs are parallel, then screw a brace across them. Attach the other arch and attach the slats.

9 **Lay out and dig holes for posts.** Dig the holes 3 feet 4 inches deep. Shovel 4 inches of gravel into the holes, tamp, then put the posts in the holes. Check that the posts are plumb, then brace them.

10 **Mix concrete.** Prepare premix concrete in a wheelbarrow following the directions on the bag. Add water a bit at a time and mix with a mason's hoe until the concrete clings to the hoe when you lift it.

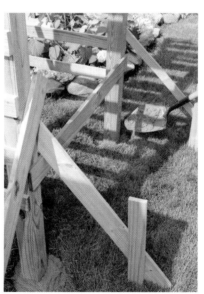

11 **Fill the holes.** Shovel concrete into the postholes. Work a 2×4 up and down in the concrete to eliminate air pockets. Slope the top of the concrete so water drains away from the posts. Allow the concrete to cure for two or three days before removing the braces.

DESIGN TIP
SLATS OR LATTICE? IT'S ALL UP TO YOU

As an alternative to putting horizontal slats on the sides of the arbor, you can place lattice panels between the posts. This design is particularly useful if you do not plan to grow tall vines or climbing plants on your arbor. The lattice panels still offer some degree of privacy and give the arbor a more finished look. Add a small lattice gate and the arched arbor becomes a Victorian-style entrance to your backyard.

CHAPTER 8

Electrical

Electricity can play an important part in your landscaping. At the most basic level, you may want power to run a hedge trimmer or a drill that you're using on one of your outdoor projects. You may want a pump for the water garden, an outlet for a bug zapper, or a light outside the garage.

Lighting can play a big role in your landscaping plan: An overhead light near your parking area makes it easier to unload the groceries at night and provides security. A series of floodlights can call attention to the landscape at night. Lights close to the ground guide you from curb to front door.

An outdoor lighting project often requires nothing more than taking down an old fixture and putting in a new one.

Getting power to another part of the yard, however, means digging a trench for the wire and somehow getting power to it. Most new homes have at least one outdoor outlet, and tapping into it to run power elsewhere is relatively easy. It's slightly more complicated if you have to bring the power from inside the house, especially if the walls are masonry.

But it doesn't have to be difficult: Low-voltage lighting systems can simplify the job. A transformer steps the voltage down to a level low enough that you don't have to dig a trench; the transformer that powers the light can be plugged in almost anywhere. The wiring is simple too. You just clamp the lights onto the cable.

Contents

Installing electric service outdoors

Even if you're an old hand at indoor wiring, you'll soon find that the electrical code is a bit more stringent outdoors than indoors. Safety, of course, is the primary concern in all wiring, and because more can go wrong outside, the requirements for 110-volt wiring are stiff.

- Cable running underground must be encased in plastic conduit, or it must be UF cable, which is approved for underground installation.

- Underground cable must be buried at the depths required by national and local codes.

- Exposed cable must be housed in conduit at depths specified by local codes.

- All electrical boxes must be approved for outdoor use. They must have gaskets and watertight fittings.

- Outlets must be GFCI protected. GFCI circuits are protected by a breaker at the service panel or in the outlet itself. Outlets are usually simplest. A GFCI outlet contains a sensor that cuts the power if it runs directly to the ground, either through a wire-to-wire short or through a person in contact with it and the ground.

As you'll see, none of the requirements are beyond the skill of most homeowners. In fact, unless you're able to tap into an existing outdoor outlet, you'll probably spend most of your time indoors, running a new circuit and getting the wiring through the wall and on its way to the great outdoors.

Electrical tool kit

Cable ripper

Diagonal cutter

Hammer drill

Neon circuit tester

Safety glasses

Voltage meter

Caulk gun

Drill and bits

Insulated screwdrivers

Percussion bit

Screwdriver

Wire cutter

Chalkline

Fish tape

Lineman's pliers

Plastic pipe cutter

Shovel

Combination stripper

Hammer

Needle-nose pliers

Posthole digger

Utility knife

TOOL TIP
A BELT'S A BELT, RIGHT?

Electrical projects will go smoother if you're wearing a tool belt.
Though a basic carpentry tool belt will keep your electrical tools close at hand, an electrician's tool belt is specially designed for keeping often-used electrical items within easy reach. Even if you work on only a half-dozen boxes and devices, a belt will save time. They are available in many styles; two are shown at right.

Materials

▶ **Cable is the heart of any electrical project.** The most common cable is NM (nonmetallic jacket) cable, used indoors. Outdoors you'll want to use UF (underground feed) cable, which is weathertight.

Cable comes in various sizes and is color coded: When it comes to indoor (NM) cable, **12-2G, or 12-gauge cable** with two conductors and one ground, is yellow; and **14-32, or 14-gauge cable** with two conductors and one ground, is white. All **UF cable** is gray. Stick with 12-gauge cable; 14-gauge wire carries less amperage. Black wires carry power, white are neutral and carry power back to the box, and grounding wires take power to the ground if there is a short. At least part of an outdoor run has to be in **plastic conduit;** the section that's above ground can be encased in **metal conduit.** The cover on a waterproof **LB fitting** is removable to make fishing wire through it easier when the cable turns a corner. Connect plastic conduit with **primer, PVC solvent cement,** and **couplings.** Use **metal fittings** on metal conduit. Attach conduit to the house with **conduit straps.** Cover exposed wire ends with **wire nuts.** Attach cable to joists with **cable staples.** For extra security, wrap wire nuts with **electrical tape** and wrap a few turns around the wire, too, to keep the nut from working loose. Low-voltage systems have **crimp-on connectors.**

Selecting the proper size cable

Wire max gauge	Amperage	Load
14-gauge	15 amps	1,440 watts (120 volts)
12-gauge	20 amps	1,920 watts (120 volts)

The higher the number of a wire's gauge, the less current—or amperage—it can carry. When you install a new circuit, make sure the wire you use has an amperage rating that matches that circuit.

Planning for voltage drop

Amperes	Volt amperes	No. 14	No.12	No. 10	No. 8
5	600	90	142	226	360
10	1,200	45	71	113	180
15	1,800	30	47	75	120
20	2,400	22	36	57	90
25	3,000	18	28	45	72
30	3,600	15	23	38	60

As electricity travels through a wire, it loses some of its strength. A voltage drop of 2 percent is acceptable, but anything more than that will affect the performance of whatever is plugged into the circuit. This chart shows the maximum number of feet a length of cable carrying a certain amount of amps can run while maintaining acceptable voltage. For example, if you want to run a circular saw that draws 15 amps 60 feet from your house, you can't use No. 12-gauge wire (maximum: 47 feet). Choose No. 10-gauge cable (maximum: 75 feet).

Materials (continued)

▶ A **ground fault circuit interrupter (GFCI) outlet** provides protection against electrical shock and is required by code for outdoor outlets. You can substitute an **indoor outlet** if it's protected by a **GFCI breaker** installed in the breaker box. A **single-pole switch** controls a light from a single location and has two terminals. It can be used outdoors, but like outlets, it must be mounted in a waterproof box made of either **metal** or **plastic**. Waterproof boxes have **gaskets** and **cover plates** to keep out the weather. Lights and other fixtures are controlled by various automatic switches, including a **motion-sensor switch**, a **photoelectric eye**, a **timer switch**, and a **time-delay switch**.

GFCI outlet · Indoor outlet · GFCI breaker · Single-pole switch · Metal box · Plastic box

Gaskets · Cover plates · Motion-sensor switch · Photoelectric eye · Timer switch · Time-delay switch

Porch light · Mercury-vapor light · Halogen light · Floodlight · Low-voltage lighting · Transformer

▲ For years, your only choices for lighting up the yard were **floodlights** and **porch lights**. You'll find a wider variety of lighting in stores these days. **Mercury-vapor lights** produce a bluish-green light, and **halogen lights** provide an intense white light. You also can buy **low-voltage lighting,** which uses an outdoor version of lamp wire to power a network of small lights. Because it works on low voltage, this network doesn't require you to dig a trench for the wire, and the fittings are very simple. A **transformer** that reduces regular 120 volts A.C. to 12 volts A.C. powers low-voltage lights. You can buy low-voltage lighting piece by piece, but you'll save money if you buy the entire system as a kit.

Amperage drawn by different motors		
Horsepower	120 volts	240 volts
1/6	4.4	2.2
1/4	5.8	2.9
1/3	7.2	3.6
1/2	9.8	4.9
3/4	13.8	6.9
1	16	8
1 1/2	20	10
2	24	12
3	34	17
5	56	28
7 1/2	80	40
10	100	50

When you want to use outdoor equipment, remember: The higher the horsepower, the more amperage the circuit draws. A 3-horsepower tablesaw, for example, running on 120 volts draws 34 amps. The circuit you plug into must accommodate the motor you run. This chart applies to motors running at usual speeds under normal loads.

Making wire connections

Skill level:
★☆☆☆

Time to complete:
Experienced | 1 min.
Handy | 2 min.
Novice | 3 min.

Materials: Cable, wire nuts

Tools: Cable stripper, utility knife, wire cutter or combination stripper, lineman's pliers, needle-nose pliers, screwdriver

ELECTRICAL

No matter what type of electrical job you're going to do, it will most certainly entail the connection of wires. Start by stripping off 8 to 10 inches of exterior sheathing. Then strip ½ to ¾ inch of insulation from the wires inside. A wire that is black or red is called hot, or live, because it is meant to carry current.

A white wire is neutral. A grounding wire may be green or bare copper. Be careful not to damage the wires while stripping them. If you do, start the process over. Make sure all bare wires are covered after connections are made. **Make sure the power is off at the main power circuit before doing any electrical work.**

Stripping cable

1 **Strip off the sheathing.** Strip 8 to 10 inches of sheathing off the end of the cable with a cable stripper or utility knife. Squeeze the stripper until it cuts into the sheathing, then pull it to slice open the cable.

2 **Cut off the sheathing.** Peel back the cable's sheathing to expose the wires. Cut off the excess sheathing with a utility knife.

Stripping wire

1 **Put the wire in a combination stripper.** Strip ½ to ¾ inch of insulation off each wire with a wire cutter or combination stripper. Fit the wire into the stripper slot that matches its gauge, then squeeze and turn the tool around the wire to cut the insulation.

2 **Remove the insulation.** Keep the jaws closed and slide the combination stripper to the end of the wire to pull off the insulation.

Making wire connections (continued)

Connecting wires

1 Twist the wires together.
Hold the wires you're connecting parallel to each other and twist the bare ends together clockwise with lineman's pliers. Once you've twisted the wires together, snip the ends so they're even.

2 Screw and tape on a wire nut. Screw a wire nut onto the end of the twisted wires. Tug gently on each wire to be sure the connection is secure. Start over if any bare wire is exposed. For extra strength and safety, wrap electrical tape around the nut and wire.

Connecting wires to screw terminals

1 Make a loop. Shape the end of the wire into an open loop with needle-nose pliers. Create the loop by stepping the pliers toward the end of the wire, making progressively smaller bends with each step.

2 Screw on the wire. Loosen the terminal screw. Hook the looped wire clockwise around the terminal and tighten the screw. Looping the wire this way causes it to tighten around the terminal when you turn the screw. If the wire end doesn't loop at least three-quarters of the way around the screw or if bare wire is exposed, dismantle, snip the extra wire, and start over.

Making pigtail connections

When more than one wire is intended for a screw terminal, code requires a jumper wire. A jumper is about 6 inches long and matches the gauge of the wires it joins. Connect the jumper and the wires with a wire nut, then connect the jumper wire to the terminal. It's good practice to use a pigtail whenever you have more than one wire going to either side of an outlet or fixture. Check local codes.

Don't use the push-in connection option

Using push-in terminals on outlets is not recommended, even though the receptacle will allow you to do so. Wires can slip out of the terminal, breaking the circuit, which disrupts power to the outlet. Electricians prefer the screws because the connection is more secure and the wire is far less likely to slip out. Checking each outlet to find out which one's the culprit isn't a great way to spend a Saturday afternoon. Screw those wires to the terminals.

ELECTRICAL

Extending a circuit

Skill level: ★★★☆☆

Time to complete:
Experienced | 1 hr.
Handy | 1.5 hrs.
Novice | 2 hrs.

Materials: NM cable, jumper wire, wire nuts, masking tape, electrical tape

Tools: Screwdriver, neon circuit tester, cable stripper, wire cutter or combination stripper, lineman's pliers, needle-nose pliers

To get power outdoors, you can either add a new circuit or tap into an existing one. Outlets, light fixtures, and junction boxes are all good places to tap into. Before you tap into a circuit, make sure what you're doing meets code. You can have no more than eight devices (ceiling lights, receptacles, etc.) per 20-amp breaker. If the circuit meets that requirement, add up the amperage drawn by each device on the circuit. If what you plan on adding to the circuit brings the total amperage to more than 80 percent of the amperage of the fuse or breaker, choose another circuit. The way you tap into a box depends on where it falls in the circuit. An end-of-the-run box—which has only one cable coming into it—is connected slightly differently from a middle-of-the-run box, which has at least two cables coming into it. Both are explained here.

Mapping circuits and loads

1 Turn off the power. To identify the electrical devices on a circuit, turn off a breaker for the circuit at the service panel. Turn on switches and fixtures to find those no longer receiving power. Check outlets by plugging a working lamp into each receptacle.

2 Add up the existing wattage. Add the wattage ratings of all devices on the circuit and those you plan to install. Divide the total by 120 volts to get a result in amps and compare it to the rating for the circuit stamped on the breaker. To prevent overloading a circuit, don't exceed 80 percent of its rating.

Joining into an end-of-the-run outlet

End-of-the-run outlet

Middle-of-the-run outlet

An end-of-the-run outlet has one cable that enters the electrical box. The black hot wire is connected to a brass screw, the white neutral wire is connected to a silver screw, and the grounding wire is connected by jumpers to the grounding screws on the outlet and the box. To extend the circuit, begin by threading a new cable into the box. Connect the new black wire to the other brass screw on the outlet and connect the new white wire to the silver screw. Make pigtails to join the grounding wires to the grounding screws.

Extending a circuit (continued)

Joining into an end-of-the-run outlet

1 Cut off the power. Determine which circuit the outlet is on and shut off the breaker for that circuit at the service panel. Post a sign to alert others that you are working on the circuit.

2 Remove the outlet. Remove the outlet cover plate, then remove the screws that hold the outlet in the box. Without touching any wires, gently pull the outlet out of the box.

3 Double-check for power. Check that the power is off with a circuit tester. Working with one hand to reduce the risk of an electrical shock, touch one probe to the wired brass screw and the other probe to the wired silver screw. The tester shouldn't light. If the tester does light, go to the service panel and shut off the correct circuit.

Calculating box capacity				
Type of box	**Box Size**	**Number of conductors**		
		No. 10	No. 12	No. 14
Switch	3"×2"×2¼"	4	4	5
	3"×2"×2½"	5	5	6
	3"×2"×2¾"	5	6	7
	3"×2"×3½"	7	8	9
Square	4"×1¼"	7	8	9
	4"×1½"	8	9	10
	4"×2⅛"	12	13	15
	4¹¹/₁₆"×1¼"	10	11	12
Octagonal	4"×1¼"	5	5	6
	4"×1½"	6	6	7
	4"×2⅛"	8	9	10

Electrical boxes are made for a specific number of wires. Add up the existing and new wires to see if the box is big enough. Count all grounding wires as one wire, no matter how many there are. Each outlet, switch, fixture nipple, or any internal clamp counts as one wire. If the box isn't big enough for another cable, change it or choose another location.

Reprinted with permission from NFPA 70-1996, the National Electric Code®, Copyright © 1996, National Fire Protection Association, Quincy, MA 02269. This reprinted material is not the complete and official position of the National Fire Protection Association on the referenced subject, which is represented only by the standard in its entirety.

WORK SMART
WHICH SIDE IS UP?

You can install an outlet with the hole for the ground at either the top or the bottom. One advantage of installing the outlet with the grounding hole at the top is that if something falls directly on the plug, it will hit the ground instead of the hot and neutral, and the outlet won't short out. But the main consideration is consistency—not alternating between hole-up and hole-down from one outlet to another—and making sure the position of the hole allows the plug you plan to install to drape down rather than stick up.

Ground wire

Neutral wire

Fastening wing

4 Disconnect the wires.
Once you're sure the power is off, unscrew the terminals and disconnect the wires from the outlet. Uncap the grounding wire connection and remove the jumper.

5 Remove the old box. Remove the nails holding the box to the stud in the wall. Slip a hacksaw blade between the box and the stud and cut through the nails. Pull the box free and remove the cable. You will replace this box with a remodeling box that has screw-driven wings to hold the box firmly against the wall.

6 Break the tabs for the cable in the new remodeling box.
Run cable for the new part of the circuit. Break the tabs in the remodeling box to provide openings for the old and new cables. Run the new cable from the end of the new circuit to the box, feeding about 8 inches of it—or enough to work comfortably—into the box through the new knockout. Feed the old cable back into the new box.

 Gotta clamp it!

If a metal box is without a built-in clamp, you'll need to install a two-piece external clamp. Slip the connector onto the sheathed cable and tighten it, then feed the cable into the box. Thread the locknut onto the connector from inside the box and tighten it by pushing against the lugs with a screwdriver.

WORK SMART NO SHOCKS

A plug-in receptacle analyzer is a handy device for checking outlets. It features lights that tell you if a wire is hot and if a circuit is wired correctly. You also can use a penlike tester that you pass along the wall. The device beeps whenever it's near a power source.

7 Install the remodeling box.
Insert the box in the opening. Tighten the box firmly to the wall by screwing the wings into place. Strip 8 to 10 inches of sheathing off the cable and ½ to ¾ inch of insulation off the wires.

8 **Connect the wires.** Connect the black and the white wires of the existing and new cables to different sets of terminals on the outlet: black wires to brass screws and white wires to silver screws. Make a loop in each wire, wrap it clockwise around its terminal, and tighten the screw with a screwdriver.

9 **Connect the ground.** Make two 6-inch grounding jumpers from the grounding wire in an extra piece of cable. Connect the jumpers to the grounding wires with a wire nut. Attach one of the jumpers to the grounding screw on the outlet.

10 **Reinstall the outlet.** Gently fold the wires into the electrical box and position the outlet. Screw the outlet onto the box, then screw on the cover plate.

Joining into a middle-of-the-run outlet

If you find two (or more) cables entering the electrical box, the outlet is in the middle of the run. Extending the circuit is likely to require a larger box to accommodate the new cable and wires (see "Calculating box capacity," page 282). In this case the total number of wires for the extension is nine (four black, four white, and one ground) so you will need a box at least $3\frac{1}{2}$ inches deep to accommodate the new wires. Because only one wire is allowed to connect directly to a screw terminal, two of the black wires and two of the white wires require pigtails. **Shut off all power to the circuit at the service panel before working on the outlet.**

Before

After

In middle-of-the-run outlets, the black wires are connected to brass screws, the white wires are connected to silver screws, and the grounding wires are connected by jumpers to the grounding screws on the outlet and the box. Add the new cable, then connect all the black wires to a jumper and connect the jumper to a brass screw. Join the white wires the same way to a silver screw. Connect the grounding wires to the grounding screws with jumpers.

1 Double-check for power.
Check that the power is off with a circuit tester. Working with one hand, touch one probe to the wired brass screw and the other probe to the wired silver screw. The tester shouldn't light. If the tester does light, go to the service panel and shut off the correct circuit.

2 Disconnect the outlet.
Undo the wires and remove the outlet. Unclamp the cables and remove the electrical box. Pry out knockout holes for three cables in a new box. Run a new cable from the end of the new circuit to the box. Clamp the new cable and the two existing cables to the box.

3 Connect the black wires.
Fasten the electrical box to the stud in the wall. Twist the black wires together with a jumper and screw on a wire nut. Tape it in place with electrical tape. Attach the jumper to a brass screw.

4 Connect the white wires. Twist the white wires together and screw on a nut. Tape the nut in place. Screw the jumper to a silver screw.

5 Connect the ground wires. Twist together the grounding wires with two jumpers and screw on a wire nut. Connect one jumper to the grounding screw on the electrical box and the other jumper to the grounding screw on the outlet. Reinstall the outlet by gently folding the wires into the electrical box. Screw the outlet to the box, then reinstall the cover plate. Restore power and test the outlet.

Extending a circuit (continued)

Joining into a light fixture

One way to get power for a new circuit is to tap into an existing light fixture and run wire for a new circuit from it. This method works well when you're adding new lights, as opposed to a receptacle used for a tool that draws a lot of current.

Start by shutting off power to the circuit at the service panel, then unscrew the fixture. Support the fixture with a length of coat hanger. Don't touch bare wires until you're sure power is off. Double-check with a voltage tester.

In the box, you will most likely find a white wire connected to a black wire. This wire goes to the switch—label it "hot" by wrapping it with black electrical tape at both ends of the circuit. Disconnect the wires from the light fixture and label all the wires. Set the fixture aside. Unclamp the cables and remove the box—the extra cable will require a larger box. See the chart on page 282 for the right size. **Shut off all power to the circuit at the service panel before working on the fixture.**

When you remove a light fixture, you'll see a black wire connected to the light's black wire and a white wire connected to the light's white wire (above left). Another black wire, the power source, is connected to a white wire marked black (it goes to the switch). To extend the circuit, connect the new black wire to the power source and black-marked white wire (above right). Connect the remaining white wires to the light. Connect all grounding wires and the grounding pigtail with a nut and attach the pigtail to the grounding screw.

1 Install a new box and cable. Turn off the power and label and disconnect the wires. Install a new box and feed in the wires. Strip 8 inches of sheathing off the new cable, feed it into the box, then strip 1/2 to 3/4 inch of insulation off the wires. Clamp the cables in place using the clamps built into the box.

2 Connect the black wires. Connect the black wire that is the power source, the new black wire, and the white wire originally marked black (this indicates it is hot in this circuit). Twist the three wires together and screw on a wire nut.

3 Connect the remaining wires. Twist the white wires together and add a pigtail for the light fixture. Connect with a wire nut. Connect all the grounding wires to a pigtail, cover with a nut, and connect the pigtail to a grounding screw. Wrap tape around all the caps and the wires running into them. Gently fold the wires into the electrical box and reinstall the light fixture.

Tapping into a junction box

A junction box—an electrical box where cables that run through exposed joists or studs have been connected—is another opportunity to extend a circuit. Shut off power to the circuit at the service panel, then unscrew the box's cover plate. Don't touch bare wires until you're certain the power is off. To make sure the power is off, touch one probe of a voltage tester to the black wire connections and the other probe to the box. **Shut off all power to the circuit at the service panel before working on the junction box.**

Three cables enter this junction box, but yours may vary, depending on the circuit. All the black wires are connected to black wires; all the white wires are connected to white wires. The grounding wires are jumpered to the box's grounding screw. To tap into the box, add a new cable to the box. Attach its black wire to those in the box. Attach its white wire to the white wires in the box. Connect all the grounding wires to the box with a jumper.

1 With the power off, undo all the wire connections. Remove the box and replace it with a larger one if necessary. Check the chart on page 282 for the proper size. Prepare the new cable and fasten all the cables into the box with the built-in clamps.

2 Twist the black wires together clockwise and screw on a wire cap suitable for the gauge and number of wires. Connect all the white wires the same way.

3 Cut a grounding jumper about 6 inches long and connect the grounding wires to it. Loop the jumper clockwise onto the grounding screw and tighten it. Wrap electrical tape around each cap and the wires that run into it. Gently fold the wires into the box and screw the cover back on the box.

Adding a GFCI circuit

Skill level:	Time to complete:	Materials: GFCI breaker, NM cable, box connector, cable staples, rubber grommet, nailing plates	Tools: Screwdriver, voltage meter, drill and bits, hammer, safety glasses
★★★☆☆	Experienced 2 hrs. Handy 4 hrs. Novice 6 hrs.		

If your service panel has a free slot (one that doesn't have a breaker in it), you can run a new circuit from the panel to take electricity outdoors. Code requires you to protect an outdoor circuit with a ground fault circuit interrupter (GFCI). This device monitors the flow of electricity and automatically shuts off the circuit in the event of a problem. Installing a GFCI breaker at the service panel provides this safety protection to the entire circuit, as well as all of the electrical devices wired into it. Alternatively, you can install a regular breaker and start the circuit with a GFCI outlet, which protects all electrical devices following it on the circuit. **Shut off all power to all circuits at the service panel before working on the new circuit.**

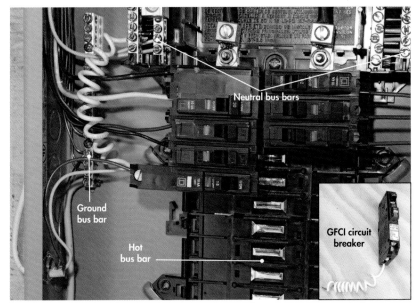

Ground bus bar

Neutral bus bars

Hot bus bar

GFCI circuit breaker

To add a GFCI circuit at the service panel, remove one of the knockouts in the side of the box and put a box connector in the opening. Feed the new cable through the box connector, then begin connecting the wires: Connect the cable's grounding wire to the panel's neutral bus bar, a metal strip that grounds the neutral and ground wires of each cable. Install the cable's black wire and white wire into the GFCI breaker. Connect the GFCI breaker's white wire to the panel's neutral bus bar.

Joining into a middle-of-the-run outlet

1 Run the new cable. Feed cable from the end of the new circuit to the service panel. Drill holes through wood studs or joists. If the studs are metal, insert a rubber grommet to protect the cable. Fasten the cable to the sides of studs or joists with cable staples every foot and 8 inches above and below the box. Each cable needs its own staples. Protect the cable by securing nailing plates to the studs before you close up the wall. (See page 293.)

2 Shut off the power. Turn off the main switch to shut off power to all the circuits. Then turn off the circuits one by one so all the circuits won't come on at once when you restore power. Unscrew and remove the panel cover. Don't touch anything inside the panel until you're sure the power is off.

3 **Make sure the power is off.** With a voltage meter or circuit tester, touch one probe to the front screw on the breaker and the other probe to the panel's ground or neutral bus bar. (In some panels, the ground and neutral will be attached to the same bar.) If the tester lights, have an electrician rewire the box.

4 **Remove a knockout.** Once you're sure the power is off, remove a knockout from the side of the panel. Install a box connector in the knockout and feed in 8 to 10 inches of cable (enough to connect the wires comfortably) through it. Tighten the connector.

5 **Wire the breaker.** Strip the cable, leaving at least one inch of sheathing inside the box. Screw the (bare) ground wire into the panel's neutral bus bar. (If your box has a separate bar for the grounding wires, attach the wire there.) Insert the white wire to a screw terminal marked "load neutral" and tighten the screw. Screw the GFCI's white wire to the panel's neutral bus bar.

6 **Connect to the GFCI.** Insert the cable's black (hot) wire into the terminal marked "line" on the GFCI. Tighten the screw to secure the connection.

7 **Snap the GFCI in place.** Put the circuit breaker into an empty slot in the panel. Press the breaker until it snaps into place.

8 **Replace the panel.** Remove a knockout for the circuit breaker in the cover of the panel. Position the cover on the panel and screw it in place.

Running conduit and cable

Skill level:	Time to complete:	Materials: Caulk, PVC conduit, metal conduit, nipple, compression fittings, rubber bushing (as necessary), wood screws, anchor shields, metal screws, LB fitting, PVC solvent cement, plastic cable staples, plastic straps, electrical tape	Tools: Shovel, hammer, insulated screwdrivers, fish tape, hammer drill, plastic pipe cutter, percussion bit, caulk gun, safety glasses
★★★☆☆	Experienced 2 hrs. Handy 4 hrs. Novice 6 hrs.		

Though you can run cable to an outdoor light or outlet several ways, the easiest is with UF cable, which is waterproof and can be buried directly in the ground. Code requires that you protect the cable above ground, so you'll have to do some basic conduit work where the cable enters and exits the ground.

Other methods require you to enclose wiring in conduit for the entire length of the trench. You won't have to bury the cable quite as deeply, but you will have to fish wires and cut conduit. It's best to stick with UF.

Inside the house, cable runs from the breaker box to a junction box near the foundation wall. Inside the junction box, each wire in the cable is attached to a corresponding wire in a UF (underground feeder) cable. A conduit nipple protects the cable's run through the wall. Outside, attach the nipple to an LB fitting—an L-shaped fitting with a removable plate that turns the cable toward the ground. The fitting attaches to conduit that goes down the house wall into an 24-inch-deep trench. The conduit then stops, and the cable continues along the bottom of the trench. At the end of the trench it reenters conduit and is routed up to the fixture it will power.

Installing PVC conduit

1 Drill a hole where you want the wire to enter the house, at a point just above the foundation. Measure and make sure the hole will go through the rim joist and not into the foundation or first floor. Make the hole wide enough to accommodate a short section of conduit, called a nipple, that protects the cable.

2 Install an LB fitting. Cut a PVC nipple to length so it extends 1 inch into the basement and test the fit. Glue it to the LB fitting and push the assembly into the hole until the fitting is against the wall of the house.

3 Dig a trench. Dig a trench for the cable below the LB fitting. Make the trench about the width of a shovel and 24 inches deep. Code requires this depth for UF cables buried without conduit.

4 Attach a piece of conduit to the LB fitting. Cut a piece of conduit to reach from the fitting to an elbow at the bottom of the trench. Spread PVC solvent cement onto the conduit and push it into the fitting.

5 Attach the elbow. Glue the elbow in place. The lower end should be at the bottom of the trench. UF cable will come out the opening and travel directly along the bottom of the trench until it reaches the other end.

USING CONDUIT

Code lets you bury UF cable directly in the ground, but you also can run conduit the length of the trench. If you do, you won't have to bury the cable quite as deep—12 inches instead of 24 inches in residential applications. You will, however, have to fish cable through the conduit. Running UF or other cable through conduit meets code, but cable adds expense and the sheathing may make it difficult to fish. Most electricians feed three single wires, known as TW wires, through the conduit instead. If you do this, run the conduit first, and glue the sections together. Once the conduit is in place, fish all three wires at once.

Using metal conduit above grade

Although PVC is flexible, rustproof, and easy to work with, some local codes won't allow PVC more than 6 inches above ground. Metal conduit, which is more durable and less likely to be damaged accidentally, is required instead. With metal conduit, all connections must be made with compression fittings, which have a compression ring (like plumbing fittings do) to keep out water. Thin-walled tubing, called EMT (electrical metallic tubing), is the easiest conduit to use. A nipple connects an interior junction box to an exterior metal LB fitting. Metal conduit extends down from the fitting to 6 inches above grade, where a compression fitting is screwed to a plastic transition fitting. An elbow is added at the bottom and then the cable runs along the bottom of the trench to the area requiring power.

Nipple
LB fitting
Compression fittings
Junction box
Metal conduit
Plastic transition fitting
PVC conduit

Running conduit and cable (continued)

6 Attach the conduit. Fasten the conduit to the house wall with plastic straps. Drill holes in the foundation for self-tapping masonry screws and screw the straps in place.

7 Apply caulk. Caulk the gaps between the siding and the conduit to create a watertight seal.

Running the cable

1 Lay cable. Remove the cover from the LB fitting. Install the fixture at the other end of the trench and uncoil enough UF cable to reach up from the trench to the fixture—plus approximately 2 feet—and leave it at the end of the trench. Then work your way back toward the house, laying cable in the trench as you go.

2 Fish the tape through the conduit. Pushing wire through a conduit by itself is next to impossible, so use fish tape—a flat, springy length of metal in a roll. Insert the end into the fitting and push the tape until it reaches the end of the conduit.

3 Tape the cable to the fish tape. To hook the cable onto the fish tape, bend the cable to form a hook and interlock it to the fish tape. Use black electrical tape to bind the fish tape and the cable together. Then pull the tape and the cable through the conduit elbow. Use conduit lubricant to make pulling easier and to prevent damage to the cable.

Cutting conduit

Running lengths of conduit often requires a fair amount of cutting. Begin by clamping the conduit in a vise. Cut PVC conduit with a hacksaw that has a 32-teeth-per-inch blade. Then remove any burrs with a utility knife and bevel the outside edges to fit the couplings. For metal conduit, use a pipe cutter or hacksaw that has an 18-teeth-per-inch blade. Wrap a piece of masking tape around the area that is to be cut to prevent the blade from slipping. Remove any burrs with a half-round file.

4 Pull the cable and feed it into the house. Pull enough cable through the conduit to reach through the wall and terminate at the junction box, plus about 8 inches. Then remove the fish tape and feed the cable into the house through the nipple.

5 Attach a junction box to the end of the nipple. Go inside the house and attach a junction box to the nipple that runs from the LB fitting. Connect the UF cable coming in from outside with NM cable that will run to the service panel. Staple the cable along the joists with plastic cable staples spaced a maximum of 4½ feet apart. If you use metal staples don't drive the staple too hard or it could crush the cable.

6 If you have to feed cable through joists, drill holes in the middle of the joists to avoid weakening them. Connect the cable to the box as described on page 287.

 WORK SMART

TAKE THE PATH OF LEAST RESISTANCE

Electricians always look for the most efficient way to complete a job. It's not because they're looking for the easy way out; it's because they know that the least amount of drilling, demolition, and pounding will yield the least amount of damage to the structures in which they're working.

For instance, instead of running cable through the foundation, you may be able to tap into an existing outdoor light or junction box. It's worth checking out because all you need to do is replace one of the screw-in seals with a fitting and conduit. Run the conduit to where you want the new outlet, then fish the cable and make the connections. The one drawback: If the new circuit is wired to a porch light, the light will have to be on to get power.

 Mounting tricks

To protect your cable from accidentally being punctured during future renovations, nail metal straps to the joists directly underneath where the cable passes through or directly in front of where it passes through a stud.

Cables tend to droop from one joist to another. To keep them running in straight lines, nail 1×3 runners between the joists and staple the cable to the runners.

Mounting electrical boxes

Skill level: ★☆☆☆	Time to complete:	Materials: Screws or shields, conduit straps, electrical box, metal conduit, receptacle, nonstick plumber's tape, 4×4 post, posthole mix concrete, soil, gaskets, in-use cover plate	Tools: Screwdriver, posthole digger, shovel

Time to complete:
Experienced 30 min.
Handy 45 min.
Novice 1 hr.

The outdoors is not a great place for an electrical box. Rain, snow, and sleet can blow into the box and cause a short. To help prevent this, boxes for outdoors have gaskets and fittings that keep the inside of the box—and the electrical wires—dry. Code also requires you to install a GFCI receptacle to help protect against shock.

It's possible to mount electrical boxes just about anywhere outdoors and on any type of siding. Mount the box close to where it will be used most often and as near as possible to where the cable exits the house.

Attaching to an exterior wall

Outdoor boxes are made from cast aluminum or PVC plastic. Both have gaskets and watertight covers to keep out the elements. If you are using PVC conduit, you can still use a PVC conduit connector to attach it to a metal box. PVC conduit attaches to PVC boxes with plastic pipe primer and solvent cement. If using a metal box, it's a good idea to wrap nonstick plumber's tape around the threads of the screw-in plugs. Outdoor boxes have flanges so you can fasten them to a structure with screws.

SAFETY ALERT
GFCI REQUIRED

To protect against shock, the National Electrical Code requires either a GFCI breaker or GFCI receptacle in all outdoor outlets.

1 Attach the electrical box. Screw through the holes or through the flanges, if there are any, to attach the box. Seal unused openings with screw-in plugs, usually sold separately. To attach the box to a masonry wall, drill holes for self-tapping masonry screws and screw the box in place. For aluminum or vinyl siding, screw directly through the siding into the framing.

2 Wire the box. Install a GFCI receptacle and make the appropriate wire connections. Fix the gasket and waterproof cover plate to the receptacle with screws.

Mounting an electric outlet on a freestanding post

In some circumstances, you may need power in a place that's not convenient to a wall or structure in your yard. The solution is to run the cable to the spot where you need it, then sink a post in the ground at that point. The post serves as an anchoring point for your electrical box. Dig a posthole that's half as deep as the desired height of the post. Then run conduit from the trench up the post. Fasten the conduit and box to the post using straps and screws. Fill in around the post with concrete.

1 Excavate for the box. Dig a trench at least 24 inches deep for the cable. With a posthole digger, dig a hole in the ground at the end of the trench. Make the hole half the exposed height of the post. Put the post in the hole.

2 Attach the box. Attach the receptacle box to the conduit first, then attach the box to the post with wood screws. Caulk the seam between the box and the post to prevent water from getting into the box. Attach the conduit to the post with straps.

3 Run cable. Fish the cable for the box through the conduit with fish tape (see Step 2, page 292). Mix up some ready-mix bagged concrete sold as posthole mix and fill the posthole with it. Fill the trench with the soil and sod you removed.

The best way to support a freestanding electrical box is with a 4×4 post. Conduit exits the box and is attached to the post with straps. The conduit runs down the post and into a 24-inch-deep trench. The cable will leave the conduit at that point and run along the bottom of the trench.

Installing a GFCI outlet

Skill level:	Time to complete:	Materials: GFCI receptacle, gasket, cover plate	Tools: Screwdriver, needle-nose pliers, wire cutter or combination stripper
★★★☆☆	Experienced 15 min. Handy 15 min. Novice 30 min.		

ELECTRICAL

National Electrical Code require you to protect outdoor outlets with a ground fault circuit interrupter (GFCI) and an in-use cover plate which allows the cover to be closed while a cord is plugged in. A GFCI shuts off the power if a short occurs and is essential for outdoor use, where dampness can make electrical shocks deadly.

GFCIs look like other outlets except for two small buttons.
One simulates a ground fault, or a short in which power runs through something (or someone) and into the ground; the other is a reset button to restore power after the test. Push the test button once a month. If it cuts power to the outlet, it's working correctly. If it doesn't cut power, check the outlet and replace it, if necessary.

Making the connections

1 Hang the box. Install the receptacle box on the wall or on a post. Use needle-nose pliers to make a loop in the end of the cable's white wire and wrap it clockwise around the silver terminal marked "line" on the GFCI. Then tighten the screw.

2 Connect the black wire. Connect the cable's black wire to the other line terminal on the GFCI outlet. Make a loop and place it clockwise around the screw. Tighten the screw.

3 Connect the grounding wires. Connect a 6-inch bare or green wire to the grounding screw on the GFCI. Connect a similar wire to the grounding screw in the box. Twist the wires together with the bare wire from the cable and cover with a wire nut.

4 Install the receptacle. Fold the wires into the box, taking care not to disconnect them, and screw the receptacle into place at the top and the bottom of the box.

5 Install the in-use cover plate. Place the gasket over the receptacle and screw on the cover plate. Make the wire connections at the other end of the cable run, if necessary, and turn on the power.

 Waterproofing

An in-use cover plate keeps rain and moisture out of the receptacle box and is now required for new installations by the National Electrical Code. This applies to items that are plugged in for extended periods, such as outdoor holiday lights or a submersible pump.

 Extending a wire run

If you want to run power from a GFCI to another outlet or light, pay attention to the labels on the terminals. Some are labeled "line" terminals; others are labeled "load" terminals. Connect the incoming cable to the line terminals and the outgoing cable to the load terminals. Then connect the grounding wires to a pigtail attached to the grounding terminal.

6 Test the circuit. Plug a radio into the outlet. Press the test button. The reset button should pop out, and the radio should shut off. If not, check the connections to the box or replace the GFCI. Press the reset button to restore power.

Installing switches

Skill level:	Time to complete:	Materials: Single-pole switch, three-way switches, three-wire cable, two-wire cable, electrical tape	Tools: Needle-nose pliers, screwdriver
★☆☆☆☆	Experienced 5 min. Handy 10 min. Novice 15 min.		

A single-pole switch has two terminals on one side and definite on and off positions. It controls one or more fixtures from a single location.

If you're replacing a switch, disconnect the wires that lead to it and reattach them to a new switch. If you're putting in a switch for a new fixture, look for an outlet or switch or tap into an existing circuit after first replacing the box with a larger one.

If the box has only one cable, it's an end-of-the run box, meaning that the power that leaves the box goes only to the light. If the box has two cables, it is in the middle of the run, meaning that the power comes into the box, then continues on to other receptacles, switches, or fixtures in addition to the light that the switch controls.

White wire recoded black

Installing a switch at the end of the run is rather straightforward. The hot wire is routed through the switch, and the white neutral wire is connected directly to the light. Both switch wires carry electricity at one point or another and, therefore, must be connected to black wires. Because there's only one black wire, however, the white wire will have to serve as a hot wire. "Recode" the wire—wrap the ends with black tape—to remind you it carries power. The switch terminals are identical: Connect the black wire to either of them and the recoded white wire to the other. Screw the bare copper wire to the grounding screw in the box.

 ## Middle-of-the-run switch

A single-pole switch in the middle of the run has two cables that enter the box: One cable leads back toward the service panel and the other takes power to another outlet. To add a switch, twist the white wires together and add a wire nut. Attach the two black wires to the two switch terminals. Connect the grounding wires to a jumper with a wire nut and connect the jumper to the grounding screw on the box.

White wire recoded black

1 Turn off the power at the circuit breaker box then recode and attach the white wire. Mark the end of the white wire with electrical tape or a black marker and use needle-nose pliers to loop it to fit around the terminal. Wrap the wire clockwise around one of the terminals and tighten the screw.

2 **Attach the black wire.** Loop the end of the black wire and screw it clockwise to the other terminal.

3 **Attach the grounding wire.** Connect the grounding wire to the grounding terminal screw in the box.

4 **Attach the switch to the box.** Fold the wires in the box. Screw the mounting strap to the box and install the cover plate. For outdoor switches, make sure you use an approved box.

Wiring a three-way switch sequence

A three-way switch sequence allows you to control a light from two locations. Unlike other switches, three-way switches do not have set on and off positions.

The term three-way refers to the number of terminals on the switch: one common terminal, which is usually dark (black or copper), and two lighter-colored traveler terminals, which are used interchangeably. When wiring three-way switches, use a cable with three wires and a ground. This cable has a red wire in addition to the usual black, white, and ground wires.

The general rule is that the power coming in from the source attaches to the common terminal of one switch. The wire carrying power to the light is attached to the common terminal of the other switch. The travelers of one switch are wired to the travelers of the other switch.

Two three-way switches allow you to turn on a light from either of two locations. Two-wire cable enters the switch box from the source. The white wire connects to the white wire of the light, and the black wire connects to the common terminal of the first switch. Three-wire cable runs between the switches, connecting the traveler terminals to each other. The black wire connects the common terminal of the second switch to the light. The second switch is a loop; the white wire is hot and must be recoded black. The grounding wires attach to the grounding screws.

Installing automatic control devices

Skill level:
★☆☆☆

Time to complete:
Experienced 15 min.
Handy 20 min.
Novice 30 min.

Materials: Timer, time-delay or motion-sensor switch, wire nuts

Tools: Screwdriver, lineman's pliers, wire cutter or combination stripper, diagonal cutters

ELECTRICAL

Automatic control devices—timers, motion detectors, light sensors— serve double duty as convenience and security devices. A timer switch allows you to go on vacation confident the lights will come on at a certain time every night. A motion detector turns on a floodlight when an intruder enters the yard or when you get home and need to find your keys. A photoelectric eye automatically turns on the light when the sun sets and comes either with the light or as a screw-in attachment. A time-delay switch shuts off a light after a certain amount of time.

Purchase a specialty switch with a manual override so you can turn the light off if the kids want to play hide-and-seek, you want to look at the stars, or the neighbors ask you to turn off the light from time to time. **Always make sure the power is off at the service panel when installing automatic control devices.**

A timer is an electric switch that you can program to turn a light on and off at selected times. General instructions for installation follow; consult the manufacturer's directions for more details.

1 Remove the existing switch from its box. Twist together the black wire from the timer and the black cable wire in the box and screw on a wire nut.

2 Connect the blue wire from the timer to the white cable wire in the box. Secure with a wire nut. Attach the incoming grounding wire to the grounding screw in the box.

3 Fold the wires into the box and mount the switch by screwing it to the box. Add a cover plate. Turn the power back on and program the switch as directed by the manufacturer.

Wiring a time-delay switch

A time-delay switch is a mechanical switch that automatically shuts off after a designated amount of time. Begin by removing an existing switch from its box.

1 Strip the wires. Pull the switch away from the box and cut off as little as possible of the old wires. Strip off insulation to expose fresh wire.

2 Attach the wires. Most switches have two push-in terminals. Push wires in the terminals. From the front, tighten the screws that hold the wires.

Wiring automatic sensor switches

Motion detectors turn on the light when something moves within their range. Photoelectric sensors turn the light on at dusk and off at dawn. You can usually buy fixtures with one or the other sensor built in. Both are wired exactly the way a floodlight is. If you want to retrofit an existing light, however, buy a sensor separately. Photoelectric sensors screw into the light socket. A motion detector has to be wired.

1 To retrofit an existing light with a motion detector, turn off the power and disconnect the light. Wire the switch module as directed: Generally, a white module wire connects to the light's white wire; the incoming black wire connects to the module's black wire, and the light's black wire connects to a red wire on the switch module. Wrap electrical tape around the wire nuts and down the wire.

2 Attach the sensor. Plug the sensor into the module. Tuck the module into the junction box and screw the sensor to the wall somewhere near the light. Let the sensor cable loop down below the sensor to keep rain from dripping along the cable and into the sensor.

Installing outdoor light fixtures

Skill level: ★☆☆☆

Time to complete:
Experienced 15 min.
Handy 30 min.
Novice 45 min.

Materials: Timer, time-delay or motion-sensor switch, wire nuts, electrician's tape

Tools: Screwdriver, lineman's pliers, wire cutter or combination stripper, shovel, fish tape

ELECTRICAL

Wiring an end-of-the-run porch light

Manufacturers offer several ways to light up your yard at night. Porch lights are one of the simplest. They provide security and shed enough light to help you unlock a door. Floodlights illuminate large areas in a yard, making it possible to use play areas even at night. A third alternative, lampposts brighten up a path and serve both aesthetic and security roles. Always make sure the power is off at the main service panel before installing any light fixture.

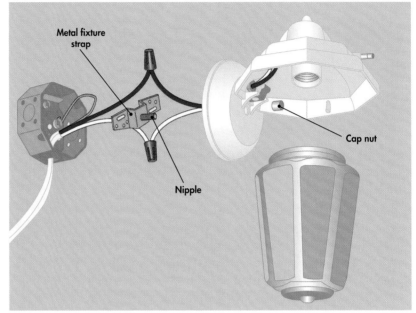

Metal fixture strap

Cap nut

Nipple

You have the option of mounting a porch light on the ceiling or on the wall. Attach a metal fixture strap across the electrical box. Screw a nipple into the strap and into the porch light's base. A cap nut screws onto the nipple and holds the fixture to the wall or ceiling. Porch lights may differ in shape, size, and fixture installation, so follow the manufacturer's instructions. The wire connections, however, should be the same.

 Middle-of-the-run porch light

A middle-of-the-run connection for a porch light is the same as an end-of-the-run connection except for three extra wires (black, white, and grounding). Twist all the black wires together and cover with a wire nut. Repeat for the white wires. Twist all the grounding wires together, add a jumper to them, and cover with a wire nut. Connect the jumper to the grounding screw in the box.

1 Install the hardware. Screw a fixture strap to the box. This strap turns so you can adjust the position of the light.

2 Attach the black wire. Hang the fixture from the box with a hook made from a coat hanger. Twist the black fixture wire to the black cable wire and cover with a wire nut.

3 Attach the ground and white wires. Twist the light's white wire and the white cable wire together and cover with a wire nut. Twist the light's ground wire and the cable ground wire to a pigtail. Cover with a wire nut. Attach the pigtail to the box's grounding screw. Wrap electrical tape around each wire nut and about ½ inch down the wires.

4 Install the light. Hold the base of the fixture over the electrical box, pushing all the wires inside. Screw the cap nuts onto the bolts in the hanger strap to attach the light fixture to the wall or ceiling.

Installing a lamppost

A lamppost and light fixture are usually sold as a unit. The majority of the work is in digging a trench and running cable from the house to the spot where the lamp will be installed. The depth of the trench depends on whether you use conduit in the trench (see pages 290–293). In this case, UF wire is buried 24 inches deep.

Anchor the post in a footing made of quick-setting concrete poured in a fiber tube form. Keep the post vertical while the concrete sets, using 2×4s staked to the ground and clamped to the post.

Lampposts may differ in fixture styles or in material used for the posts. However, the electrical connections are the same for all types of posts.

When working with electricity, always turn off the power by shutting off the appropriate breaker at the service panel.

What you don't see when you look at a lamppost is the work that went into it. Here, waterproof UF (underground feed) cable is buried in a trench 24 inches deep and runs from the house to the location of the post. (If you run conduit, you can dig a shallower trench. See pages 290–293.) A concrete footing made with a tube supports the lamppost. Wire connections are made by joining three pairs of wires with wire nuts.

ELECTRICAL

Installing a lamppost

1 Dig the trench. Dig a trench 24 inches deep and a hole deep enough for the lamppost and wide enough for a fiber tube form. Cut a form that reaches the bottom of the hole and cut a slot in the bottom for the conduit elbow. Fish cable from the trench through the conduit and lower the post into the form. Fill the form with quick-set concrete. Brace with 2x4s staked in the ground and clamped to the post until the concrete is set.

2 Wire the light. Strip the cable wires and connect them to wires in the light. Twist and connect the black wire to the black wire, the white to the white, and the ground to the ground. Tuck the wires into the post.

3 Attach the light. Screw the cap to the top of the post, then mount the light socket in the cap. The mounting method depends on the type of fixture. Check the instructions that come with the lamppost.

Installing a halogen floodlight

Halogen floodlights are made of fused-quartz tubes filled with pressurized halogen gas. The filament inside gives off a very bright white light. When it comes time to replace the bulb, however, don't touch the new one with your fingers; the oil from your skin actually causes the bulb to burn out. Wear gloves or use a cloth.

Installation of a halogen fixture is straightforward—attach the light's black wire to the cable's black wire; the light's white wire to the cable's white wire, and ground wire to ground wire. You can also add a light-sensitive sensor that turns the light on at dusk and off at dawn. The fitting screws into a hole in the light fixture covered with a removable plug. Wire the light so that power goes through the sensor before it goes through the light. When wiring, always turn the power off at the service panel.

Halogen bulb

Photoelectric eye

Halogen floodlights come in various sizes and often are sold in pairs on one base. Add a light sensitive fitting to automatically turn the light on at dusk and off at dawn. **Halogen lights are extremely hot when they are on.**

1 Add the sensor and wire the light. Remove the screw-in slug from the light, and replace it with a sensor. Twist the black cable wire to the black sensor wire. Twist the red sensor wire to the black light wire. Twist the white wires together. Attach the ground wire from the light and the cable to a jumper and connect the jumper to the grounding screw in the box. Connect the wires with wire nuts. Wrap electrical tape around the caps and about 1/2 inch of the wires.

2 Hang the light. Assemble the fixture, if necessary. Push the wires to the back of the box and screw the base of the fixture to the wall.

3 Test the circuit. Turn on the power. Test the photoelectric eye by covering it with black tape. Once the eye is covered, the light should turn on. If it doesn't, check the wire connections for problems or return the light.

Installing a mercury-vapor light

Mercury-vapor lights belong to the family of high-intensity discharge lamps. They give off a distinctive bluish-green light. Mercury-vapor lighting is energy-efficient and often is used in street lamps. It's also popular for lighting large areas of a yard. Your local home improvement store sells a variety of models designed for homeowners. One disadvantage is that the light is intense. Make sure your light doesn't shine onto other people's property, or you may end up with an irate neighbor.

Always make sure you turn off the power at the source before installation. For added security turn off the power at the service panel by shutting off the appropriate circuit breaker. **In any installation, the last thing you do is attach the wires to power.**

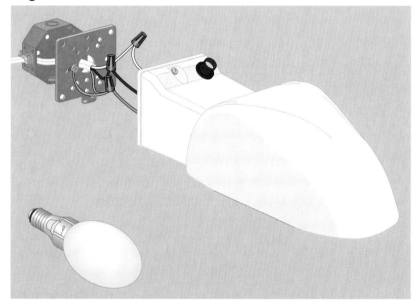

Mercury-vapor lights tend to be large and powerful. Like an incandescent lightbulb, the bulb usually is screwed into a socket. Mercury-vapor lights come in a variety of fixture styles, each of which may have different installation instructions. **Mercury-vapor lights are extremely hot when they are on.**

Installing low-voltage lighting

Skill level:
★ ☆ ☆ ☆

Time to complete:
Experienced 2 hrs.
Handy 3 hrs.
Novice 4 hrs.

Materials: Wood screws or shields and screws, low-voltage lighting kit with transformer and cable

Tools: Drill and bits, screwdriver, shovel

ELECTRICAL

Low-voltage landscape lights—those that are 12-volt AC—literally are a snap to install. The lighting parts snap together, and the connectors snap into place. Some cables looks like lamp cord.

Landscape lights are available in a kit that contains the transformer, the lights, and the connectors that you'll need. You also can buy the system piece by piece so you get exactly what you want. Talk with the sales staff to make sure you get the right transformer.

If necessary, splice low-voltage wires. Strip the wires, put in a silicone-filled cap (sold as a grease cap), and attach the new wire. Some caps are brand-specific, so make sure you buy a cap designed for your wire.

Most low-voltage lighting systems include a transformer that is plugged into a regular outdoor receptacle. The transformer steps the 120-volt household current down to 12 volts. Most transformers are rated to handle a load of 100 to 300 watts. The higher the rating, the more cable and light fixtures you can connect. A timer in the transformer turns the system on at dusk and off at dawn. One end of the cable connects to the transformer; you can attach lights to the cable anywhere you want.

1 Wire the transformer. A transformer steps the voltage down from 120 volts to 12 volts. Attaching the cable for the lights is an easy task of screwing the wires in place. Details vary by manufacturer, so follow the directions that come with the transformer.

2 Hang the transformer. Mount the transformer on the wall next to a GFCI outlet. For most types of siding, you can make the attachment with a wood screw. Drive it into the plywood or the sheathing underneath the siding. For masonry, drill a hole for a lag shield, then screw into the shield.

3 Assemble the lights. Light fixtures usually require assembly. You'll need to snap the sockets in place at the very least, and you may need to do some simple wiring. Follow the manufacturer's directions.

4 Place the lights. Lay the light fixtures in the approximate spots they will be installed and run the cable across the ground from light to light.

5 Connect the lights. Attach the cable connectors. For this light, put half the connector on each side of the cable and snap it together to connect the lights.

6 Dig for the cable. Dig a 6-inch-deep trench alongside the cable and place the cable in the trench, but do not bury it yet.

7 Set the timer. Plug the transformer into the outdoor receptacle and set the timer. Cover the GFCI outlet with a plastic cover, usually sold separately. Test the lights; if they work correctly, bury the cable.

 Get enough power

If you have a long garden path to light, don't just buy the least expensive low-voltage kit and a few extra lighting fixtures. You may end up underpowering all the fixtures and not having enough light—a fact you're not likely to discover till after you've gone to all the work of installing the system. Make sure you plan for an adequate number of lights and get a system whose transformer is rated to power them.

CHAPTER 9

Plumbing & drainage

Outdoor water can be a blessing or a curse, depending on where you find it. If you're running water to a garden or a pond, it's a blessing. Water that's building up in the yard, however, can turn the yard into a muddy bog, erode foundations, wash away plants, and eventually work its way into the basement.

Like indoor plumbing, outdoor plumbing involves two systems: supply and drainage. Indoors, the job is split between the two. What comes in must go out, and for every dripping faucet there can be a plugged drain.

Outdoors is a different story: For every person who runs a pipe out to the horse barn, countless others watch water build up in their yards. For those who plan to run pipes to the shed, the rules are simple: Use plastic pipes so they won't corrode, bury the pipes below the frost line so they don't

freeze, and slope the pipes toward the house so you can drain them if need be.

For drainage problems, few rules but numerous options exist. If water is working its way into your basement, start with the gutters. Make sure they're working, they're not leaking, and water is directed away from the foundation by a splash block at the least. Better yet, route the water away from the foundation with drainpipes.

The problem may be geography: If you live at the bottom of a hill, water will run there when it rains. Solve problem geography with geography: Long, low berms direct water to a new path. Low, shallow depressions channel the water where it won't be a problem. Note, however, that directing water toward the neighbor's yard in order to dry out your own may create more problems than it solves.

Contents

Making connections

The process of joining pipes is easy, and a few guidelines help guarantee success. If you work with PVC, the pipes are glued together, or more properly, they're solvent-welded together. The solvent, which you brush on both the pipe and the fitting you're attaching it to, melts the surface of the plastic. When you put the pipe in the fitting, the two melt together and once the solvent evaporates, they become a single solid surface. Here are a few tips to make sure the joint you make is a good one:

- Cut the pipe with a cutter made for cutting PVC. Copper cutters won't work, and although handsaws will, they leave a ragged edge.

- Cut and fit all the pipe before you glue any of the joints together. If you do, the pipe will be the right length and go to the right place. You'll also solve any problems you run into—such as a joist that's in the way—before you spend time making connections.

- Prime. For a good joint, apply a PVC primer to the pipe before gluing it. The primer helps clean the pipe and softens the PVC before you apply the glue.

- Turn the pipe. Brush on the solvent first, then put the pieces together. Give the pipe a ¼ turn to spread the solvent evenly over the entire surface.

You may use copper to get the water outdoors but once outside, always use plastic pipe. Copper and plastic are joined with special connectors, but copper pipes should be soldered to each other. (Plumbers call it sweat soldering, but it's safe to think of it as soldering.) Cut the pipe with a pipe cutter made for copper, and assemble the entire run before you solder anything. Some tips for a good joint:

- Clean the pipe and fitting. Rub the pipe with emery cloth until the surface is shiny. Clean inside the fitting with a small wire brush made for the job.

- Apply flux. Flux is an acidic paste that further cleans the joint, and if the joint isn't clean, the solder won't stick. Brush flux on both the fitting and the pipe before you put the two together.

- Heat the joint with a torch and remove the heat before applying the solder. If the metal is hot enough to melt the solder, it will flow inside the fitting and seal the joint. If you melt the solder onto a cold pipe, the solder won't flow into the joint and may not even stick to the pipe.

Plumbing & drainage tool kit

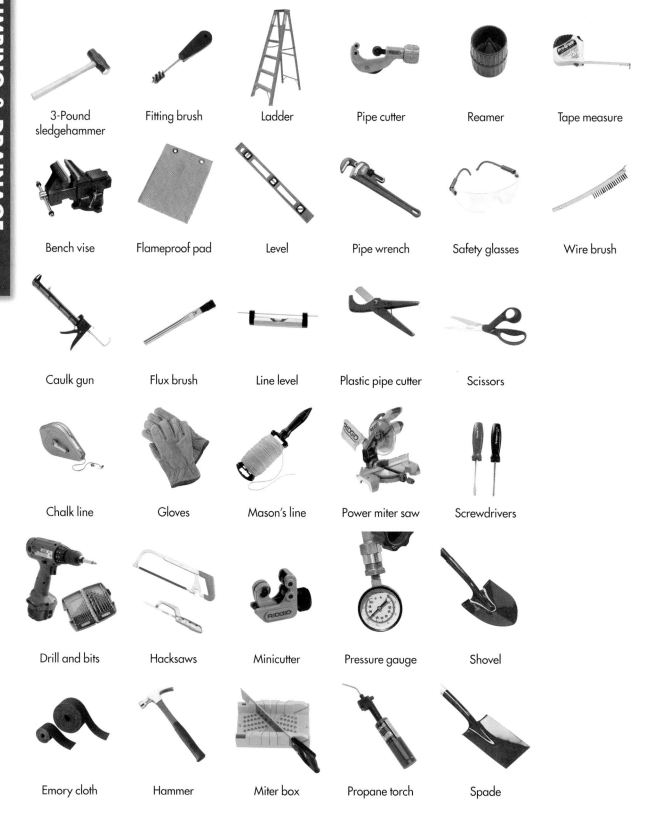

3-Pound sledgehammer

Fitting brush

Ladder

Pipe cutter

Reamer

Tape measure

Bench vise

Flameproof pad

Level

Pipe wrench

Safety glasses

Wire brush

Caulk gun

Flux brush

Line level

Plastic pipe cutter

Scissors

Chalk line

Gloves

Mason's line

Power miter saw

Screwdrivers

Drill and bits

Hacksaws

Minicutter

Pressure gauge

Shovel

Emory cloth

Hammer

Miter box

Propane torch

Spade

Materials

▶ The main types of plumbing pipes are **copper, galvanized steel, PVC, CPVC** and **PEX.** Attach them to joists or other supports with **pipe straps.** To connect two pieces of copper pipe, clean them with **emery cloth,** then join them by applying **soldering paste** or flux, heating the pieces with a torch, and applying **lead-free plumber's tape.** To join plastic pipes, apply **plastic pipe primer,** then glue with **solvent cement,** designed for the plastic you're using. Wrap **nonstick plumber's tape** around the threads of steel pipes when joining them. Prevent pipes from freezing by draining them through a **stop-and-drain valve.** Attach a **vacuum breaker** to a **faucet** on the outside of your house or a freestanding post. The breaker will prevent water from backing up into your water system. A **freezeproof faucet** drains automatically. **Sewer-and-drainage pipe** is laid hole-side-down in the ground to dispose of water underground. You also can use **perforated drainage pipe.**

Galvanized steel · Copper · Sewer-and-drainage pipe · Perforated drainage pipe · PVC · Stop-and-drain valve · CPVC · Lead-free plumber's tape · Faucet · PEX · Vacuum breaker · Pipe straps · Plastic pipe primer · Freeze-proof faucet · Soldering paste · Emery cloth · Solvent cement · Nonstick plumber's tape

PEX · PVC or CPVC · Copper · Galvanized · T fittings · Adapters

▲ Each type of pipe has its own fittings. Connect **PEX flexible plastic pipe** with T fittings, crimp rings, and barbed splicers. (The connectors also come in plastic for residential applications.) Connect plastic pipes with **PVC** or **CPVC** fittings, choosing the same type of plastic for pipe and fitting. Connect copper pipe with **copper fittings,** solder, and flux. **Galvanized fittings** have threads that screw the pipes together. There also are **adapters** for reducing the size of a pipe or changing from one pipe material to another. Each fitting comes in different diameters to fit the different-size pipes. To go from ³/₄-inch pipe to ¹/₂-inch pipe, for example, use a ³/₄×³/₄×¹/₂ **T fitting,** which has two opposing ends with ³/₄-inch diameters and an exit source with a ¹/₂-inch diameter.

Types of pipes and tubes

Types	Uses	Joining method
PVC (Polyvinyl chloride)	Cold water supply; outside irrigation systems; indoor drainage (SCH40PVC)	PVC primer and solvent cement
CPVC (Chlorinated polyvinyl chloride)	Hot and cold water supply, indoors and out	CPVC primer and solvent cement
PEX (cross-linked polyethylene)	Indoor and outdoor supply	Crimped or compression fittings on flexible pipe
Copper	Indoor supply	Soldering with lead-free solder and copper or brass fittings
Galvanized steel	Indoor supply	Threaded pipe to threaded steel fittings

Making supply-pipe connections

Skill level:	Time to complete:	Materials: Copper pipe and fittings, galvanized metal pipe and fittings, CPVC/PVC pipe and fittings, PE pipe and fittings, lead-free solder, solvent cement, lead-free flux, thread-cutting oil, rag, nonstick plumber's tape, band clamps	Tools: Pipe cutter (copper, galvanized pipe, or PVC), fitting brush, propane torch, pipe threader, pipe wrenches, reamer, bench vise, flux brush, leather gloves, marker, flameproof pad, wire brush, screwdriver, emery cloth, safety glasses
★★★☆☆	Experienced 30 min. Handy 45 min. Novice 1 hr.		

Fitting pipes together is to plumbing what driving nails is to carpentry—you can't do much without it. For outdoor plumbing, tap into an indoor line and make connections to run pipe outside. Generally, indoor pipe is ½ or ¾ inch in diameter and made of copper or plastic, although you'll sometimes find galvanized piping in older homes. Outdoor lines must always be plastic. Special adapters make connecting copper and plastic easy. Before you start tapping into the system, turn water off at the main shutoff valve and open all faucets to drain the system.

Galvanized metal pipe is threaded and screwed together.
Connecting—or sweating—copper pipe involves heating the pipe before touching it with lead-free solder. Plastic pipe comes in three varieties: PVC, CPVC, and PE. Both PVC (polyvinyl chloride) and CPVC (chlorinated polyvinyl chloride) are used outdoors for supply lines. PVC is more practical, but you can use CPVC for hot-water lines. Connect plastic pipes with the solvent cement designed for the type of pipe; never substitute. PE (polyethylene) pipe is connected with barbed fittings and band clamps. You can purchase adapters to join two different types of pipe.

Connecting copper pipe

1 Cut the Pipe. Place a pipe cutter over the pipe and tighten the handle. Rotate the cutter around the pipe. As you do, the cutting wheel scores a straight line. Tighten the wheel and cut again. Continue until you cut the pipe.

2 Remove the burrs. Pipe cutters have a triangular blade called a reamer. Twist it back and forth inside the end of the pipe to remove the burrs that cutting it created. Remove burrs from the ends of all pipes to be joined.

3 **Clean the ends of the pipes.** Rub the ends with emery cloth until they are shiny. Clean the inside of the fitting with a fitting brush. Avoid files or steel wool; they are too rough. Don't touch the ends after cleaning them— the oil in a fingerprint can ruin the joint.

4 **Apply flux.** With a small, stiff brush, apply lead-free soldering paste (called flux) to the last 1 inch of the pipes and the inside of the fitting. **Wear gloves—flux is caustic.** Insert one pipe into the fitting and twist it to spread the flux.

5 **Apply Heat. Protect wood and wiring with a flameproof pad and keep a spray bottle filled with water nearby in case anything catches fire.** Slide the second pipe into the fitting. Light a propane torch and adjust the flame until the blue part is 1 to 2 inches long. Hold the torch so the flame is vertical and heat the pipe and fitting until the flux begins to sizzle.

6 **Apply solder.** Remove the torch and touch the joint with the end of a length of lead-free solder. It should melt evenly and completely around the joint. Use ½ to ¾ inch of solder for each joint. Although it may seem as if more is better, don't overdo it, or solder will flow into the pipe and reduce water flow.

7 **Clean the joint.** Wipe off the excess solder with a clean, dry rag. If you don't, the pipe will oxidize and turn green. **Be careful—the pipes are still hot at this point.** Wait until the joints have cooled completely before turning on the water and testing for leaks.

$ BUYER'S GUIDE
ORDERING PIPE

Plumbing, heating, and refrigeration pipes have confused many customers. Make sure you buy plumbing pipes. The common size for most outdoor projects is ¾ inch, but you can use ½-inch pipe to install outdoor faucets. If you are replacing a pipe, you'll need to know both its outside and inside diameters so the new pipe will fit in the same fitting. You can do it with a tape measure or set of calipers, but the safest method is to take a sample to the store. Remember to include the distance the pipe extends into the fitting when calculating the length you need.

Making supply-pipe connections (continued)

Connecting threaded pipe

1 Cut the pipe. Clamp the pipe in a vise. Cut it with a rented iron pipe cutter that's equipped with a blade designed for metal. Tighten the handle after every two or three rotations. Cutting with a hacksaw is not advisable because the cut needs to be perfectly straight so the end threads properly.

2 Clean out the inside of the pipe. Put the reamer attached to the pipe cutter inside the cut pipe end and twist it to scrape away any burrs that might restrict water flow.

3 Thread the pipe. Rent a pipe threader that handles the diameter of the pipe. Fit the threader onto the pipe. Apply generous amounts of thread-cutting oil as you rotate the handle clockwise until one thread extends beyond the end of the threader. Remove the threader and clean the threads with a wire brush.

4 Apply nonstick plumber's tape. Before you thread the pipe into a fitting, wrap nonstick plumber's tape 1½ turns clockwise around the male threads, pulling the tape tight. The tape seals the joint, preventing leaks and helping prevent rust.

5 Twist the pipe into the fitting. Turn as far as possible by hand. Then clamp one pipe wrench on the pipe to hold it and another on the fitting, as shown. Place a short piece of pipe in the fitting so it doesn't collapse. Turn the wrench on the fitting clockwise and apply force only toward the open mouth of the jaws.

WORK SMART

THE TURN OF THE SCREW

The problem with removing threaded pipe from a fitting is that it's next to impossible: As you turn the pipe to remove it from a fitting at one end, you're driving it into the fitting at the other end. Soon you've driven the pipe all the way into the fitting at the far end without freeing it at the other end. To solve this dilemma, cut the pipe first. Then clamp one wrench on the pipe and another on the fitting. Turn only the wrench attached to the fitting, applying force toward the open mouth of the jaws. Be sure to use the proper size of wrench for the job: a 12- to 14-inch wrench for ½- to 1-inch pipes or an 18-inch wrench for 1¼- to 1½-inch pipes.

Connecting PVC and CPVC pipe

1 Cut the pipe. Make a straight cut in the pipe with a pipe cutter made for plastic or cut it in a miter box. Use a reamer to remove burrs from the cut end. When you cut a pipe to length, add an extra 1/2 inch at each end for the pipe that slips inside the fitting.

2 Put the pipe in the fitting. Test-fit the pipe in the fitting and mark the pieces so you can align them during installation. Test-fit the entire run of pipe. Apply primer to the end of the pipe and inside the fitting. Spread solvent cement on the end of the pipe, following the manufacturer's directions. Apply more lightly inside the fitting.

3 Put the pipe in the fitting. Slide the pipe completely into the fitting and give it a quarter-turn to help spread the solvent and remove bubbles. Adjust the fitting so the marks are aligned. Hold the joint for 10 seconds. Wipe off excess cement with a dry rag. Wait two hours before running water through the pipe to check for leaks.

 PEX pipe

PEX (cross-linked polyethylene) is a flexible plastic pipe used for hot and cold supply lines. While it is gaining wide national acceptance, some local codes may prohibit or restrict its use. Be sure to check with your building code department before using it.

PEX pipe attaches to fittings with copper or stainless steel crimp rings compressed by a crimping tool. No tape or pipe compound is required.

 Connecting irrigation pipe

1 Put the fitting in the pipe. Polyethylene pipe is a flexible plastic pipe intended for outdoor use in rock-free soil; it is often used for irrigation systems. Cut the pipe with a knife or fine-tooth saw. Slide a loose band clamp onto the pipe, then fit the pipe over the ribs on the fitting. You can heat the end of the pipe with a hair dryer to expand it and make it easier to insert the fitting.

2 Tighten the band clamp. Move the band clamp so it is 1/4 inch from the end of the pipe and beyond the ribs in the fitting. Tighten the screw on the clamp with a screwdriver.

Tapping into supply pipes

Skill level:	Time to complete:		Materials: CPVC pipe, CPVC T fitting, PVC pipe, PVC T fitting, copper pipe, copper T fitting, adapters, lead-free plumber's solder, flux, solvent cement, plumber's tape	Tools: Minicutter, small hacksaw, emery cloth, plastic pipe cutter, pipe wrenches, propane torch, flux brush, flameproof pad, pressure gauge, fitting brush, safety glasses, work gloves
★★★☆☆	Experienced	30 min.		
	Handy	45 min.		
	Novice	1 hr.		

To get water outdoors, you need to work from indoors. Start by cutting through an existing pipe, adding a T fitting, and attaching the pipe that goes outdoors.

Before you cut, make sure you do two things:

■ Connect a water pressure gauge to the outdoor hose faucet. You'll need a minimum of 40 pounds of pressure to take the water any distance. Take an average of readings made at different times of the day.

■ When you're ready to cut into supply lines, turn off the house's main shutoff valve and open the faucets in your house to drain the pipes. Have a bucket handy, just in case.

Attaching CPVC

1 Cut the existing line. Turn off the water at the main shutoff valve. Cut through the cold-water supply pipe at the desired location with a plastic pipe cutter. Cut off an additional ½ inch for ½-inch pipe and ¾ inch for ¾-inch pipe.

2 Glue on a T fitting. Insert a T fitting and turn the stem in the direction of the new run. Mark the T and pipes with reference lines. Remove the T and apply pipe primer and cement to both cut pipe ends and the insides of the T. Apply a second coat of cement to pipe ends. Fit the T back onto the pipe, align the reference lines, and hold for 10 seconds. Glue the new run into the fitting.

Attaching copper to copper

1 Cut the pipe. Cut out a piece from the cold-water pipe at the desired location with a pipe cutter—cut off an additional ½ inch for ½-inch pipe and ¾ inch for ¾-inch pipe. Use a close-quarters pipe cutter (a minicutter) like the one shown here if the space is cramped. Buff the cut ends with emery cloth and clean the fitting with a fitting brush.

2 Solder the fitting. Brush flux to the last inch of the cut pipe and the new pipe and to the inside of a T fitting. Put the fitting on the cut pipes and insert the new run of pipe in the opening. Solder the joints one at a time, starting with the lowest and working up. Heat the joints until the flux sizzles. Remove the torch and touch lead-free solder to each joint until it melts around each evenly.

Attaching PVC plastic to galvanized pipe

1 Cut and remove the pipe.
With a small hacksaw or mini-reciprocating saw, cut through a section of the cold-water pipe. Clamp a pipe wrench to the fitting and another wrench next to it on the cut pipe. Turn the wrench that is clamped on the pipe counterclockwise.

2 Screw on transition fittings.
Wrap nonstick plumber's tape around the threads of two male ¾-inch transition PVC fittings. Screw them onto the fittings at each end, tightening them one turn beyond hand-tight.

3 Glue on pipes and a T fitting. Cut pipe to run between the adapter and the T fitting; put it and the fitting in place without gluing. Measure the length of pipe needed to fit between the T and the second adapter. Cut and test it, then apply pipe primer and glue to attach the new pipe into the adapters and the T. Glue the pipe for the new run into the remaining hole in the T.

Attaching copper to galvanized pipe

1 Cut and remove the pipe at a coupling or at a valve.
Galvanized pipe comes in 8-foot lengths so you will find a coupling every 8 feet. Cut through the galvanized pipe with a small hacksaw or mini-reciprocating saw. Twist each section out of the coupling or fitting using two pipe wrenches. Hold one on the fitting and the other on the pipe and twist the wrench that is on the pipe counterclockwise.

Dielectric fitting

2 Attach adapters. Solder threaded brass fittings to two lengths of copper pipe that will run to a T fitting for the new riser pipe. Connect one side of a dielectric fitting to the copper and another to the galvanized steel pipe. A washer between the two pipes prevents corrosion that otherwise occurs between dissimilar metals. Wrap nonstick plumber's tape on the threads of the adapters, screw them in place, and tighten. Repeat on the other side.

3 Extend the run. After connecting the copper pipe to the galvanized steel, you're ready to extend the run. In this example a T fitting is soldered between two lengths of copper pipe to extend a new run upward.

Running supply pipes

Skill level:	Time to complete:		Materials: Pipe, elbow fitting, stop-and-drain valve with a waste drain, pipe straps, lead-free flux, silicone caulk, lead-free solder	Tools: 3/8-inch drill and bits, hammer, pipe cutter, tape measure, propane torch, flameproof pad, flame retardant work gloves, caulk gun, tape measure, safety glasses
★★★★★	Experienced	1 hr.		
	Handy	2 hrs.		
	Novice	3 hrs.		

The next step in getting water outdoors for whatever application you want to install is to run supply pipes. Drill through the rim joist or concrete foundation to create an exit point for the pipe. Then tap into the supply line with a T fitting. If you live in an area with freezing temperatures in the winter, install a drainable valve—called a stop-and-drain valve—somewhere above the T but below the faucet. As winter approaches, open the drain on the valve to drain the faucet and the outside pipes. Once the valve is in, run pipe from it to the outdoors.

Rim joist

Waste plug

Stop-and-drain valve

T fitting

Supply pipe

To transport water out of the house, cut into an existing supply line and insert a T fitting. The two openings opposite each other on the T fitting must be the same size as the existing pipe, but the third fitting can be any size. Use 1/2 inch for a faucet and 3/4 inch for all other fixtures. When you're deciding where to run the pipe through the wall, look for a rim joist—it's easier than going through a masonry wall. You can use copper or plastic pipe for faucets that attach to the house. Any pipe buried in the ground, however, must be plastic, so consider using plastic for every pipe that comes after the T fitting.

Extending the supply line

1 Drill through the rim joist. From inside the house, locate a spot on the joist just above the foundation where you want the pipe to exit. Drill a 1/4-inch test hole at a slightly downward angle. Go outside and find where the bit went through the house. Drill a hole for the pipe at this point. Use a bit that's the same size as the pipe.

2 Attach the fitting. Solvent-weld, or solder, the fitting or faucet to the pipe while you can still slide it away from the house to work. Start by cutting a pipe a few inches longer that the thickness of the wall and attach a fitting to it. Slip the pipe, or nipple, through the hole. In colder climates install a frost-free fitting.

3 Install a T fitting inside. Tap into the supply pipe with a T fitting. Add a section of pipe and install a drainable valve, called a stop-and-drain valve. Water must flow through the valve in the direction indicated on the valve for it to work properly. The waste plug is the valve's drain: When you turn off the valve and open an outdoor faucet, you can unscrew the plug to drain the pipes.

4 Attach an elbow. Install an elbow on the end of the nipple so it faces toward the stop-and-drain valve. For $\frac{1}{2}$-inch pipe, measure from $\frac{1}{2}$ inch inside the elbow to $\frac{1}{2}$ inch inside the valve to determine the length of pipe needed. For $\frac{3}{4}$-inch pipe, measure $\frac{3}{4}$ inch inside each fitting.

5 Connect the fittings. Cut pipe to the right length and sweat or solvent-weld it between the elbow and valve. Caulk around the outside of the hole you drilled to keep water from entering. On a faucet, caulk the flange; on a fitting, caulk around its perimeter. **Protect walls and ceilings with a flameproof pad and wear glasses and flame-retardant gloves when using a propane torch.**

 Supporting pipe

 Drilling concrete

To support pipe, run it along a joist and fasten it with pipe straps. Use a strap of the same size and material as the pipe. Slip the strap over the pipe and nail it to the joist.

If you are running pipe across joists, drill a hole slightly larger than the diameter of the pipe in the center of each joist. Don't drill closer than 2 inches from the edge, or you will weaken the joist.

You may need to drill through a masonry wall to install pipe below grade. The pipe must fit inside a PVC sleeve to prevent abrasion, so drill the hole large enough for the sleeve. It's hard work; you may want to call in a pro. If you are doing it yourself, rent a hammer drill with a $\frac{3}{4}$-inch carbide-tipped percussion bit.

Adding outdoor faucets

Skill level:	**Time to complete:**	**Materials:** Lead-free solder, lead-free flux, vacuum breaker, faucet or frost free faucet, nonstick plumber's tape, scrap 2×4, silicone caulk, PVC pipe, PVC connectors, PVC elbow, solvent cement and primer, threaded PVC-to-metal adapter, sand, galvanized pipe, pipe clamps, steel rod	**Tools:** Caulk gun, propane torch, flux brush, ³⁄₈-inch drill and bits, pipe wrench, 3-pound sledgehammer, screwdriver, shovel, safety glasses, work gloves
★★★☆☆	Experienced 30 min.		
	Handy 45 min.		
	Novice 1 hr.		

When choosing a location for an outdoor faucet, pick a spot that is close to the indoor cold-water pipe you plan to tap into. If possible locate it high enough on the wall to clear a bucket. If the faucet is freestanding, run the pipe through the foundation at the same level you'll run it through the yard—somewhere below the frost line. In colder climates install a frost-free faucet to prevent water from getting trapped in the pipe and freezing. Purchase a model with a vacuum breaker, which keeps the hose from sucking in water if the water pressure drops. If your faucet doesn't have one, you can screw one to the threads.

Installing a wall-mounted faucet

Caulking

Faucet

Nipple

Flange

Vacuum breaker

An outdoor faucet valve handle turns water on and off. It is connected to a nipple that is attached to the supply pipe inside the house. The spout is usually male-threaded to accommodate garden hoses, although some models are female-threaded or unthreaded. Screw a vacuum breaker to the threads. The faucet has a flange that sits against the exterior wall of the house. Apply caulk to the flange before pressing it to the wall to ensure a weathertight seal.

 ### Before you run any other pipes

Fit the flange over a nipple and solvent-weld, or sweat, the faucet onto it, leaving the valve open to protect the washers. Apply caulk. If you are using plastic pipe inside, use a plastic nipple and a plastic faucet. Insert the assembly in the wall and screw the flange to the wall.

A frost-free faucet

In climates where frozen pipes are a concern, install a frost-free faucet, which has a long body that extends through the exterior wall into the basement. A long stem runs through the body and into the

house. When you turn the handle to turn off the water, a washer on the end of the stem stops the water inside the house, where it won't freeze. Install the faucet so it slopes downward toward the outside; excess water then can drain out. Some faucets have threaded fittings; others have to be sweated onto ¹⁄₂-inch copper pipe.

Installing a freestsanding faucet

A freestanding faucet brings the source of water closer to the plants and flowers that need it most. Plan its location so the faucet doesn't get in the way of the traffic flow in your yard. It will take longer to install than a wall-mounted faucet. How long, of course, depends on how far from the house you want to install it—you'll have to dig a trench below the frost line for the pipe. Use PVC pipe underground (it won't corrode), but support the faucet riser on a separate piece of steel rod driven into the ground for stability.

Install a stop-and-drain valve indoors so you can drain away standing water in the pipe before the first freeze.

You can use dirt or sand to support the pipe in the trench. Sand will fill voids beneath the pipe more effectively but the dirt is already there from digging the trench. It's your choice.

Run PVC pipe from the house to the end of the trench, where it's attached to a galvanized riser and the faucet. Support the riser with a steel pipe. Drive the support pipe 2 feet deeper than the trench bottom. The support should end about 2 inches below the faucet and be attached to the pipe with pipe clamps.

1 Dig a trench. Make the trench about 12 inches deep and slope it uphill 1 inch for every 8 feet as it moves away from the house. Lay out lengths of PVC pipe from the house to the outlying faucet location and support them with scraps of 2×4. Solvent-weld the pipes together using couplings.

2 Support the pipe with dirt or sand. Fill the trench below the pipe with dirt or sand, removing the 2×4 pieces as each section of pipe is supported. Attach a plastic elbow with one threaded end to the end of the PVC pipe. Test the pipe for leaks before filling the trench.

3 Wrap teflon plumber's tape around the threads of a galvanized pipe and screw the pipe into the elbow. Drive a piece of steel support rod 2 feet below the bottom of the trench next to the riser. Brace the riser to the support rod with pipe clamps. Screw on the faucet without damaging the fitting by placing a screwdriver in the spigot and turning clockwise until tight.

Gutters and downspouts

Skill level:	Time to complete:	
★★★☆☆	Experienced	1.5 hrs.
	Handy	2 hrs.
	Novice	3 hrs.

Materials: End cap, hangers, gutter, drop outlet, downspout, elbows, diverters, screws

Tools: Ladder, drill with screwdriver bit, chalkline, hammer, mason's line, hacksaw or power miter saw, line level, tape measure, safety glasses

For gutters to carry water, make sure they slope toward the downspouts. For installation, vinyl is easier to use than metal. It cuts easily with a hacksaw or power miter saw. You must allow for expansion and contraction, however, because vinyl expands with the heat and contracts with the cold.

In fact, vinyl gutters are designed to allow for expansion. Each system is a little different, so follow the directions that come with your gutter carefully. At some point you'll need to skip a section of gutter, install the drop outlet, and then measure for and cut the missing piece of gutter, minus an allowance for expansion. You find the proper length by measuring from the last section of gutter installed over to a mark in the drop outlet that corresponds to the current temperature.

1 Stretch a level line. Drive a nail into the fascia at the end of the gutter that will be farthest from the downspout. Tie a mason's line to it and attach a line level. Stretch the line to what will be the other end of the gutter, level it, and mark the end of the line.

2 Lay out a slope. Measure down from the mark 1/8 inch for every 10 feet of gutter and drive a nail. Stretch a chalkline between the two nails.

3 Snap the chalkline to mark what will be the top of the gutter.

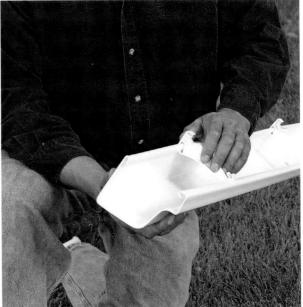

4 Partially assemble the gutter. Working on the ground, put an end cap in what will be the high end of the gutter. Slide the hanging hooks inside the gutter, spacing them 1 foot from each end and every 2 feet in between.

5 **Hang the gutter.** Hold the middle of the gutter and put it up against the fascia. Align the top with the chalkline and screw the center hook in place.

Keep the gutter aligned with the chalk line and screw the rest of the hooks in place. Make sure the gutter will slide back and forth on the hooks; if it won't, find out which hook is either too high or too low and reposition it.

6 **Hang the drop outlet.** Hang the drop outlet next, before you install any more sections of gutter. Position the outlet so the downspout will run along the corner of the building. Screw the outlet in place before you install the gutter between the drop outlet and the first section of gutter. Lines inside the gutter are labeled for various temperatures. Mark the fascia above the one corresponding to the temperature at time of installation. Measure from the mark back to the first section of gutter. Cut a piece of gutter to this length.

7 **Hang the second section of gutter.** Slide one end of the gutter you just cut into the drop outlet. Butt the other end against the first section of gutter, and put a two-piece connector across the seam. Start with the inner section, positioning it so it spans the seam. Then put the outer connector across the seam and snap it in place. Screw the connector to the gutter to keep it from moving.

8 **Connect gutter to the other side of the outlet.** Cut a piece of gutter to reach from the outlet to the end of the soffit. Put an end cap on it, slide the assembly into the drop outlet, and screw the hanger hook in place.

9 **Put an elbow on the downspout.** Hold an elbow against the wall 6 to 8 inches below the first. Measure the distance between the two, subtract the amount the manufacturer recommends for expansion, and cut a piece of downspout to this length. For a tight seal, make sure the gutter is clean when attaching connectors.

10 **Hang the downspout.** Measure from the elbow to the ground, subtract 6 inches, and cut a piece of downspout to this length. Hold it temporarily in place and mark the location of the downspout clips. Attach the clips and downspout. Put an elbow in the bottom and a diverter on the ground below to direct water away from the house.

Installing outdoor drainage systems

Skill level:	Time to complete:	Materials: 4-inch nonperforated drainpipe, 2×4,	Tools: Shovel, level, line level, spade, hand saw,
★★★☆☆	Experienced 4 hrs.	1×2 stakes, 90-degree drainage bend, downspout adapter,	scissors, wheelbarrow, mason's line, tamper,
	Handy 6 hrs.	patio block	3-pound sledgehammer, safety glasses, work gloves
	Novice 8 hrs.		

A mushy yard is hard on plants and not particularly easy on the feet. One of the biggest culprits is the gutter, which takes water that falls on a few hundred square feet of roof and dumps it onto a few square inches of lawn. Corrugated pipe buried underground channels the water away from the house, the plants, and even the basement.

Make sure you use nonperforated pipe—perforated pipe is intended for use along the bottom of a basement wall.

Channel water from the downspout with nonperforated pllastic pipe. Dig a trench from the downspout sloping down 1/8 to 1/4 inch per foot. Run the trench to a point where the bottom reaches the surface or to a dry well. To gauge the slope, place a 1-inch spacer between the end of a 4-foot level and a 2×4. The slope is correct when the bubble is centered.

Controlling downspout runoff

1 Lay the pipe. Line the trench with a corrugated plastic pipe 3 or 4 inches in diameter. Align the pipe with the downspout. Lay nonperforated pipe so the water from the downspout will be channeled away and won't soak into the soil near the house.

2 Attach the pipe to the downspout. Snap a 90-degree elbow to the end of the pipe that's nearest the downspout. Use a hand saw to cut enough pipe to reach from the elbow to the downspout. Snap one end to the elbow; snap the other to a downspout adapter. Slip the adapter over the downspout and fill in the trench.

Constructing a dry well

Despite its name, a dry well collects water. In this case the well takes water from a drain line when it isn't possible to drain it into a storm sewer or some other suitable spot. Dry wells are typically 2 to 4 feet wide and about 3 feet deep. Check local code for the appropriate size of well for your area; size usually is related to average rainfall. The well must be situated at least 10 feet from the house to keep water away from the foundation. Dig the drainage trench, then dig the dry well. Line the well with landscape fabric and fill it with gravel. Cover the well with a patio block to prevent it from filling up with water from above, rather than from the seepage trench. Then conceal the slab with earth and sod.

Your local home improvement store may carry an optional fabric cover or "sock" that fits over the corrugated pipe to prevent debris from entering the pipe through the drainage holes.

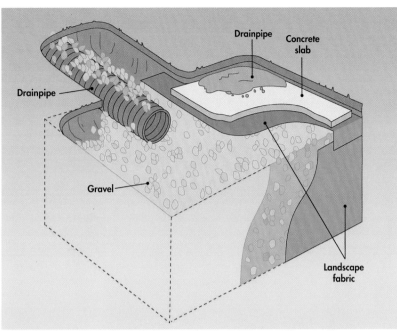

A dry well is a hole that serves as an outlet for a drainage trench. Put the well at the low end of the trench at a minimum of 10 feet from the house. After digging the well, cover the inside of the hole with landscape fabric and fill it with gravel. The landscape fabric keeps the soil from mixing with the gravel. Cover the dry well with a patio block to keep rain from seeping into the well. Cover the slab with soil and sod.

1 Dig out the trench. After you dig the trench, dig the dry well at the low end of the trench. Check local code for the proper width and depth of the well.

2 Slope the bottom of the trench. To work properly, the trench must drop ⅛ to ¼ inch for every foot it travels on its way to the well. To gauge the slope, slip a 1-inch spacer between a 4-foot level and a straight 2×4 that is at least 4 feet long. When the bubble in the level is centered, you have the right slope.

3 Lay drainage pipe. Shovel in enough gravel to cover the bottom of the trench. Lay 4-inch-diameter drainpipe along the bottom of the trench and a few inches into the dry well. If you are using PVC, lay it with the perforated side down. Dry assemble the lengths of pipe with couplings.

4 **Line the dry well.** Landscape fabric keeps soil from mixing with gravel. Line each side of the dry well with a piece of landscape fabric, leaving enough extra to fold over the hole later. Use scissors to cut a hole in the landscape fabric for the drainpipe.

5 **Fill the trench.** Shovel enough gravel into the trench to cover the pipe and lay landscape fabric over the gravel. Backfill the trench with soil and cover the soil with sod.

6 **Fill the well.** Fill the well with gravel. Leave enough room at the top for a patio block cover, a topping of 2 to 3 inches of soil, and a layer of sod. Fold the ends of the landscape fabric over the gravel.

7 **Cover with a patio block.** Place a concrete patio block on the gravel and landscape fabric to prevent water from the soil from filling the well. Leave enough room on top of the cover for 2 to 3 inches of soil and a layer of sod.

8 **Replace the sod.** Put a 2- to 3-inch layer of soil over the block and lay down the sod you removed earlier.

Building a berm to divert water

A berm is a small earthen barrier that redirects the flow of water. It's usually paired with a shallow ditch, called a swale, which helps drain away the water.

1 Remove the sod. Cut through the sod with an edger, removing a strip of sod as wide as a shovel. Pull up the sod and set it aside.

2 Build up the surface. Use a wheelbarrow to dump loads of soil along the path of the berm. Smooth it out with a spade and a rake and create a small mound. Tamp. Cover the mound with the sod you removed and seed any bare patches.

Building a swale to carry water

Swales are shallow trenches that catch water and channel it away from the house and toward a more suitable spot, such as a storm sewer. The swale should run along the bottom of the slope to catch water and drain it away. Allow the swale to follow the natural slope of the land.

1 Lay out the slope. Remove the sod and drive a stake at each end of the swale. Stretch mason's line between the stakes and level it with a line level. On what will be the low end of the swale, lower the line ¼ inch for every foot that the swale is long.

2 Excavate to create the swale. Work your way along the line, digging so the bottom and the line are a constant distance apart. Throw the dirt to the downhill side as you go, then rake it to form a small berm. Tamp the berm and seed it. Cover the trench with the sod you removed.

CHAPTER 10

Concrete

Concrete wears many hats in the construction trades. It's used to anchor fence posts, decks, piers, and basketball hoops. Concrete is used for sidewalks, driveways, the foundation for walls and sheds, and the base for patios—sometimes it *is* the patio.

Concrete is a mixture of cement, sand, and gravel. Masons refer to sand as a fine aggregate and gravel as a coarse aggregate, but no matter what you call them, concrete is a mixture, and that greatly affects the way you pour a pad.

When you first pull a board, or screed, across the top of the forms to level the concrete, the stones are spread evenly through the mixture, including along the surface. This look is fine for a foundation.

To get the smooth surface you're used to seeing on a patio or sidewalk, however, you'll need to do some more work. Use the darby and bull float, two trowels used in the initial finishing phase of concrete. As you slide the trowels over the surface of the concrete, the stones on the surface of the cement sink, and the sand and cement rise, forming a thin layer of mortar.

Once the mortar surface forms, you'll need a different tool to create the finished surface. A broom creates a nonskid surface; a wood trowel creates a surface that, while flat, still has enough texture to help prevent slipping. If you use a metal trowel, you'll get a smooth, almost slippery surface—just the sort of thing you don't need outside.

Contents

Concrete evidence

Concrete may dry hard and stay hard, but it's not the rock-solid surface it appears to be. Unlike wood, which has fibers running the length of the board, the structure of concrete runs every which way. Its random nature needs to be reinforced, or it's bound to crack.

Steel reinforcing mesh does the trick. Put mesh across the entire bed before you pour, supporting it on wire supports, sometimes called chairs. (The old practice of supporting the mesh on brick pulls moisture from the concrete.)

Concrete will, of course, stick where you least want it to, namely to adjoining structures. All structures are moving— slowly perhaps, and not enough to see, but enough to cause concrete to crack. Expansion joints, which are thick, wide strips made of petroleum-impregnated felt or paper, help solve the problem. They're the black tarlike strips you see between a patio and the house. Because they are so

oily, concrete won't stick to them, and the walk and the house can each move at their own rate without cracking the patio.

Once the mesh is in and the concrete poured, all large concrete surfaces need control joints. Control joints are the lines that run across the width of a sidewalk, and their purpose is to introduce a weak spot in the walk. If the ground under the walk settles for any reason, the resulting cracks are most likely to occur in the control joints. The result is not only neater, it's stronger than it would be if cracks ran all over the face of the concrete.

Think of a concrete pad as a system—parts of which are designed to make the pad stronger, others to make it weaker. Even the rounded edges you see on concrete are structural— rounded edges are less likely to chip than square ones. For the best results pay attention to the entire system while you work.

Concrete tool kit

3-pound sledgehammer

Caulk gun

Garden hose

Mason's line and powdered chalk

Power tamper

Tape measure

Brick and cold chisels

Chalkline

Hammer

Mattock

Rake

Trowels

Broom

Control jointer

Handsaw

Mixing tub

Safety glasses

Utility knife

Brush

Finishing trowel (Darby)

Levels

Paint brush

Shovel

Wheelbarrow

Bucket

Dust mask

Magnesium and wood floats

Paint roller with extension

Spade

Work gloves

Bull float

Edger

Mason's hoe

Posthole digger

Tamper

Materials

▶ Concrete pads start with forms made of **lumber** and **duplex nails** — the double heads are easy to remove. Form curves with **tempered hardboard** or **metal flashing.** Install **expansion joints** along adjoining surfaces so new concrete moves independently. Add strength to slabs with **6×6-10/10 wire mesh** — 6-inch squares of 10-gauge wire. Prop mesh and rebar on **wire supports** (sometimes called chairs). If you're pouring piers, either as a foundation or to hold sports equipment posts in place, use **fiber tube forms.** Use bags of **premix concrete** for jobs needing up to 1 cubic yard. Additives in **fast-set concrete** speed the curing process. Add color to concrete with a **dye.** Cover fresh concrete with **plastic sheeting** or **burlap** to keep it from drying too quickly. Seal concrete with **non-yellowing sealer.** Fill small cracks with **vinyl patching compound. Anchoring cement** expands as it dries to create an extremely secure bond with regular concrete. A **bonding agent** helps repairs adhere to damaged surfaces.

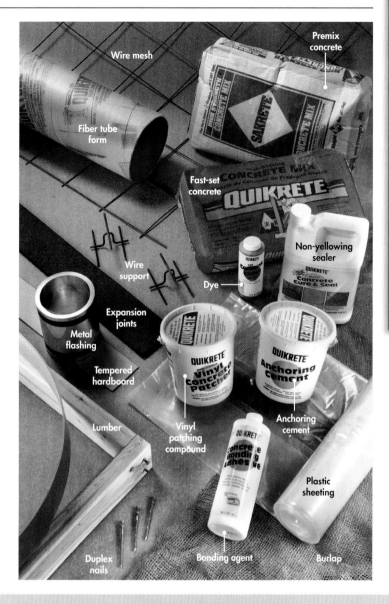

Wire mesh — Premix concrete — Fiber tube form — Fast-set concrete — Non-yellowing sealer — Wire support — Dye — Metal flashing — Expansion joints — Tempered hardboard — Lumber — Vinyl patching compound — Anchoring cement — Plastic sheeting — Duplex nails — Bonding agent — Burlap

Defining terms

Concrete is made of three materials: **Cement,** usually portland cement, **sand,** and **gravel. Mortar,** which is used elsewhere in the book, contains **lime** instead of gravel. Concrete works both as an underground foundation and as a slab poured on the surface. Mortar is used to bond materials together, such as bricks and stone. Both concrete and mortar can be hand-mixed from dry ingredients, but it is easier to buy them in **premix bags.** Always mix concrete and mortar with clean, clear water — water that is clean and clear enough to drink.

Premix bags — Cement — Gravel — Concrete — Lime — Mortar — Sand

Assembling forms for a concrete pad

Skill level:	Time to complete:	Materials: ¾-inch gravel, 2×s, ½-inch plywood, 10d (3-inch) duplex nails, ½-inch expansion joint, 6×6-10/10 wire mesh, chairs, construction adhesive, form-release agent or vegetable oil, tie wire, concrete	Tools: Mattock, spade, power tamper, shovel, wheelbarrow, rake, line or water level, tape measure, chalkline, hammer, 3-pound sledgehammer, handsaw, caulk gun, paintbrush, safety glasses, dust mask, work gloves
★★★☆☆	Experienced 14 hrs. Handy 17 hrs. Novice 20 hrs.		

In most areas a concrete slab begins with 4 inches of compacted stone, which provides drainage below the concrete and helps prevent flooding and perhaps cracking as the ground shifts. Areas with excellent drainage don't need a stone base, so check with your local building office to see what's required locally.

To keep the slab from cracking, the pros put mesh in the middle of the pour to help tie the slab together. Next they put a strip of tar-impregnated felt, called an expansion joint, between the new pad and any existing structures. If an adjacent structure, such as the house foundation, stays stationary while your new pad shifts, the expansion joint allows them to move independently, thereby preventing cracks in the slab or foundation.

Control joints act as magnets for cracks. The joints are lines that are weaker than the rest of the slab. Cracks are more likely to form along the control joints, where they are hidden, than in the middle of the pad.

A concrete pad is a system of stone, metal, and concrete. The top 4 inches is a concrete slab. A wire mesh running through the middle of the pad supported by metal supports called chairs, ties it together to help prevent cracks. Beneath the concrete is a gravel bed, which improves drainage and is easier to level than soil. An expansion joint between the pad and house allows the two to move independently of each other when the ground shifts. Forms hold concrete in place as you pour and act as guides when you drag a board across the forms to level the surface. The forms usually are removed after the concrete cures.

1 Lay out and excavate the pad. Lay out the pad with batterboards and mason's line. Remove the sod and dig out 8 inches of soil across an area that is 1 foot larger than the pad in each direction. Compact the surface with a power tamper.

2 Add gravel and compact again. In areas that require gravel beds (most do; check local code), spread gravel on the surface in 2-inch layers, compacting the layers and adding gravel until you get a bed 4 inches thick.

3 **Lay out the outside edge of the forms.** Install a second set of layout lines, putting them on stakes. Position the stakes outside the first set of lines, offset from the first set by the thickness of the forms you'll use. Level them with a line level or water level.

4 **Drive stakes along the new layout lines.** Drive stakes along the layout lines, putting them at the corners of the pad and every 2 feet in between. Drive the stakes so they're plumb and firmly bedded in the ground. Don't worry about their height; you'll trim them to height later. Remove the first set of layout lines; you don't need them anymore.

5 **Mark the stakes.** The pad must slope away from the house at a rate of $1/8$ to $1/4$ inch per foot—check local code for the proper amount. Measure down from the batterboards and mark the corner stakes at the finished height of the pad. Hold a chalkline tight at the marks you made and snap the chalkline to mark the rest of the stakes.

6 **Nail the first form in place.** Align the form with the mark on the stakes and nail it in place with two duplex nails. You can hold a 3-pound sledgehammer against the back of the form board to make nailing easier. Nail the rest of the stakes to the form board the same way.

7 **Cut off the stakes.** Cut the stakes flush with or slightly below the top of the forms. You will use the tops as a guide to level the concrete surface, and any stake rising above the surface will keep you from getting a smooth result.

CONCRETE

8 Install the remaining boards. Cut the boards long enough to span each of the remaining sides. Position them one at a time so their tops are level with the marks you made on the stakes earlier. Nail them to the stakes with duplex nails.

9 Splice boards together, if necessary. On sides too long for a single board, butt two boards together. Cut a strip of 1/2-inch plywood and nail it across the joint. Drive a 2×4 stake at each end of the plywood strip and nail it to the forms with duplex nails.

10 Install the expansion joint. With construction adhesive, attach a 1/2×4-inch expansion joint to the foundation of the house and any other existing concrete that meets the pad. The joint will prevent the pad and foundation from bonding and cracking if they shift or settle at different rates.

BUYER'S GUIDE

$ A MATTER OF FORM

As most do-it-yourselfers discover sooner or later, 2×4s are not actually 2×4 inches. In the process of planing and drying, they lose 1/2 inch in each direction to the planer. Not a problem in most cases, but what if you're using a 2×4 as a form to pour a 4-inch slab?

Not a problem here either. When you nail the forms to their stakes, just make sure the top of the 2× lies on the plane of the proposed pad. There will be a 1/2-inch space between the 2× and the gravel below it. The concrete will flow out through the cracks a bit. This doesn't affect the quality of the job, however, and in the end, you'll bury the edge, hiding the ooze forever.

11 Coat the forms with release agent. Coat the form boards with a commercial form-release agent or vegetable oil to prevent the concrete from sticking to the form boards.

12 Place the mesh. Reinforce the concrete with 6×6-10/10 wire mesh (6-inch squares, made of 10-gauge metal). Put the mesh on wire supports, called chairs, and sold separately, so it sits roughly in the middle of the slab's thickness. Keep the mesh a few inches away from the edges of the forms to prevent rust. Overlap sections by 4 inches and tie them together with wire. Wire the mesh to the chairs.

Mixing and pouring concrete

Skill level:
★☆☆☆

Time to complete:
Experienced 4 hrs.
Handy 5 hrs.
Novice 6 hrs.

Materials: Concrete (portland cement, sand, gravel, water), wood and concrete block for ramp, nails, plastic sheeting

Tools: Wheelbarrow, concrete mixer, broom, mason's hoe, bucket, shovel, control jointer, rake, pointing trowel, screed, bull float, darby, edger, wood or magnesium float, safety glasses, dust mask, work gloves

Concrete is sold three ways—premixed in bags, cement mixed with aggregates on site, or concrete ordered premixed in volume from a ready-mix company. The easiest method for small jobs—under 1 cubic yard—is to buy premixed bags. All you have to do is add water. Mixing the concrete from ingredients—portland cement, sand, gravel, and water—is very labor-intensive so you'll have to decide if it's worth the savings and the time to mix the concrete yourself. If you're dealing with more than 2 cubic yards, consider ordering the concrete from a ready-mix company. You'll have to round up the amount you order to the next full yard or possibly pay for a minimum amount of cubic yards even if you don't plan to use it all.

Concrete recipe

Material	Parts
Portland cement	1
Sand	3
Gravel	2
Water	½

Cubic yards of concrete needed

Area (Sq. ft.)	3" slab	4" slab	5" slab	6" slab
10	.10	.14	.17	.20
25	.25	.34	.42	.51
50	.51	.68	.85	1.02
100	1.02	1.36	1.70	2.04
200	2.04	2.72	3.40	4.07
300	3.06	4.07	5.09	6.11
400	4.07	5.43	6.79	8.15

The chart above tells you how much concrete you'll need for some typical jobs. If the chart doesn't apply to your job, some simple math will tell you what you need. Talk to a sales associate at your local home center to figure out how much you'll need. Always add 10 percent for subgrade variations and waste.

BUYER'S GUIDE
$ CHOOSING CONCRETE

A variety of specialized concretes are available: vinyl concrete, fast-setting concrete, surface-reinforced concrete, sand-mix concrete, and anchoring concrete.

Vinyl concrete, also called patching mix, is used generally for repairs. To make your own vinyl concrete, add a bonding agent to the mix of dry ingredients.

Fast-setting concrete (or quick-setting) dries faster than regular concrete. This allows you to get back to work on your site more quickly. Use fast-setting concrete for postholes.

Surface-reinforced concrete is expensive and normally not used in do-it-yourself applications.

Sand-mix concrete has no gravel, only sand and cement. It is useful as a grout and for repairs two inches thick or less. Sand-mix shrinks more than regular concrete because it has no gravel.

Anchoring concrete contains an epoxy cement that allows it to adhere to regular concrete. Also, it is 2½ times stronger than regular concrete.

WORK SMART
☑ FAST IN, FAST OUT

If you decide to order your concrete ready-mixed, make sure you're prepared to unload the concrete as quickly and efficiently as possible. The longer the truck is at your site, the more money you'll pay. This is the time to call in a few friends to give you a hand. To keep costs down, prepare the site as thoroughly as possible. Lay a pathway of 1×8 planks from where the truck will park to the site. Make sure all forms are in place and secured. And don't overfill the wheelbarrow: Concrete is heavy, and a top-heavy load is more likely to tip.

Mixing and pouring concrete (continued)

Mixing concrete

For small batches, fill a wheelbarrow no more than three-quarters full with premix concrete or dry ingredients. Pile the ingredients into a mound and make a small crater in the center. Pour water into the crater a little at a time. Mix well with a mason's hoe or shovel, then test the consistency. The concrete should cling to the side of the tool.

If you need larger amounts of concrete, rent a concrete mixer. Fill the mixer no more than half full with premixed concrete from bags or add each dry ingredient separately. Turn on the mixer and mix the dry ingredients, then add the required amount of water from a bucket. Let the mixer rotate for about five minutes, then test the consistency.

To tell if the consistency is right, slice through the mixed concrete with a spade. If ready, the edges of the slices should hold straight, not crumble, and be the consistency of oatmeal. If the edges crumble, the concrete is too dry and you need to add some water. If the edges fall over, it is too wet and you need to add more dry ingredients.

Pouring concrete

WORK SMART
EVEN AIR DISTRIBUTION

Air-entrainment agents may sound like unnecessary extras, but they make your concrete much stronger, especially in climates with frequent freezing and thawing. Air-entrainment creates evenly distributed air bubbles in the concrete, which strengthen the mix and increase its workability. Air-entrainment agents for dry, premixed concrete— usually sold in liquid form—are available at home centers. For ready-mix concrete, consult your supplier. Whatever method you choose, talk to a pro. The necessary amounts may vary from brand to brand and affect the quantities of sand and water needed.

1 Pour the concrete in the forms. If you're using a wheelbarrow, build a temporary ramp over the forms so the wheelbarrow won't displace them. Dump the loads of concrete against each other, starting on the side farthest away from the ramp. Have a helper with a shovel spread the concrete into corners and against the forms and expansion joints.

2 Remove trapped air. Lay a wide board across the forms so you can reach the interior of the pour. If the concrete causes the wire mesh to sink, pull it up with a rake so it's in the middle of the slab. Work a shovel or rake up and down to remove air pockets, especially alongside the forms.

Flatten the surface. With a helper, pull a screed (a long, straight 2×4) across the form to level the concrete. Tilt the screed forward and slide it from side to side as you push it forward. Stop to shovel off excess concrete in front of the screed or to fill in low spots. Then make a second pass with the screed.

4 Float the concrete. On large slabs, work a bull float back and forth across the surface with the leading edge of the blade slightly raised to smooth and compact the concrete. Work the concrete until water forms on the surface.

For smaller pads, float the concrete with a large float called a darby. The technique is the same even though the tool is different. Slide the darby across the concrete, smoothing and compacting it, until water forms on the surface.

Finishing concrete

DESIGN TIP
GETTING THE RIGHT SURFACE

Function often dictates how a pad should be finished. For a smoother finish, use a magnesium float instead of a wooden one. Avoid finishing concrete with a steel trowel because it will create a finish so smooth that it becomes slick and dangerous when wet. A skid-free broomed finish is an especially good idea around pools.

1 Round the edges. When you've finished floating, separate the concrete from the forms by running the tip of a pointing trowel between the two. Then slide the cutting edge of an edger along the forms to round over the pad edge to make it less likely to chip. Tilt up the leading edge of the tool to avoid marring the concrete.

2 Cut control joints. Cut shallow grooves, called control joints, in the wet cement pad. The joints provide a line along which the concrete can crack if the ground shifts, You need a joint every 8 feet, so mark the forms every 8 feet. Place a jointer at the mark and guide it against a board that spans the pad.

CONCRETE

Mixing and pouring concrete (continued)

3 Float the surface. After you've cut the control joints and once any water sheen leaves the surface, run a wood or magnesium float over the surface for a final smoothing. Raise the leading edge of the float slightly as you work to avoid making lines on the surface of the concrete.

4 Brush the surface. For improved traction, pull a stiff-bristled broom toward you over the concrete. Draw the broom in either straight or wavy lines. If you don't like the pattern or if it is too coarse, trowel, wait, and broom again. The longer the concrete dries, the finer the broomed surface. Make another pass along the perimeter with an edger.

5 Let the concrete cure. Lay plastic sheeting over the finished surface. The moisture trapped inside eliminates the need for watering during the curing stage. Let the concrete cure at least 48 hours, then remove the form boards. For more information, see "Curing concrete," below.

 Curing concrete

Concrete is not like glue, which hardens as the water in it dries out. A chemical reaction called hydration causes the concrete to harden. Let a slab dry out as it cures, and it's liable to crack. One way to keep it wet is with a sprinkler. Turn it on whenever the concrete appears dry.

You can also cover the slab with plastic sheeting to trap evaporating moisture. Keep the wind from blowing the plastic off the concrete by stapling the edges of the plastic sheet to the forms.

A final option is to cover the slab with clean burlap and keep the burlap wet with a hose or sprinkler for the duration of the curing. Adjust the flow of water so it doesn't puddle on the burlap. Turn the sprinkler on for a few minutes every few hours, as needed, to keep the burlap damp.

Anchoring posts for sports equipment

Skill level:	Time to complete:		Materials: 6-inch diameter fiber tube form, duct tape, 2×2 stakes, 1×4 braces, gravel, concrete	Tools: Posthole digger, 3-pound sledgehammer, shovel, hammer, trowel, level, utility knife, tamper, mason's hoe, wheelbarrow, safety glasses, work gloves
★ ☆ ☆ ☆	Experienced	3 hrs.		
	Handy	4 hrs.		
	Novice	5 hrs.		

Some sports equipment—basketball hoops, for example—work best with posts that are firmly anchored in concrete.

Dig a hole half as deep as the exposed height of the post. Set the post in the hole and plumb and brace it before adding concrete. You can pour concrete directly into the hole or set the post in a fiber tube form. A form results in consistent strength throughout the base, and you are guaranteed not to waste concrete because of a hole that is too wide. **Locate all underground utilities before excavating.**

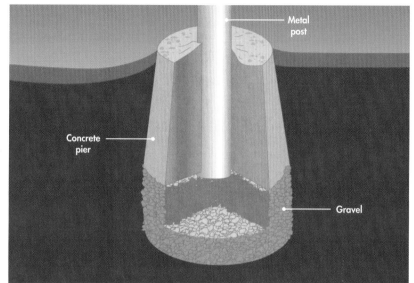

The size of the hole depends on whether the post you're setting is for a tennis net, volleyball net, or basketball hoop; follow the manufacturer's instructions. The easiest way to anchor the post is to pour concrete directly into the hole. Put gravel in the hole before pouring the concrete to provide better drainage.

1 Dig a hole for the post. Using a posthole digger, dig a hole half the exposed height of the post. Add 4 inches of gravel at the bottom of the hole for drainage.

2 Put the post in the hole. Drive 2×2 stakes into the ground and nail 1×4 braces to them. Plumb the post and tape the braces to the post with duct tape.

Anchoring posts for sports equipment (continued)

3 Mix the concrete. Pour bagged concrete mix into a wheelbarrow and add half the recommended amount of water. Mix with a mortar hoe, adding water a little at a time until the desired consistency is achieved.

4 Put concrete in the hole. Shovel 6 to 8 inches of concrete into the hole, then tamp it with a 2×4 to remove air bubbles. Continue, adding 6- to 8-inch layers and tamping until the hole is filled.

5 Tamp again and crown the top. Once the hole is filled, give it a final tamping. Add a bit more concrete, then crown the top so water will drain away from the post. Let the concrete cure for 48 hours.

Anchoring posts with a fiber tube form

1 Put the form in the hole. Place a 6-inch-diameter fiber tube form in the hole. Support the form about 6 inches above the bottom of the hole by nailing two 2×4s to it, as shown above. Shim under the 2×4s to level the form.

2 Put the post into the form. Drive stakes into the ground and nail braces to them. Plumb the post and tape it to the braces with duct tape. Fill the form in 6- to 8-inch layers. When you finish pouring a layer, work a scrap 2×4 up and down in the concrete to remove trapped air. When the form is full, crown the top so water can drain away.

3 Remove the 2×4s and cut off the exposed section of the form. Let the concrete cure for at least two days, then backfill around the form with soil. Use a utility knife to cut off the part of the form that sticks out of the ground.

Making a molded concrete walk

Skill level:
★☆☆☆

Time to complete:
Experienced 2 hrs.
Handy 3.5 hrs.
Novice 5 hrs.

Materials: Dye, concrete, level, concrete sealer, stakes, pavers

Tools: Mason's line, tape measure, concrete mixer, spray paint or powdered chalk, edger or spade, shovel, concrete mold, mason's hoe, mason's trowel, metal trowel, wheelbarrow, paintbrush, stiff bristle broom, safety glasses, dust mask, work gloves

Concrete molds simplify the job of creating a decorative walk. The mold is usually 2-foot plastic square with interior dividers that create a stone or brick pattern in wet concrete. You put the form on the ground, fill it up with concrete, and trowel the surface flat. Next you remove the mold, put it next to the concrete you've poured, and pour again. If the walk curves, angle the form to get the shape you want.

An 80-pound bag of concrete fills the mold, simplifying mixing and measuring. You can pour and mix more concrete one square at a time with no worries about a large batch of concrete drying while you work. Pour and move the mold as many times as it takes to lay the walk, or stop whenever you like.

If you're using a mold with a stone pattern, you can use the concrete right as it comes out of the bag. If you're using a brick pattern, such as the one shown here, mix dye with the concrete to give it a brick color.

The job requires some digging. You'll need to remove the sod so that the walk has a firm base. But once you've removed the sod, leveling the walk is much simpler than it is with traditional forms. In fact you may have a choice: You can let the mold follow the contour of the ground, the same way a footpath would, or you can level the mold before pouring, giving you the level surface of a city sidewalk. The choice is yours. Leveling instructions are included here to give you an idea of what's involved.

1 Lay out the walk with stakes and mason's line. Lay out any curves as described on page 116. Spray paint or sprinkle powdered chalk along the lines to mark the ground.

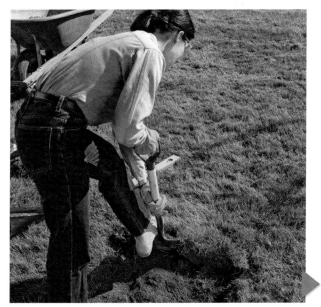

2 Remove the sod. Cut along the edge of the walk with an edger or spade. Hold the handle of the spade low to the ground and kick it to remove a strip of grass. Repeat until you've removed all the sod.

CONCRETE

Making a molded concrete walk (continued)

3 **Remove about 1 inch of soil.** Dig a trench about 1 inch deep, checking from time to time with a 2-foot level to make sure the surface is level. The soil need not be flat because the concrete will conform to any irregularities. It must, however, be firm: Shovel out any soil you knock loose, or the concrete may crack.

4 **Mix the concrete.** If you're using a brick pattern, such as the one shown here, dye the concrete red before putting it in the mold. You'll need one 80-pound bag of fiber-reinforced concrete per 2×2-foot section of walk and about 10 ounces of liquid color per 80-pound bag. If using a mixer, pour in color and water before you pour in the concrete.

If mixing by hand, mix the color and water together, then add it to the concrete mix. If you're using a mold that imitates stone, mix the concrete following the directions on the bag but leave out the dye.

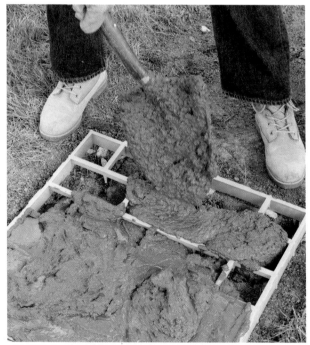

5 **Put the mold in place.** Put the mold on the ground and check it for level. Prop it on small stones, as needed, to level it.

6 **Fill the mold to the surface.** Shovel concrete into the mold, filling it to the top. Smooth the top with a mason's trowel.

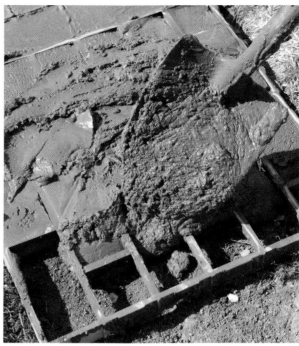

7 **Remove the mold.** Lift the mold from the wet concrete. The edges of the concrete will be somewhat rough. Trowel lightly to remove imperfections.

8 **Reposition the mold.** Turn the mold a quarter-turn and put it next to the concrete you just poured. Check for level and shim with small stones, as before. Mix and pour concrete, and trowel it smooth. Work your way down the walk, section by section.

9 **Position the mold to make a curve.** Start a curve by putting the mold at an angle so it overlaps a straight section of walk. The angle should position the edge of the mold along the curve you've laid out, and the overlap should be just enough to accommodate the angle.

10 **Fill the mold.** Shovel concrete into the mold. Trowel until smooth all the concrete within the mold, including any concrete from the previous section. Move the mold as often as needed to create the curve, keeping the angle and overlap constant from square to square.

11 **Seal the concrete.** When the concrete is fully cured (approximately 72 hours), brush on a concrete sealant to protect it from oil, grease, and salt. Fill the gaps around the edges of the walk with soil.

Special surface finishes

Skill level: ★★★☆☆	Time to complete: Experienced Variable Handy Variable Novice Variable	Materials: Concrete, rock salt, aggregate, plastic sheeting	Tools: Concave jointer, concrete stamp, stiff nylon-bristle broom, floor roller, hose and nozzle, wooden hand float, bull float or darby, work gloves, safety glasses, knee pads

CONCRETE

Specialty surfaces offer variety from the well-known broomed surface. Stamped or tooled surfaces create the appearance of brick or stone. In areas not subject to freezing, a rock salt finish or an exposed aggregate finish creates a dressier slip-resistant surface.

A salt finish is easy to apply. Scatter salt on the surface, press it in with a roller, and wash out the salt after the concrete has cured.

An aggregate surface is one in which you cover the surface entirely with small stones. Although not difficult, applying an aggregate surface is time-consuming. Plan for it to take about three times as long as a broomed surface. Because of the time involved, you may want to break the walk into several small pours. Divide the forms into smaller sections with 2×4 dividers. Put expansion joints against one side of the dividers, pour one of the sections, and apply the finish. When you're done with the section, remove the divider but leave the expansion joint in place. Work your way along the walk one section at a time, always leaving an expansion joint between sections to help avoid cracking.

Creating a stamped surface

Screed and float the surface as you normally would. Stamp the surface with a commercially available plastic, metal, or rubber mold that creates a brick or stone pattern. Depending on the mold, it may be easier to stand on the mold to make the impression in the concrete. When using a mold that imitates brick, dye the concrete a brick color before stamping.

Creating a pattern by hand

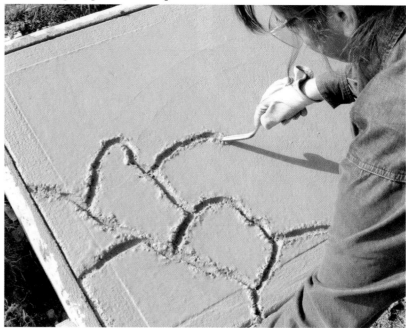

Screed, float, and then pull a concave jointer across the surface, carving simulated irregular flagstone joints 1/2 to 3/4 inch deep. When finished remove the concrete ridges along the joints by floating with a magnesium float.

Making a rock salt surface

1 Screed and float the surface. Finish the surface as you normally would: Screed it flush with the top of the forms and float with a darby or bull float until water forms on the surface.

2 Scatter salt. Scatter rock salt over the surface of the concrete at a rate of about 5 pounds per 100 square feet.

3 Roll the salt into the surface. Push the salt into the surface of the concrete by rolling with a 90-pound floor roller. In a pinch you can roll the salt with a pipe or push it below the surface with a trowel. The floor roller will give you the best surface with the least amount of effort, however.

4 Let the surface cure. Cover the surface with sheets of plastic and let it cure for five days. To avoid discoloration, keep the plastic flat and wrinkle-free on the surface of the concrete. (Don't use curing compounds or sprinkle the surface with water as it cures. Let the plastic do its job.)

5 Wash and brush away the salt. Once the surface has cured, hose it with water and scrub with a stiff-bristle broom to remove the salt.

Special surface finishes (continued)

Making an exposed aggregate surface

1 Screed and float the surface. Prepare the surface as you normally would: Screed the surface flush with the top of the forms and smooth it with a darby (finishing trowel) or bull float until water appears on the surface.

2 Spread the aggregate. Spread gravel (which masons call aggregate) evenly over the surface of the wet concrete with a shovel and by hand. Cover the surface with a single, even layer of stone.

3 Embed the aggregate. Push the gravel into the concrete with a wooden hand float, darby, or 90-pound floor roller. Once the aggregate is most of the way into the concrete, float the surface with a magnesium float, pushing the stone the rest of the way in. Keep floating until about $1/16$ inch of concrete—but no more—is on top of the stones.

4 Brush off the concrete. Wait until the surface is hard enough to support your weight while you kneel on a board placed on it. If the board leaves an impression, wait longer. Brush the concrete off the top of the stones with a stiff nylon-bristle broom. If brushing dislodges the aggregate, let the concrete harden more before continuing.

5 Brush and flush. As soon as you finish brushing the surface, brush it again, this time washing off the concrete with a fine spray of water. You can use either the broom and a hose and nozzle or a special aggregate broom that you attach to the hose.

6 Repeat. Let the slab harden a bit, then brush and flush again. Let it harden further, then repeat as often as necessary to get the desired surface.

Index

Index (continued)